THE LAST CAPTIVE

Testimonials

We, the undersigned, who make the following remarks, know Mr. Lehmann to be the man (Indot, Alaman, Montechina, Charley Ross) that was a captive among the Indians from 1870 to 1878 and brought back to Loyal Valley by the soldiers.

I have known Mr. Lehmann several years and find him to be a faithful, law-abiding, patriotic citizen.

J. H. JONES
Loyal Valley, Texas

I have known Mr. Lehmann for twenty years. I saw him the day he met his parents, brothers and sisters, after his long captivity among the Indians. It was a joyful meeting and a touching incident—a scene never to be forgotten by me. It was like one coming from the dead, for his parents had thought him to be dead.

H. M. DYE
Loyal Valley, Texas

I have cow-hunted with Herman and been with him in all kinds of weather, and I find him ever the same. He never forgets a friend, but quickly forgives an enemy.

HENRY KOTHE
Cherry Springs, Texas

Herman Lehmann has been my friend for twenty years and many happy hours have we spent together drinking beer and telling stories.

OTTO MARSCHALL
Cherry Springs, Texas

I can testify that Herman is the boy who was stolen on Squaw Creek in the early '70's, and he has been O. K. since he returned.

C. F. W. LANGE
Cherry Springs, Texas

We were neighbors to Mr. Lehmann, the father of Herman, and have known the family for a long, long time and since Herman's return he has been a faithful citizen and a good neighbor.

AUG. ELLEBRACHT
Cherry Springs, Texas

I, the undersigned, can say that I have known my old friend, H. Lehmann, for twenty years. It is now twenty years ago Herman returned from the Indians, where he had to go through many, many hard days and when he returned home he went right to work and has tried ever since to go through the world honest, and by that Herman got to be the friend to everybody that knows him.

AD. MARSCHALL
Cherry Springs, Texas

Herman is just what he claims to be.

A. R. EVERS
Cherry Springs, Texas

We believe Herman to be O. K.

H. LANG   WM. MITTEL
PAUL NIXON   *Cherry Springs, Texas*

Herman can entertain a whole crowd with his Indian stories, and the beauty of it is, we believe them.

LOUIS WELGE   W. L. MUND
CONRAD MUND   CHARLEY FRIEDRICH
EMIL GREENWELGE   ADOLPH EVERS
G. E. NIXEN   *Cherry Springs, Texas*

Herman Lehmann is my half brother and I have known him nearly all my life. I was very small when he returned. I love to watch him plug the drummers' hats and hugely enjoy his stories.

HENRY W. BUCHMEYER
Loyal Valley, Texas

We have been (and are yet), old neighbors of Herman and are proud to state that he is all right. We wish him God's speed, and many sales for his valuable book.

CARL GREENWELGE	ERNEST DAUNHEIM
LUDWIG P. GREENWELGE	CHARLES LEHMANN
C. C. SCHNEIDER	WM. BRATHERICH
MAX MARSCHALL	G. L. FLORA
MAX A. KRIEWITZ	EDW. OHRENS

Cherry Springs P. O., Gillespie Co., Tex., Feb. 26, '99.

Dear Sir:

I know Herman Lehmann for about ten or twelve years, and always thought that he was and would be a good and honest man, which would not be the case of other fellows who were stolen by the Indians like Herman Lehmann and stayed with them as long as H. Lehmann did. But when he first got back from the Indians Herman Lehmann was as friendly to everybody as any other man could be. That showed that he is a good neighbor and nothing wrong with him. Afterwards he started a saloon on the main road between Fredericksburg and Mason at the Cherry Springs postoffice, where all the people in the neighborhood have their enjoyments now. If it would not have been for Herman Lehmann to start that saloon and dance hall at Cherry Springs, all the young folks had to go a long ways to amuse themselves. And another thing, if H. Lehmann kept that place instead of selling it, the people would see still more fun yet. For now I must close my writing, it is getting late and time to go to bed. Good night to you, my dear friend H. Lehmann. Your true friend,

EMIL CRENWELGE.

Fort Sill, O. T., April 16th, 1898.

We the undersigned Comanches know Mr. Herman Lehmann to be the man (Montechina, as we called him) that was a captive in our tribe about four years, from 1873 to 1877 or 78. He was taken from us forcibly by the soldiers at Fort Sill.

Witnesses:

D. A. GRANITHAM.

A. R. HOLCOMB.

QUANAH PARKER,

PAT-CHA-NO,

CHIWAT,

an Apache and brother to Carnoviste.

CARTE,

PUEBLO,

Quassucheka.

THE LAST CAPTIVE

The Lives of Herman Lehmann, Who Was Taken by the
Indians as a Boy From His Texas Home & Adopted by Them;
His Career as an Authentic Wild Warrior With the
Apache & Comanche
Tribes;
His Subsequent Restoration to the Bosom of His Family
& the Difficulties & Confusions
Faced in Adjusting His Savage Training to
A Civilized Society;
His Experiences Carrying Him from the
Time of the Scalping Knife
To the Very Threshold of
Our Atomic Age;
Together With Verifying Accounts by Members of
His Family and Others
Who Shared Some of Those Extraordinary & Historical Events.
Now Published by The Encino Press, Austin

By A. C. Greene

FIRST EDITION

© 1972 : THE ENCINO PRESS
2003 SOUTH LAMAR : AUSTIN

FOR DAVID, THE UNCAPTURED

Preface

THE SOUTHWEST, and Texas in particular, has made ample contribution to that minor American literary form, the Captive Narrative.

This literature came from the mouths and pens of those who had been taken prisoner by the American Indians and lived to tell about it. Some were kept in slavery, some escaped or were traded back to the white world, and a few became "white" Indians. The captive narrative is an old form, at least as old as Captain John Smith's *Generall Historie of Virginia* of 1624, and it has honored its constants, not the least of them being Captain Smith's Pocahontas figure who saves the white captive from doom by throwing herself between him and her people.

I do not believe that a purely literary study of the captive narratives has been made, although Carl Coke Rister's *Border Captives* brings together many of the Southwestern accounts for historical analysis. I would like to see a psychiatrist or psychologist do something with the genre. But psychiatrists—the licensed kind—shy away from the frontier, for some reason, although it would seem a legitimate field for their speculation, seeing how much of it we have inherited that drives us to the couch.

My personal inclination in captive narratives has been toward those which tell of white prisoners who lived with their captors until they, too, became Indians. Cynthia Ann Parker has assumed the ritual role in this part of the field. Captured at a tender age—nine years in her case—the captive comes to accept, then embrace, the savage life, despite its cruelties and hardships. Contacted by friends or family from the white world, the captive refuses to go back, or if forced to return to civilization, continues to yearn for the old, free life with the tribe. Cynthia Ann Parker lived only a few years in her white captivity and died, not yet forty years of age, from what was popularly held to be "a broken heart." Thus, her story served the double myth of white superiority—the white captive is always preferred by the chief and produces a yet greater chieftain, Quanah Parker—and Noble Savagery—somehow the Indian life is basically preferable to civilization.

Other forms of the captive narrative have assumed their own stereotypes. Few were written by the subject him- or herself, therefore, most of the accounts are filled with a kind of secondhand sensation, calculated to thrill the reader rather than enlighten him. Virtually all the captive narratives concentrate on the terrors and degradation of captivity, the barbaric inhumanities of the captors, and the inferiority of the red men. Very few stories make any attempt to give an unprejudiced account of Indian social customs or beliefs—things we now consider valuable but which, a century ago, were thought of as irrelevant or, worse, indecent. It is not hard to understand why this was true. The Indians, at the time most captive narratives were produced, were a problem of another sort, not anthropological. They were a social nuisance which had value only when it was eliminated.

But of all the captive narratives, I believe the finest story is Herman Lehmann's. Taken, at age eleven, from the family farm in Mason County, Texas, by the Apaches, Herman underwent the brutal realities of Indian life and became a warrior, eventually leaving the Apaches and joining the Comanches. When the Kwahadi remnant he was a part of surrendered and went to the reservation, Herman was among the most reluctant to go. And when he was returned to his white family he was reluctant to stay. Yet Herman did stay and lived to be an old man in the white world without ever giving up the red. He became a bridge between an ungraspably remote age and our own—from the flint knife almost to the atomic bomb in time. He was ancient-modern in a way a Western man cannot ever be again.

One of the main differences between Herman's story and that of the other captives is that Herman's is told good-naturedly. Although Herman himself didn't put the story down (in fact, from my investigations I have come to believe Herman could scarcely read or write) his sense of humor and fairness must have been so evident that those who wrote the story for him couldn't keep from stressing these qualities in their manuscripts. His disability at reading may help account for the alarming contradictions, errors and misapplied assumptions of the 1899 version of his story. While the 1927 version is more carefully done, it too has parts one feels reluctant to accept as Herman's own account.

The purpose of this present volume, however, is not merely to edit or rewrite the first two. I hope to have created a third Herman Lehmann story, utilizing the others but becoming something separate and individual, involving a comparative study of the texts but with additional accounts of specific events and the evidence of more accurate or later history.

Herman Lehmann's story was first told in an 1899 publication written by Jonathan H. Jones, who later became a well-respected judge of Mason County. It was published by Johnson Brothers Printing Company of San Antonio. The cover bore the name *Indianology*; however, the title page carried a wholly different name, in that finely effusive style of pre-twentieth century literature:

> *A Condensed History of the Apache and Comanche Indian*
> *Tribes. For Amusement and General Knowledge Prepared From*
> *the General Conversation of Herman Lehmann, Willie Lehmann,*
> *Mrs. Mina Keyser, Mrs. A. J. Buchmeyer and Others.*

The fact that the book is in no way a history of either tribe makes little difference. It is a captive narrative done in the manner which the time dictated and is valuable for this reason, or despite it.

The second edition, or version, came in 1927 with J. Marvin Hunter, a publisher of historical magazines in Texas, as amanuensis. While the recital is calmer and the prose more readable, this edition lacks a great deal of investigative conclusion and includes various inaccuracies. Again we have one name used on the cover and as the running title throughout the book, *Nine Years With the Indians*, and another on the title page: *Nine Years Among the Indians 1870–1879*. Either way seems to be in error. Herman was captured May 16, 1870, and returned May 12, 1878, according to family records.

Hunter modestly lists himself only as editor of this edition, which was published by the venerable Austin firm of Von Boeckmann-Jones. Forty-odd years later the company reported that orders for the book still came in, although it had been out-of-print since the early 1930s.

The 1927 version, which I shall henceforth refer to as *Nine Years*, has generally been the book in mind when a reference has been made to Herman's experiences. The 1899 version is not only quite rare but seems not to have excited any bibliographers. Outside of the introduction to the 1927 edition I have found no references to it. That introduction, by the way, calls it *Indianology* and gives it much too brief a dismissal, editor Hunter noting merely, "from this book I have obtained valuable material which is used in this volume. But most of the facts were related to me by the ex-captive, who, at this date, May 28, 1927, is with me and telling me of his harrowing and hair-raising experiences."

Indianology, or as I shall call it from now on, *A Condensed History*, is owed a much bigger debt than that. Virtually all of *Nine Years* was derived from the earlier narrative.

The 1927 edition is also scarce. J. Frank Dobie termed it "the finest of the captive narratives of the Southwest" in his *Life and Literature of the Southwest* (1952), but adds nothing to that simple statement. Sister Agatha's *Texas Prose* (1935) doesn't mention it, and it is not listed in any of Ramon Adams's three western bibliographies; *Six Guns and Saddle Leather* (1954), *The Rampaging Herd* (1959), and *Burs Under the Saddle* (1964). William Morrison's *Texas Book Prices* records one sale of *Nine Years* but nothing on *A Condensed History* or *Indianology*.

There is another, smaller item which concerns itself to some extent with Herman Lehmann's story. It is a 24-page pamphlet by Henry W. Buchmeyer, printed by Triangle Publishing Company, Dallas (n.d), titled *The Life and Hardships of My Mother, Augusta Johanna Buchmeyer*. This account, by one of Herman's half-brothers, offers few additions to the story of the captivity but it does give some dates and a great deal more on the history of Herman's mother and her parents, not all of it accurate.

It is of interest to note that in 1963 the *Frontier Times* magazine, a vestigial survivor of J. Marvin Hunter's publications, carried a two-part version of *Nine Years*, edited for brevity but without any factual corrections or additions.

A major importance of the Herman Lehmann story is that it gives a realistic picture of Indian life. It is realistic, at least, to the point that it accepts the Indian way of doing things as having as much validity as the white world's way. The reader gets to know the routine of Indian life and what motivated the Indians so that the continual raid, kill, steal, flee cycle becomes more than just a dull horror story. It becomes explanatory and, in a statistical sense, enlightening.

And although Judge Jones's book is a maddening collection of inappropriate poetry, awkward Victorian circumlocutions, and nice-nellyisms, it also contains the best examples we have of sexual experiences by white captives. It was unthinkable, certainly, for a restored white wife or daughter to admit she had had sex with Indian bucks, although we know very well that this was most likely the first thing that happened to a captured female. And it is just as likely that what began as rape became accepted as part of their slave existence by the women and girls who survived. The white Texans could never quite be reconciled to the obvious sexual facts about Cynthia Ann Parker, even though her relationship to her Indian husband was as "legal" as tribal custom could make it.

But Herman, being a male, could be more explicit. He tells of several sexual incidents among the tribesmen and relates some of his own affairs with Indian girls. One of his stories is of a quality to make it a candidate for Boccaccio or Chaucer. Herman even hints that he was forced to practice what might have been considered, in white society, some form of homosexual activity for his captor. It is from these flashes of reality that the reader comes to understand that Herman is not just another frontiersman with an adventure story, but a frank, free and naive spirit—a truly unusual personality on or off history's pages.

Herman has another virtue which is not always present in early Texas memoirists. He is honest. He is not infallible—the Indians win a suspiciously large number of times when they engage in battles with the whites—but he is not reluctant to cast himself as a murdering, scalping redskin. He does not attempt to appear heroic at any time.

There are inconsistencies in Herman's stories, nowhere more so than in the use of Indian names. It is hard to say whether the inconsistency is Herman's or his collaborator's. For example, in the 1899 edition he calls his Apache captor-father "Chivatateto" but in the 1927 version the name becomes "Carnoviste." This switching of names—not just an adjustment of phonetic spellings—goes right down the line. I have generally accepted the 1927 name system because it is more inclusive and also because in the instances where historical checking is possible it seems more accurate. For an instance of the latter, in the 1899 edition the famed Apache chief is called Victory instead of Victorio. In another example, Herman's Indian lover is named Willamena (or Willamina) in the 1899 version and Ete in the later work. I chose Ete for ethnic reasons, if nothing else! But the 1899 edition carries its inconsistency with names past all reason. Herman's owner is given four different names—never with an explanation—sometimes using two or three different names for him in the same chapter. It goes without saying that Jones is also capricious in the spelling of all the names in his book, both white and Indian. The only possible explanation is that Herman couldn't read and neither Jones nor anyone else ever proofread the book before it was printed and bound.

In the Jones version of the mother's story there is the rather amazing error of having her refer, in the first person, to her then present husband as "Mr. Lehmann," not once but several times. As Mr. Lehmann had been dead for more than twenty years and her husband was Phillip Buchmier and had been for many years, we must also put this down to a complete lack of editing or proofreading by Jones.

Even in the matter of the names which Herman says he was called by the Indians we find confusion. In parts of the 1899 book he is addressed as "Alaman" by the Apaches and in other parts he is called "Enda" or "Indot." The Comanches call him Montechina (or Montechena, or Montechema), and at Fort Sill, after he had surrendered and come to the reservation, he was known as Charley Ross— after a white boy from Kansas who Herman was thought, by the troops, to be.

Alaman is fairly easy to figure out, it being the Spanish word (rendered phonetically in English) for German—*alemán*. Herman being of German descent and speaking only German when captured, this name is plausible. However, Indot or Enda pose other problems. I don't believe this is what the Apaches called him, even though Herman says it was. I think this may have been what the Apaches called him *after* he had left their tribe and become a Comanche. John R. Swanton's authoritative book *The Indian Tribes of North America* gives a list of names by which the other tribes called the Comanches and "Indá" was the Jicarilla Apache word that meant Comanche. Since Herman had been captured by a Jicarilla band, it seems logical that after he left them they should call him "Indá" (variously rendered), or Comanche, because they saw him many other times, especially on the reservation. Herman says that Montechina is Comanche for "white boy." At any rate, this was the name the Comanches called him, as evidenced by letters written by the tribe to Washington on Herman's behalf.

There is a certain charm to the effusiveness and digressions of Judge Jones in the 1899 edition. However, one also wearies of the tiresome string of prolixity and pietism which clogs it and the ridiculous pedanticism which, for example, has a wild Apache warrior turning to Herman, on the occasion of Herman's first sight of a buffalo, and saying, "See alaman? Bos americanus!" Spanish we can accept, but Latin . . . ?

Herman, who candidly admitted that at the time of his capture he had had little instruction in the Christian religion—had never even been to Sunday school, horror of horrors—has an insufferable number of pseudo-pious sentimentalities thrust into his defenseless mouth by his 1899 co-author. This is even more egregious than ordinarily because Herman repeatedly expresses his Indian religious beliefs throughout the narrative. Well, religious hypocrisy is nothing new to Texas history. The times may have demanded it, in Jones's view.

Herman was conscientious about dates and facts where he could be. The Indians, of course, kept no calendars and knew little of what was going on in the white world.

There are some peculiarities of the 1899 edition which are part of Jones's style. He uses the word "camps" for "camp," for instance. He must have had some reason for this, because the camps-camp business occurs dozens of times. Jones also uses words in archaic and rare senses—"recruit" in the sense of recuperating, for example. I have left a couple of these in for flavor. Incidentally, most of the drawings that illustrate the 1899 edition, outside of family portraits, are as inaccurate and inappropriate as the poetry, so that one is convinced that the illustrator never so much as saw the manuscript before doing the artwork.

But with all its flaws the 1899 edition contributes greatly to our understanding of the Herman Lehmann story and we may thank the memory of Judge Jones, despite the unkind remarks I have made.

Throughout this book I have inserted my own running commentary, my intention being to clarify or illustrate and not simply to contradict or fuss. I have also declined, after much consideration, to put footnotes in the narrative portion of the book, trusting to the accompanying commentary to show sources of outside information. I have not mentioned such obvious reference works as the *Handbook of Texas*, the *Texas Almanac*, or various editions of the Spanish dictionary.

Herman Lehmann's story, I think, goes far beyond the standard captive narrative. It reveals the terrible frustration of a people coming to realize that they are doomed. Not just their way of life, but themselves. It also gives us incidental insights into the incredible carelessness and ignorance of some of our pioneer forefathers—the stupidity of innumerable parties who forgot to carry guns in Indian country, who blundered their way into doom by sheer perversity or arrogance. Herman wastes little sympathy on them in his story and seldom do we, as we read.

In following Herman's accounts of intertribal wars and hatreds, we may also see that if the Indians of North America had had any semblance of organization or understanding of the broad social community they might easily have kept the white man away from their hunting grounds for several more decades, or possibly have thrown him off the continent to begin with. But the end of the American Indian story, as even Herman eventually accepts it, was inevitable.

History is what comes to pass; it is not what might have been . . .

A. C. GREENE

San Cristobal
Austin, Texas

Herman Lehmann

Introduction

IN 1842 a group of titled Germans, motivated by democratic ideals despite their personal aristocratic notions, formed the *Adelsverein*, or Society of Noblemen.[1] Their purpose was simple: to purchase land in the Republic of Texas. Their grand plan was more majestic. They wanted to offer the freedom of the New World to worthy European families by means of a colonization scheme. There is evidence they quite possibly hoped eventually to see a separate Germanic state set up which would act as a gateway to trade with Mexico.[2]

Like most such dreams, this one was much too unrealistic. The *Verein* members knew little of the true nature of Texas and the enormous costs involved in establishing settlers there. But by 1844, despite some extraordinary instances of bad luck, worse judgment, meager funding, incompetence, and local chicanery, the *Verein* was bringing hundreds of families to Texas under auspices of its *Verein zum Schutz deutscher Einwanderer in Texas* (Society for the Protection of German Immigrants to Texas).[3]

Although the *Verein's* original intention was to settle a huge tract it had bought called the Fischer-Miller Grant, the Europeans soon discovered this would have to wait. The grant, between the Llano and Colorado rivers, amounted to raw Comanche hunting grounds, not only dangerous but too remote for supplies or marketing. Therefore, to take care of the incoming families, a smaller piece of land was bought at the juncture of the Comal and Guadalupe rivers, some one hundred fifty miles closer to Texas civilization. On this location, in the spring of 1845, the city of New Braunfels was established, to become the first stopping place for most of the *Verein* immigrants.[4] In May, 1846, John O. Meusebach, commissioner-general of the *Verein*, established Fredericksburg as a halfway place between New Braunfels and the Fischer-Miller Grant.[5]

On October 12, 1846, Jacob Adams, age 40, and his family sailed from Bremen on the ship *Johanna* among the one hundred twenty-five *Verein* immigrants bound for Texas.[6] The Adams family, when applying for a certificate of colonization, had listed Culm, Pomerania (now Chelmno, Poland) as its home.[7] The wife and mother, Petronelle, was age 30 and there were five children: Augusta Johanna, age 13; August Jacob, 11; Petronelle Dorothe, 8; Emilie Marie, 2; and Gustav Adolph, three months. All were listed as being members of the Evangelical Lutheran Church.[8] The voyage was a miserable one and family tradition says the mother died at sea.[9] The bereaved family reached Galveston on December 22[10] and transferred to a smaller ship to sail to Carlshafen (Indianola).

The immigrants had little idea what faced them on the Texas frontier and most of them hadn't the money to spend for arms and equipment to make survival easier. Another family tradition says that on the one hundred fifty mile journey from the coast to New Braunfels several deaths occurred when the hungry strangers ate poisonous berries growing along the trail.[11]

Despite her age, Augusta had shouldered the responsibility of mothering the family. They settled near New Braunfels and not long after, again according to family tradition, Jacob Adams too died.[12] The children were split up and sent to live with and to work for other families.

In September, 1849, Augusta married Moritz (or Maurice) Lehmann.[13] Moritz was the son of Gottfried and Anna Lehmann, of Laubnitz, Prussia, who had arrived in Texas just a few weeks before the Adams family. The Lehmanns brought two other sons and a daughter with them and they were also accompanied by Gottfried's twin brother, Gottlieb, and his wife, and a single brother, Samuel Lehmann.[14] All the Lehmanns had moved to Fredericksburg by 1847.

Several years after their marriage, Augusta and Moritz moved to Squaw Creek in southeastern Mason County. There their son F. Herman[15] was born on June 5, 1859,[16] the middle child of seven. Not long after Herman's birth, Moritz became very ill, and by the time of his death in 1864 Augusta had assumed the role of family provider, working in the fields as well as keeping the house.

In 1866 she married Phillip (or Philipp) Buchmier (or Buchmeier), a stonemason.[17] Family tradition says he knew nothing about farming, so Augusta continued to oversee the fields while Phillip seems to have been rather successful at his craft.[18] Six children were born to this marriage.[19]

The Lehmann-Buchmier family spoke only German and saw few people because the farm was situated several miles off the only road through the area—that between Fort Mason and Fredericksburg.[20] The Civil War had heightened this separateness, for most of the German settlers around either remained loyal to the United States or avoided having much relations with the Confederacy. Loyal Valley, the nearby community which became the home of Meusebach after the war,[21] got its name from the attitude of the residents toward the federal government.[22]

The Lehmann children lived pretty much the life of all frontier youngsters in that farming and ranching area. There was no school for them to attend and no neighbor to play with so they hunted and explored the bluffs, creeks and hills around their home. Herman once broke a leg tumbling from a high cliff on Squaw Creek.[23] His mother remarked, on another occasion, that a rattlesnake's rattles, worn on a hat or bonnet, would ward off headaches. A few days later, Herman and his younger sister, Mina, presented their mother with an impressive set of rattles. She asked where they had killed such a big snake but Herman told her they hadn't been able to kill it, that he had held the rattler with a forked stick while Mina cut off the rattles.[24]

Another family story involved Mina and Adolph, a brother older than Herman. When their mother told them that heaven was a place where one found everything his heart desired, the children decided this meant heaven was full of candy and apples. They devised a system to obtain some of the delicacies. Adolph would kill Mina who, being a good child, would automatically go to heaven. Then she could throw down the candy and apples to her brother on earth. Anxious to get their scheme underway, Adolph had Mina lie on her back while he brought a large rock smashing down on her stomach. Hurt, but not badly injured, Mina leaped up screaming and decided heaven wasn't worth it.[25]

Herman, speaking of those times, later said: "Schools were scarce in West Texas in those days, so I grew up there to be eleven years old without even so much as knowing my letters. I could not speak English and never went to school a day. I had never been to church or Sunday school and had seen very few people, and when visitors came to our house, I ran away and hid. Thus I spent the first eleven years of my existence."[26]

But then his life changed suddenly and completely, and nothing was ever again the same for Herman Lehmann.

---

[1] Rudolph L. Biesele, *The History of the German Settlements in Texas 1831–1861*, 65–69.

[2] John A. Hawgood, *The Tragedy of German-America*, 166–178.

[3] Chester W. and Ethel Harder Geue, *A New Land Beckoned*, 5–7.

[4] *Ibid.*, 8.

[5] Irene Marschall King, *John O. Meusebach, German Colonizer in Texas*, 74.

[6] German Immigration Contracts, General Land Offce, Austin. (For alphabetized listing of families see also Geues, *A New Land Beckoned*, 73–164.)

[7] Solms-Braunfels Archives (transcripts), Vol. 15, List 52, University of Texas Archives, Austin.

[8] *Ibid.*, Vol. 6, 75–77.

[9] Henry Buchmeyer, *The Life and Hardships of My Mother, Augusta Johanna Buchmeyer*, 3.

[10] German Immigration Contracts.

[11] Buchmeyer, *The Life and Hardships of My Mother*, 4.

[12] New Braunfels church records show a Jacob Adams as witness to a family wedding in 1860 but this is possibly the son, Augustus Jacob Adams.

[13] Buchmeyer, *The Life and Hardships of My Mother*, 5.

[14] German Immigration Contracts.

[15] Name on gravestone, Loyal Valley, Texas, cemetery.

[16] Jonathan H. Jones, *A Condensed History of the Apache and Comanche Indian Tribes*, 10.

[17] *Philipp* and *Buchmeier* are spellings from gravestone, Loyal Valley cemetery. *Buchmeyer* seems to have been used by the family after the turn of the century. Prior to that there was no consistent spelling.

[18] Buchmeyer, *The Life and Hardships of My Mother*, 7.

[19] *Ibid.*, 7.

[20] Jones, *A Condensed History*, 12.

[21] King, *John O. Meusebach*, 163.

[22] W. P. Webb and H. B. Carroll (eds.), *Handbook of Texas*, Vol. II.

[23] Jones, *A Condensed History*, 12.

[24] Buchmeyer, *The Life and Hardships of My Mother*, 8.

[25] *Ibid.*

[26] Jones, *A Condensed History*, 12.

THE LAST CAPTIVE

Chiwat, Herman's captor and Apache "father"

1

ON MAY 16, 1870, my brother Willie Lehmann, my two sisters, Caroline and Gusta, and I, were sent out into the field about three hundred yards from our house to scare the birds away from the new wheat. I was nearly eleven years old, Willie was just past eight, and Caroline was just a little girl. Gusta, no more than two years old, was being taken care of by the rest of us.

We sat down in the field to play and were absorbed in our games when the first thing we knew we were surrounded by Indians. We saw their painted faces and oh, how frightened we were. Some of us pulled for the house, but Willie was caught right where he was sitting. They chased me for a distance and caught me. I yelled and fought manfully when the chief, whom I came to know as Carnoviste, laid hands on me. He slapped me, choked me, beat me, tore my clothes off, threw away my hat—the last one I had for more than eight years—and I thought he was going to kill me. I locked my fingers in his long, black hair, and oh, how I did wool him! I kicked him in the stomach, I bit him, and I almost succeeded in getting loose when another Indian, Chiwat, who had seized Caroline, dropped her and hurried to Carnoviste's assistance. Caroline immediately ran toward the house and had reached the fence surrounding the field before the Indians realized she was gone. However, just as she sprang over the fence the Indian who had been holding her raised his rifle and fired. Although the shots were wild, Caroline fainted from fright and fell to the ground. The Indians had no time to dally with her so they passed on, thinking she was dead, and they often told me she was killed, and I believed it for years, until I came home. Baby Gusta must have been overlooked, otherwise they would certainly have killed her.

Between the two Indians, I was quickly overcome. Carnoviste caught me by the head and Chiwat by the feet, and they conveyed me to a rock fence nearby. They gave me a sling and my face and breast plowed up the rocks and sand on the other side.

I was so completely stunned by the jolt that I could not scramble to my feet before the two Indians had cleared the fence and were upon me. They soon had me securely bound, and I was seated astraddle a forked stick firmly attached to the back of a bucking broncho and so strapped and lashed that though the last bit of life were extinct, I would still remain astraddle of that pony. I was naked, with the exception of the cords and straps that held me on, and as we raced through the brush and undergrowth, my flesh was pricked and torn by the thorns of the catclaw, mesquite and cactus. The sun, which had just passed its zenith, blistered my naked back and limbs and I felt death, just then, would have been a relief to me. My brother, Willie, was in the same distressing predicament as I, but he didn't murmur.

3

We crossed Squaw Creek west of Loyal Valley and went up on the bluff and signaled, then came down, recrossed the creek and drove the horses, which the party had stolen, east. The band went through Loyal Valley and on to Moseley's Mountains. There they located some more horses down in the valley. All of the Indians except Carnoviste went for the horses, and he was left to guard us two boys. The Indians down in the valley fired several shots and made quite a noise, and Carnoviste went over to a point to see what was happening. Willie and I tried to run away, but Willie was so afraid that he was unable to run fast, and Carnoviste soon caught us. He beat us and gagged us so we could not scream, and threatened by his countenance and actions to torture us more if we made another attempt to get away.

Soon the rest of the party returned with the stolen horses, having frightened away the whites. We turned west and traveled for a ways, and the Indians picked up a gray horse and a sorrel. One had William Kidd's brand and the other Mr. Stone's. Then we turned northwest, passed by Keyser's ranch and on to the Llano River.

At the river they took me from the pony, tied me securely, and hobbled Willie. The Indians all lay down on the ground to rest, but they neither made a fire nor ate anything here. Willie and I had had nothing to eat since breakfast early that morning. Late in the night we were aroused and set out up Willow Creek, passing to the right of Mason, where the band scattered out and Willie and I were separated. The Indians sent back scouts to see if we were being followed and to destroy all signs of our march.

Carnoviste had me with him. We found a young calf lying down. The Indian made signs for me to catch the calf, sicking me on it with the same sounds you would make to a dog. I was afraid not to go, so after the young bovine I went. The little fellow butted me over, but I went for him again and succeeded in catching him. Carnoviste jumped down off his horse, stabbed the calf then cut it open. He plunged his knife into the calf's stomach, got out the soured milk it had drunk, and ate that nasty stuff with zest. I turned away disgusted and sick at the stomach. He made signs for me to eat some, but I made an effort to escape doing so. He grabbed me and soused my head into that calf's paunch, rubbing that nauseous stuff all over my face, in my eyes, up my nose, into my ears and forced some down my throat. He held my nose and made me swallow, but the stuff would not stay on my stomach and I vomited. He then cut out the kidneys and liver and compelled me to eat them while they were warm with the animal heat. I would throw the mess up, but he would pick it up and make me swallow the same dose again —and again I would vomit. He would soak it in the warm blood and make me swallow it down again. The blood settled my stomach, and he loaded me with warm dung. Then Carnoviste took me to a hole of water, washed my face, put me on the horse with him, and we went to rejoin the other Indians of our party.

AS IS GENERALLY THE CASE when several eye-witnesses describe the same event, there are contradictions, confusions and additional facts offered in the various accounts of the capture of Herman and Willie Lehmann.

The version given to this point is mainly taken from Herman's recollections in *A Condensed History* and in *Nine Years*. But even these offer discrepancies. Herman, in the earlier book, says Caroline picked up the baby, Gusta, and ran toward the house, but he never mentions Gusta again. In *Nine Years* he says Gusta was being taken care of by Caroline and that she left the baby and ran toward the house.

Willie, in a newspaper interview given when he was seventy years old, said of the capture: "I had a baby on my lap [when the Indians appeared]." Willie fled and the Indians picked up the child "but when they had gone a short distance one came back after me, leaving the baby behind unharmed."

Henry Buchmeyer, in *The Life and Hardships of My Mother*, says Gusta was being cared for "by the other children" and adds only that she "was overlooked" by the Indians. The details of Caroline's escape also differ in the three accounts. Neither *A Condensed History* nor *Nine Years* mentions the fence but it figures in both Henry's and Mrs. Buchmeyer's account. Incidentally, although nobody bothers to say so, can't we take for granted Gusta is a short form of her mother's name, Augusta?

I have taken a few facts from other accounts and added them to Herman's story where there is no reason to challenge them. For example, the distance of the wheat field from the house and the date of the month. Herman, telling of his capture, merely says it was May, or as Jonathan Jones, in a singularly inappropriate use of the cliche, puts it, "the merry month of May, 1870."

There are interesting, and conflicting, accounts of what the mother did at the time of the capture. First, from the chapter, "A Mother's Experience" in *A Condensed History*:

Rushing to the door, I saw they [the children] were pursued by men whom I supposed to be cow-boys. I was by my oldest daughter [Mina?] who said, "Mamma, I think it is Indians." My husband, my daughter and myself rushed toward them, but alas!

Too late, too late! . . . I fell, overcome by the thought that my poor children were gone. . . ." (Here Judge Jones tosses in a mixed-metaphor about the children having no one to care for or protect them "except the All-seeing Power of God" which seems to nullify his many sanctimonious allegations that "God is all one needs, His power alone can save," *ad inf.*)

I was carried into the house and lain on my bed where I remained for seven weeks. My husband raised the alarm, and all the neighbors were assembled in pursuit of the Indians, and all the forts were notified, but all in vain. . . . Nothing could comfort me until I happened to think of a conversation I had overheard a few days before he [*sic*] was stolen. The children were all talking about what they would do if the Indians were to get them. Some said "they would just cry themselves to death," but Herman said, "I would not; I would try to be friendly to them until I got a good chance to run away, and then I'd come home." This childish prattle was the only comfort I could find.

Henry Buchmeyer tells it thusly:

MOTHER was at the house when the attack occurred. As soon as she heard the screams and shouts of the struggle, she ran frantically to the wheat field to help. She was half-way to the fence when the shot intended for Caroline rang out. By the time Mother reached the field it was too late to help. . . .

Mother desperately attempted to find help to follow the Indians and save her children. Father and the older boys, however, were working at the time. The hired man refused to help; he hurried to his own home to protect it. Mother was helpless; she could not leave the homestead to find other assistance for fear the raiding party would return. She was powerless to attempt to rescue her boys until Father returned. When Phillip came home, he attempted to pick up the trail of the Indians, but it was too late. Even if the trail could be found, Phillip had no one to help him fight the Apache band. Indeed if the marauders were forced to fight they would probably kill Herman and Willie—if the two were still alive.

So it may be seen that the stories, while they differ, are not irreconcilable.

Two Apaches at about the time Herman was captured

2

AFTER TRAVELING SOME DISTANCE, we went up on a hill and made a big fire. Indians began to come in from all quarters but they approached cautiously. They had captured quite a bunch of horses. When they discovered our identity they drew ropes around the horses and sat down to a hearty meal of raw and barbecued bull.

The other six Indians, who had Willie with them, had gone farther north. We destroyed all signs as nearly as we could, sent back scouts, then proceeded northward, too. There was water all along the way but we were not allowed to drink, although I was real thirsty. We scattered again, Carnoviste again taking charge of me. He took the cartridges out of his pistol and gave it to me to see if I knew how to shoot. We played with the weapons for some time, and I began to think the old boy was a pretty jolly companion, although I could not exactly understand him— and then he would beat me.

The entire band of twelve suddenly came together and a consultation was held. Again they divided into two parties, six, Willie with them, going north. Six went west; I was in that company. That afternoon our party stole nine more horses. When we came together again, the other party had not captured anything.

They selected a wild pony, roped him and caught me and tried to put me on that wild animal. I screamed and the pony reared. I was afraid of him and he shied from me, and by a continuity of effort we stayed apart and baffled the Indians' skill, patience and strength. The pony fought and so did I, and confusion reigned for a while. Even the Indians failed this time, but they were rather talkative for a while after we left camp.

We traveled together, thirsty and dry, until we came to a pond; muddy, full of flies, bugs, and laden with the essence of frog. The Indians dismounted, unbound us and helped us down. They pulled up a lot of nice, clean grass, spread it over the water and used it as a strainer. I went off a little way from the Indians and threw myself on the ground and began to suck up the muddy water through the debris, and was enjoying the cool, refreshing breeze that was then blowing— wetting my palate and thinking of home—when stealthy old Carnoviste came up to me, soused my head into the mud, and every one of the tribe laughed, while I secretly swore vengeance.

From this water hole we went north, and about 4 o'clock in the afternoon we killed a steer and made a fire on a hill. The Indians were very careful what kind of wood, and the quantity, they used lest the smoke ascend in too great a cloud and thus reveal to the white people our presence.

My Indian master, Carnoviste, staked out his horse and escorted me back some distance. He had a mirror made of a bright piece of steel (the other scouts had similar mirrors) and this he used to throw the reflection of the sun in a certain manner. These flashing signs were signaled from one to another of the scouts back down the line, and an answer came that all was well.

Carnoviste motioned to me, but I did not understand him. I went forward a little way and came back. He motioned and growled again. I went again and returned. Then he got mad that I did not understand, and he pulled his pistol and pointed it at me. He even cocked it and leveled on me, but I still could not understand what he wanted.

Finally, in disgust at my stupidity, he lowered his pistol and went for his horse, and I understood then that this was what he had wanted me to do. He threw me up on the horse's back, jumped on in front of me, and we rode to join the others on the bank of a small stream. Willie was there. Our sores were washed and dressed, the old hide and blood peeled off. We were painted up like Indians and placed on the same horses we had ridden the day before, between the forked sticks that made the Indian saddle, and doomed to another naked ride in the hot sun. The reader can imagine the sufferings of a child who had, up to a day before, been tenderly cared for by a kind father and loved by a devoted mother, now cut off from all hope of recovery and not knowing but that each moment was to be the last. His face blistered by the scorching sun, the skin all peeled off his back and breast, his feet and hands tied, and where he rubbed against that forked-stick saddle the meat was worn away nearly to the bone. Could the sufferings of Job have been greater?

3

WITH A DROVE OF HORSES we were traveling northwestward, and on the fifth day after our capture, while near Lipan Creek in the Concho territory, we ran into a party of rangers while they were dismounted at a water hole, watering their stock or preparing to camp.

We were not discovered by the rangers, and the Indians hastily withdrew and turned back the way we had come, leaving the drove of horses, and lit out at top speed. One of the Indians was walking because he had a sore leg and it pained him to ride. This Indian jumped on the horse which Willie was riding and followed the other fleeing Indians. The horse began to show signs of giving out when this Indian threw Willie off into some brush and continued his flight after his comrades. He urged the horse on for some distance, when the poor animal fell exhausted and another Indian went back and took the warrior up behind him and they hurried on. Willie had been abandoned.

After we had run for many miles, the Indians keeping me in the lead, they finally halted and held a pow-wow. As they had lost their herd of horses, they decided to go back into the settlements and get some more, as it would not speak well for them to go back to the tribe without some stolen horses. Accordingly, ten of the number took the back trail while two, Chiwat and Pinero, agreed to take me and pull for Indian headquarters, somewhere to the northwest. I was still tied to the horse and riding very uncomfortably, and as we rode forward my thoughts were on my little brother. I did not know what had become of him, and I feared our captors had killed him. I wept bitter tears, and oh, how lonesome I felt, and I yearned to know what had happened to him. Something seemed to tell me he had escaped, but how on earth could he, just a little boy eight years old, ever hope to find his way so far back home across that howling wilderness? And I thought of home, my happy home, and of my dear mother and my little sisters. These unhappy thoughts occupied my mind during the weary hours as we rode along, and I was downcast and sad.

FOR THE REST of his captivity, Herman was never sure what had happened to his young brother, Willie. As he says, he felt that Willie had escaped, and there was no evidence that the Apaches, at least, had killed him. They would certainly not have hesitated to tell Herman if they had.

Willie told his own story on his capture and escape in *A Condensed History*. There are some differing points between his and Herman's recollections, which is proper enough when we recognize the difference in their ages at the time and the even vaster differences in their experiences over the intervening years. We may also ask ourselves if Willie, telling his story long after Herman's return, isn't perhaps a bit more "understanding" of his treatment at the hands of the red men because he knows how Herman feels about his red brothers.

At any rate, here is Willie speaking, telling us what Herman was not to know until years later:

THAT DAY in May 1870, about twelve o'clock as we sat in the wheat, someone said: "Look at the Indians!"

We all jumped up and some ran, but I was too scared to run much. I was caught before I realized my danger. I was placed on a horse behind a warrior and I saw Herman put on a horse. We went east in a fast gallop over the rocks and the forked-stick saddle in front of me gored me. We ascended a hill, or mountain, but I don't know how far we had gone. Two Indians (one with a bright silver breastplate on his chest and a big rooster feather in his cap: this was Victoria) went forward afoot. They traveled in a zigzag manner as if they were trailing something. They went on out of sight. Another Indian climbed a tree and watched. He had field glasses that no doubt he had bought from the Mexicans, or stolen. These foot Indians came running back and got more bows and arrows and went again. They caught two horses—a sorrel with a star in his forehead and a gray.

While they were standing near a little live oak thicket talking a white man passed right near us. The Indians scattered and rode away, but watched and tried to cut the man off as he went around the point of a hill. This man was riding a gray horse and leading a dun. He got off of the gray and tried to bridle the dun, but the dun seemed to be wild and would not take the bits. He remounted the gray and rode, jumping over rocks and down steep places. The Indians tried to cut him off as he went around another hill but he passed before we got there, never realizing how near death he had been all the while.

We rode some more, then all the Indians except one left Herman and me. We were on a high hill and the Indians were fighting down in the valley. Our guard went out to watch them and Herman and I started to run away. The Indian came back to us and put Herman on a horse and me up behind the Indian himself and we rode down the mountain, rejoined the rest and all rode away. The other Indians had captured several horses of Stark Moseley.

Herman was on a sorrel horse and he would ride out of the herd and just leave the

9

whole crowd and circle around. But the horse would just go so far from the Indians and then he would come back every time. Had this horse been manageable, Herman could have left the Indians easily.

After riding fast for a little while, they stopped and tried to put me on a wild horse, but the pony was too wiry, so they failed. The first day the Indians killed several hogs (which meat they would not eat) and came up to a yearling and ran it, one Indian on each side, and lanced it as they ran. I can remember seeing the blood on the grass and ground. We rode up and the Indians stuck their spears in its little tender feet to see it flinch. They tortured the little fellow to death.

After the fight down in the valley I could not see the Indian with the silvery breast-plate, and I supposed that he was killed, but he may have merely taken his armor off. I never counted the Indians for I was too small to think of that.

We crossed a river after dark and camped. Herman was tied, but I was just turned loose. Our horses were corralled. We got up the next morning and started before day. I don't know which away we traveled, for I was lost all the time.

The Indian I was riding behind gave me a small, peculiarly made cap. It had ears standing straight up over it like a frightened jack-rabbit. It was made of fur or some curious substance. He stopped and put a small pair of moccasins on my feet. The Indians separated and the one I was with killed a panther and several domestic animals. He ate raw meat, but never made me eat any of it, although he offered me some. He never did beat me or abuse me, but he often frightened me.

Some of the Indians had on shirts and navajoes [blankets] around the loins, but after we came together again my Indian motioned to his breast and then at my shirt. (I had on a new shirt.) I could not understand him, but Herman said, "He wants your shirt." I pulled it off and handed it to the Indian. He tried to put it on but could not. He laughed all the time. I took the shirt and put it back on.

We rode on and separated again. My Indian rode back and dismounted, cleaned his pistol and primed his arrows. While we were sitting there, I saw two white men pass on

horses. I don't think the Indian saw them. He went up on a high point and looked around and came back and pointed at his horse. I walked out to his horse and came back. He looked mad, drew his gun, scolded and growled, while I was scared to death and had no idea what he wanted. Eventually I saw he wanted me to untie his horse, but he did it himself, helped me up then sprang up himself, and soon we were gone. That night we camped on a hillside, and I rolled away down the hill from the Indian, but crawled back. The next morning I heard chickens crowing nearby, so we must have been near a settlement or a house.

The next day we were riding along with the other Indians and one of my moccasins dropped off. I thought sure they would beat me for that. I began punching the Indian in front of me, but I could not get his attention for some time. When I did I pointed down at my bare foot. This Indian and the one who was riding by us laughed and talked and looked at my foot and laughed again and again.

Several cattle were killed that day and the Indians ate the meat raw. That night we camped in a thicket, for it rained—no, I believe it was just thick cloudy and looked like rain.

The next day they tried to put Herman on a wild horse but failed. I think maybe they were just scaring him. That evening we came to an old muddy pool of water and we all got down to drink. An Indian sneaked up and pushed my head in the mud and laughed. Herman was treated likewise.

Our sores were greased and we were painted. They had old black looking rocks that they would spit on, run their fingers over the spit and smear the rock on our faces. It would give us the savage hue, a kind of brightly yellowish red. They cooked us some meat and we rode on, pretty tired, stiff, and sore. That night we camped near some water.

I think it was the sixth day we were going leisurely along. One Indian had a crippled leg and could not ride on horseback without irritating the place, so he was walking.

Suddenly soldiers came upon us and stampeded the whole outfit. I was on a little brown pony. This Indian on foot tried to catch one of the loose horses—several had long ropes on them—and failed. So he

10

jumped up in front of me. The other Indians had left us, but we were going at a breakneck speed. The Indian goaded the pony but we got further behind because of the load. The Indian tried to crowd me off, but I held on tight. He kept pushing me and finally got me off in spite of my tenacity.

I fell among the rocks and lay there, but if any soldiers passed me I never saw or heard them. I got up and wandered through the chaparral, expecting to be torn to pieces by panthers or devoured by wolves.

I was very hungry and almost famished for water, so I found a little ravine and went down that in hopes of finding water. I traveled on and the deer would come up to me to see what I was. I would climb a tree. Two or three large, vicious looking animals passed right close to me. They were wolves or panthers. I climbed a tree and stayed up there a long, long time. Night came on and I lay down to dream of home. Tired and exhausted I soon fell asleep, to be aroused the next morning by two big old bucks as they sniffed the air nearby. I arose and climbed a tree to be out of danger. That morning the deer often ran me up trees, for they were traveling toward the sun and couldn't tell what I was until they came real close. I guess I was a funny looking aspect with that cap on.

That ravine led me to the stage road where I found a piece of cornbread that some freighter had thrown away. I blew some of the dirt off of it and devoured it. That was the best bread I ever ate. I toiled on that day without seeing anybody.

I found a tree in the middle of the road—the road passing on either side of the tree—so I lay down there and went to sleep. Away in the night I heard the stage pass, but I was afraid to hail them in the dark, lest they kill me for an Indian.

I was still painted and had but one moccasin on, and that cap. I was so weak I could go only a few steps without rest and my mouth was dry. Along about noon I saw a man and I thought it was Papa. I waited until he came up and I spoke to him. He said something to me, but he spoke English and I spoke German, so he passed on without even so much as stopping. I thought that cap was the trouble and supposed he took me for an Indian, so I said to myself, "I'll throw that cap away the next time I see anybody." But I

sure liked that cap and wanted to keep it.

In a little while I saw a man coming in a wagon. I went out of the road to hide my cap. The man saw me and spoke German to me and told me not to hide. I am satisfied the other man told this man about me. He talked to me, hugged me in his bosom and wept, and I cried. I told him of how I was stolen, my hardships and starvation, so he gave me all the food and water I wanted. I ate and drank so much it nearly killed me.

This man carried me to a settlement at Kickapoo Springs, where there was a stage stand. He left me with a family by the name of Flannagan and told me to stay there until he came back and then he could carry me home. He had a load of freight for Fort Mc-Kavett, up above, and was gone several days. The stage from Fort Concho to Fredericksburg and San Antonio came by and the driver wanted to take me on home, but I wouldn't until my freighter came back by.

Mr. Flannagan and his family nursed me gently, treated me kindly and I was well and stout when my man came for me. I don't know the man's name who picked me up, nor where he lived. The only pay he would take for his trouble was that moccasin on my left foot, and that was freely given. My cap I left behind the bush where I had tossed it when I was found.

During my stay with the Indians I was never whipped or beaten, and besides scares, hard rides, and starvation, I was treated well.

Willie was gone from home nine days, according to Herman, although that sounds a trifle short, considering the events that seem to have taken place. At any rate, the young brother was restored to his family and created a hope in his mother's breast that she would see her other captured son someday.

We wonder, of course, just what sort of person that first man was who, beholding an eight-year-old boy in the midst of, in Herman's terms, "the howling wilderness," could keep walking without even attempting to find out who he was and why he was there.

Willie's explanation that he took him for an Indian is too kind, regardless of its accuracy; although the traveler may have thought Willie, being a young Indian, was a sign that there was a camp nearby and was frightened. Herman, in his 1927 account, says the man was on horseback and accepts the idea that the boy "evidently presented a ludicrous appearance, being painted as an Indian and decorated with a cap made from the scalp of a calf's head." Herman also points out that Willie, "being of a very timid nature," did not talk much to the man.

Modern readers are forgetful of how cut off from people the early settlers could be, and when this natural timidity was compounded by an inability to speak the language being used around them it naturally resulted in strange behavior.

That much of the tale, at least, had a happy ending, and later, when Herman returned to white civilization, Willie became his closest companion, the one person, perhaps, who understood something of the Indian life and could relate to Herman.

But for Herman, all this was only to be known many years later.

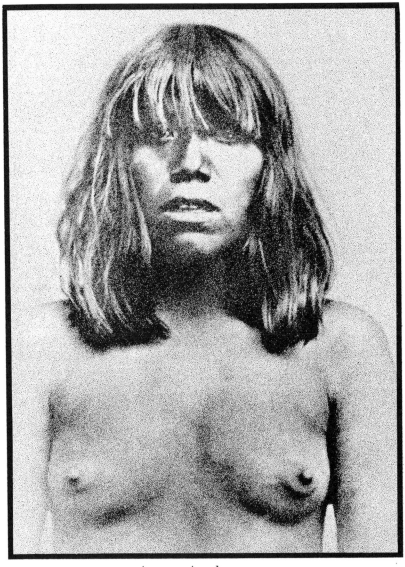

A young Apache squaw

12

4

WE WENT OUT ABOVE FORT CONCHO AND SAN ANGELO, traveling three days and nights without sleep, water, or anything to eat. About dark on the third evening we came to a little creek and stopped there. My bounds were loosened by Chiwat and I slipped away and crawled right down into the water. I was so dry I wanted to feel the water. I drank and bathed in it for some little time. The Indians missed me and began looking for me. I heard them all around, but they never thought of looking in the water for me. They finally gave up the search and went on. By that time I had my thirst thoroughly quenched, but I stopped and studied what I must do. I knew I could never find my way back home; the wolves and wildcats and other wild beasts would certainly tear me up and devour me, and we were far beyond the last line of settlements. If I followed the Indians, I thought, they will see that I don't want to leave them, so I will be treated better.

With that decision, I ran forward to try and overtake them. They looked back and saw me and waited for me to catch up. Pinero grabbed me by the hair and lifted me on the horse, and we rode on until about 9 o'clock that night, when we made camp.

The Indians usually selected a high place for their camp. Being refreshed to some extent by the bathing and drinking water, I observed how they made their fire. Chiwat took two sotol sticks and rubbed them together until they began to smoke. This was done by cutting little notches in the sticks and adding sand to cause friction when they were rubbed together rapidly. After getting fire, they lighted their cigarettes and covered the fire up in order to keep it and also to keep the smoke down. They sang a weird song while sitting there smoking the cigarettes they had made.

Then they caught me, tied a rope around my neck, and fastened the other end to a bush. They strapped my arms behind me and tied my feet together. This done, they secured a pole, each end of which was placed in a forked stick driven into the ground. These sticks were about six feet apart, so that I was suspended from the horizontal pole, face down, so near the ground that my breast barely touched the sand and the least pressure would draw the cords deep into my flesh.

Not content with placing me in this extremely painful position, they then placed a heavy stone on my back, pressing my face and nose into the sand, and there I was compelled to stay all night long, with no covering except that large rock on my back.

It was damp and cool, and I suffered all the agonies of death, but when I would groan an Indian would jump up and pull my hair and ears and beat me. How I lived through that awful night I do not know, but I was so frightened that I did fall asleep only to be visited by nightmares and bad dreams.

13

About daybreak next morning Pinero removed the rock, unbound the cords and drew his gun on me. Chiwat strung his bow and fitted an arrow and motioned for me to get up and evacuate. I did not care if they killed me, for I was willing to die right there where I lay. I could not stand at first. I was a perfect scab. A little moving soon made the worst sores run, and the corruption and bloody water covered me. We had no breakfast—the fourth day without food and the water I drank the day before had increased my fever. I was so dry I could not spit. They put me on a horse and we rode on.

We had then come to the Llano Estacado, so the country was open, but not exactly a desert, as early novelists would say. I heard little dogs barking and I didn't know what to make of it. We were in the midst of a prairie dog town. I had never seen one before.

We traveled three or four hours when all at once Pinero stopped and pointed down in the grass. I saw something there that had keen little eyes. The Indian made the same sign that had been made when I caught the calf, but I was afraid, because I did not know what they were. He jumped down and gathered them in his arms. They were little antelope. He put a rope around my neck and attached the other end to the antelope and tried to hang all of us on the saddle. I fought and cried, the antelope kicked and bleated. After having all the fun he wanted, he untied me and put my end of the rope on the other antelope, threw them on his pony, put me up, mounted the horse himself, and away we rode.

We rode some distance, ascended a hill and met Gray Wolf, another Apache, who also had an antelope. We built a big fire, arranged sticks so as to hold something above the embers, and threw on our antelopes alive; hair, guts and all. We were hungry, so we had no time for niceties or butchering. That was the first eating we had had for four days and we ravenously pulled away the hair and picked the bones of those pretty little animals.

There is a peculiarity about the antelope. They sometimes leave their young for hours at a time hidden in the grass, but if anything disturbs them the mother is inquisitive enough to follow to see what becomes of her young and is sure to trail you up if you carry her young away. So we watched our back trail and soon had two older antelope for supper. One Indian went back near our track about half a mile from camp and hid in the long grass. His vigil was soon rewarded and one loud report broke the stillness of the plains. He returned and watched me, and the other went back and slew the mother of the fawn he had brought. We camped that night hard by, but I was not treated so cruelly as on the night previous. I was only corded and not weighted down with a rock.

5

AFTER WE CLEANED UP THE ANTELOPE we traveled two days without food. Then we

"See, Alaman! bos americanus!" The Apaches stripped the entrails and ate the food they found in the Buffalo's stomach as well as the lining of the stomach.

came in sight of a large, woolly animal that I am quite sure would weigh a ton. He was very bulky, but nevertheless fleet, and had short horns. Both Indians charged him on their steeds and after a spirited race, he turned and made fight. This was the first buffalo I ever saw, although I had heard my father speak of them.

Gray Wolf shouted, "See, alaman! bos americanus!" Chiwat soon buried a ball in the heart of the bison and Pinero broke his neck with an arrow. Then came the reverential part. I knew nothing about the different modes of worship so I stood and watched with fear, awe and wonder at the red men's maneuvers. They made signs to the sun and marched around, smoking and gesticulating.

They cut the buffalo open, took out the entrails, and ate the food they found in his stomach as well as the lining of the stomach, which abounds in pure pepsin. Then they cut off a piece of the liver and smeared gall over it and gave it to me to eat. I swallowed it but it came back up. I swallowed it down again, and again it came back. This swallowing process was continued and each time an additional amount of gall was added until I held it down. From then on we found game in abundance and I learned to eat what was given me without vomiting.

We traveled for at least ten days and one day came upon a little knoll. Chiwat raised a red blanket and waved it a half-circle and returned it the same way. The process was repeated several times. I watched their countenances and at first they seemed perplexed but soon their faces brightened and their smiles broadened into a grin. They seemed to have forgotten me entirely. Keen yells escaped their lips and they began urging their horses forward into a sweeping gallop, and at that

15

speed we rode into the village that was located somewhere near the New Mexico line by a beautiful lake—a rare thing to find on the Staked Plain.

Yells, whoops and various sounds greeted our ears as the Indians swarmed to meet us. This village must have contained 2,500 Indians. Chiwat jumped off and left me, while Pinero led my horse on to Carnoviste's tent and halted. The squaws and children were yelling, hooting and making so much confusion I didn't know anything of what was going on and was badly frightened. Several of them rushed at me, and I thought my time had come. One fat, squabby, heathenish, hellish wench grabbed me, pulled me from the horse, pinched me, slapped me, beat me, wooled me, threw me down on the ground and wallowed me, but sometimes I was on top and again it was she. This exhibition continued for some time, greatly to the glee of the onlookers, but to my mortification, for in those days I could not endure much hugging and banging, especially from a woman. At last this tiresome old profligate let up on me and the whole camp came marching around me, dancing and yelling. The old squaws were in the front, the braves in the second squad, and the young girls and boys brought up the rear. The women chanted their incantations, the warriors fired their guns and yelled, the young ones danced and sang ditties and such another jubilee I never saw.

This storm finally passed over and out came an old squaw with a big knife and caught me by my hair. I thought she was scalping me, but she was only shingling my hair. Of course, she occasionally cut a plug out of the scalp, and the blood trickled down my back, over my face and covered my shoulders, but I kept a stolid countenance and tried to conceal my fright. Another of the men had been heating a small iron rod, so he came up and stuck that hot rod through my ear, burning a hole as it went. He took the iron out and tied a buckskin string in the hole he had made. He then repeated the process in the other ear, while others held me. He then turned his iron rod to my arms and burned great holes there. I have the scars yet, as proof of these assertions. I fought, kicked and raved, but still they beat and burned me until I became exhausted and wanted to die. I grew very sick, everything went black, and I fell to the ground and lay still.

How long I lay there I have no way of telling, but after they had punished me to their soul's desire, they took me up and were washing me when I came to.

I HAD BEEN WASHED, BATHED AND OILED and in many respects felt better, after regaining consciousness, but I little knew what the future had in store. Pinero came and carried me to where the food was spread for a feast. The warriors had at some previous time bartered with Mexicans and the table—which was a blanket spread on the ground—was well supplied with civilized food such as cakes, breads, piloncia (as sugar loaves were called) and coffee, as well as cooked and raw meat. Either on account of my intense hunger or Divine Providence, I seized the raw meat and began to eat. That pleased the Indians and they immediately began to pat me. Had I first touched the cooked foods—the foods of civilized man—I would likely have been tortured to death. The Indians laughed, cut many capers, and made many signs so that I understood that I had pleased them. I was then adopted by Carnoviste, and all again engaged in merry dances. This time I was led through the ordeal of an Indian religious festival and thus initiated into the tribe, but my trials, hardships and vicissitudes were by no means at an end.

After the feast the Indians gave me a large jug and sent me to a lake nearby for water. This jug, or keg, was made of dogwood, plaited or woven close together and cemented with pine pitch. It was strapped about my neck and I was sent into the lake to fill it. Several little Indian boys went with me. They showed me how to fill the jug by stooping down and allowing the water to flow in at the mouth of the jug until it was full, and then they helped me up, but the water was so heavy and I was so small and weak that it pulled me over and I fell, getting a ducking. When I tried to rise the water jug held me down. The boys laughed and assisted me to rise again, but just as I was up straight they turned me loose and over the jug pulled me. Several times in succession I was ducked and I was so strangled that I could not stand, even without the jug. Chiwat came and carried the water keg out of the lake and led me back to camp. I then lay down and rested for about three hours.

I was aroused, painted, and made to wrestle and fight awhile with the boys. They would get me down, but I would scratch, bite, kick and knock until I got on top. Then we would have another fall.

Such was our camp life from day to day. After wrestling, fighting and racing until we were totally exhausted, we were washed, greased and painted. A squaw made me a buckskin jacket, moccasins, and a little cap with a red feather in it. Any time we had rested a little the severe exercise was continued. They gave me food nearly every day, but they were by no means regular about it.

Amid all these hardships I thought of home and my loved ones. Sister Mina being my favorite. I thought a great deal of her, and often thought if she were with me we could whip the whole tribe.

Food became scarcer, and one day I went down a little creek that had almost dried up so that only stagnant pools remained, and caught fish. I was so hungry that I wanted to eat the fish, but my companions told me that would offend the Great Spirit. I tried to argue the question when the chief came up and, getting the meaning of my talk, picked me up and tossed me over into the creek, probably with the invitation for me to help myself to the forbidden game. While wallowing in that mud I found a hard shelled turtle. The Indian boys were delighted with that, and soon joined me in catching turtles. When we had secured about fifty of these we took them to camp where the squaws built up a big fire and threw the turtles on the hot coals. Some would crawl out, only to be picked up and thrown back into the fire. They were roasted shell, entrails and all, and we ate them and they were good.

7

I WAS ENTRUSTED with a herd of horses and shown the way to water, quite a long distance from camp. I was left by myself with the horses away out on the lonely prairie. I looked away to the east over the blue hills on the horizon, and tears came trickling down my cheeks. While my physical being, although somewhat scabby from recent sores, was comparatively at ease, yet there was a constant choking emotion, "an inward inexpressibility and an outward all-over-ness," which I had never felt before. Civilized people call it homesickness. I sat there on my pony and cried.

I never cried while I was being tortured, nor when I ran the gauntlet, nor when I nearly drowned. In those times I gave a yell of defiance or a snarl of vengeance, but now in my loneliness and desolation, I wept.

Then a new thought struck me. My tears vanished and a smile flitted over my face. I made up my mind to escape. I carefully concealed what provisions I had in a buffalo robe, strapped a jug of water to my pony's neck, carefully surveyed the surrounding country, and mounted the pony allotted to me and started east in a sweeping gallop.

On I swept over the buffalo licks and prairie dog towns, but had I viewed the western horizon with the telescope of an Indian's eye, I would have seen a cloud of dust rising and known that they were giving chase. In fact, I did just what I was expected to do—made an effort to escape. I rode manfully for a boy of my age, but soon the pony stumbled and fell and I struck the ground heavily, and breath and hope deserted me. It was only a matter of a few moments until I was overtaken.

One of my feet was sticking out and as one of the warriors named Somepanther rode up he roped that leg, jerking me around and several feet from where I had fallen. He whipped me severely with a rope, bound me tightly, and carried me back to camp. They all assembled around me, held a long council, spoke loud and vociferously, making many fierce gestures, then whipped me again and burned me. I was tied securely and put under a close watch for some time.

After this a boy accompanied me to keep me under his eye, but he also kept me from being so lonesome. He taught me the Indian language and showed me how to fix arrows and make bows. We herded the horses and I waited on my master, Carnoviste, the chief. He stole me so I belonged to him. I would do various things; get his horse, bring his food, light his pipe, bathe his feet, paint his skin, tighten the points on his arrows and make a solution of rattlesnake venom, skunk musk, and a kind of weed to poison some of the arrows. I would catch lice for him to eat and attend to what other chores he required—some not decent to put in this book. Which did I do, work or drudgery? Yet I never suffered as I did those times I was left entirely alone.

I worked hard, and when I was not watching the herd or administering to my master's needs, every old squaw in the village had me trotting to her whims and fancies. I had to pound up the corn, skin the game, rub sotol sticks for fire, carry water, drag away dung, dress wounds and do many loathsome things. Life became a burden to me, and once more I longed for death as relief, but to me no ray of hope could come.

After serving the vilest of the base for a while, my thralldom was somewhat modified. I was permitted to associate more with the boys and girls of the village. Carnoviste began to teach me to ride wild horses, to jump from the ground astraddle the horse as he ran by, and dodge an arrow at the same time. I was taught to crouch closely to the neck of the horse so an enemy could not hit me, and how to use the shield and ward off arrows.

I have often been asked how the Indians made their shields, and I will try to tell it now.

To make a shield required several days' time. The Indians took the hide of an old buffalo bull, cut a round piece from the neck and shoulders and threw this over the fire and heated it while green. When it was as hot as it would stand without burning it, it was rubbed on a rough rock until the meat was erased, then a smooth stone was used until the hide became very smooth, soft and pliable.

A rattan or hickory withe was made into a hoop and the rawhide was strapped on it and sewed with thongs of more rawhide. Then it was given the necessary "dish" by stretching over stakes and left to dry. After it is thoroughly cured it is set up as a target, and if an arrow pierces it or a bullet goes through it, it finds a place among the debris of the camp. But if it proves warproof, it occupies a place with the warriors. A strong string is placed through each side so it can be held on the arm, the hairy side next to the arm and the slick side facing the enemy. The moon, sun, serpents, turtles and other designs are painted on the shield and in such a location as to serve as a compass to guide and direct its owner on a rainy or cloudy day.

I was given a shield and placed off about fifty yards while four braves took bows and blunt arrows and began to shoot at me. I knew what I had to do, for I had seen the performance before. I began moving the shield up and down, from right to left as a snake when it tries to charm its prey. The arrows poured against my protector and I managed to ward them off for a while with the wavy motion, but torrents of blunt arrows came and I was too slow. One passed over the shield and took me in the forehead. I saw stars, not those painted on my shield but fiery flashes. It downed me, and my comrades let up on the shooting for a while, but soon it reopened, and I knew that I *had* to learn to use that shield. I was knocked down several times before I became an adept. All Indians were thus trained.

After this they taught me to ride races. I was tied on the horse the way I was expected to sit, nearly straight, leaning a little forward, with my knees clamping the horse so as to cut the wind. After they quit tying me on I fell off several times. The horse would sometimes fly the track and would have to be run down on the prairie with me sometimes swinging under his belly, when I was tied on. In training we would run around a lake, but in the gambling races a straight track was used so neither horse would have the advantage of an inside track.

All Indians tried their luck in games of chance. They had a game called *plava-penyole* which was played with five sticks painted red on one side and blue on the other. One of the sticks also had a red cross on it. They would cast them up like dice. All one color up with the highest tally, and the cross was the "king." They would bet on these sticks, on foot races, horse races, or anything of chance that came along. Sometimes luck would run against a brave and he would lose all his earthly possessions, including his wife and children.

Apache women gambling with their clothes as the stakes

The Apaches were mean to their squaws and indulgent to their children. At the age of twelve, boys were taught to pilfer, rob and steal.

It was the custom of the Indians that when an Indian captured a white child that child became the property of that particular Indian. Therefore, according to tribal custom, I belonged to Carnoviste and was called his son. He gave me an Indian name, En Da, or Indot, meaning "white boy." His squaw, Laughing Eyes, was very good to me and treated me as her own. At that time she had no child of her own and she lavished affection upon me. And in my childish way I returned her caresses. Later when her baby, Straight Bow, was born she did not cease to bestow motherly affection upon me, and when she died a year later I felt that I had lost my best friend among the Indians.

THUS HERMAN LEHMANN became an Apache Indian. We cannot be certain how long this process took, but it seems a remarkably short period. It was not more than a year, and we may find it amazing that in less than twelve months all the environmental training of eleven years could be so altered. But in recent historical times we have seen similar conversions in cases of what we term "brainwashing" among prisoners of war. It becomes a case of survival and the substitution of value systems so that the victim—if we want to call him that—feels not only that he must do specific things to stay alive but begins to feel that the new standards of conduct are not only more practical but have a better moral framework than his old ones. From the almost universal results of young captivity by the Indians we must acknowledge their expertness as psychological revisionists. The Indians succeeded with their white captives much better than white society did with the Indians it inherited.

One factor was that Indian society was much less complicated than white, where various levels of social intercourse had to take into account all sorts of complicated relationships. The Indians had a few simple units which a person had to understand, and within or without these units his conduct was governed by a standard set of responses. Basically he had friends or he had enemies. Members of his tribal unit were the only certain friends and persons outside the unit must always be presumed to be enemies, but even if they proved not to be enemies they were not often held to be friends. In fact, there is no Indian relationship which precisely matches the "friend" of white society. Among the Indians one became kin—blood brother or son—or one was still a potential enemy.

It is also to be noted that Herman came from a peculiar segment of his society: an isolated family which saw few outsiders and did not even speak the language of the world around it. He was more easily assimilated into the simple structure of Indian society because he was used to a simply-structured society already. This thesis can't always be applied, of course, but it seems safe to assume that a white child taken from a large city, even of that period, would have had more involved ties to remember and to draw him back if, under the circumstances, he had survived.

Meanwhile, after Herman's capture and the restoration of Willie, the Lehmann-Buchmier family found its exposed position on the Texas frontier to be past enduring. So within a few months changes took place. This chapter is the summary of what the family was doing while their son was becoming an Apache. These accounts, the reader should remember, were written years after Herman himself had come back to white society.

First is sister Mina's story, told after she had become Mrs. Keyser, in *Nine Years:*

ON JULY 18, 1870, two months after Herman was stolen, my stepfather, Philip [sic] Buchmier, and my brother, Adolph Lehmann, were about a mile from home irrigating land. My other brother, Willie Lehmann, and I drove the horses to water. On the west side of the creek was a high bluff and while the horses were drinking a big rock rolled down

21

the bluff and struck near me. I told Willie that we must run home; that it might be Indians. We waded into the water and drove the horses out. Not having enough water, they went reluctantly, but we hurried them to the pasture and then ran to the house.

Mother had to do all of the sewing for her large family by hand in those days, so she put me to sewing up the long straight seams. We had not been sitting there long until the dog began to bark. I looked out to see what he was barking at but could see nothing. In a few minutes he set up barking again, and we thought father was coming home with the sows and calves, and as he always scolded if the gate was not opened, I rushed out toward the gate, and to my horror there came twelve big Indian warriors in a gallop, holding their shields before them, weaving to and fro like snakes, their long hair dangling in the air. . . . They did not yell or make any more noise than was necessary. [Silence is a characteristic trait of the attacking Apache, while the Comanche always shouted, yelled and made all the noise possible. H. L.]

They rode around the house about fifty yards away the first round, but kept circling, coming a little nearer each time. I fetched in the axe and we closed and barred the doors. The smaller children were terribly frightened and some were screaming. Mamma was nervous from excitement. She had never shot a gun in her life and we little knew how we were to defend ourselves against such odds. . . . At first I trembled and a sense of fainting came over me but all this soon passed off and I felt bold and determined— even furious.

By this time the Indians had closed in on us and began throwing rocks and sticks through the windows until the debris and broken glass covered the floor. The children being barefooted, they could not walk on the floor, so I threw them under the bed. But they kept trying to crawl out to see what was going on. One little fellow made his escape from the bed-prison and unlatched the door and started out before I seized him and put him back. Sugar was a scarce article in those days and Papa had just bought four-bits worth. I grabbed that up, tore open the paper and scattered sugar under the bed for the children, but they didn't lick any up that day.

The Indians would dress up sticks to look like people and throw them in at the windows, trying to get us to waste our ammunition. There was a large goods box on the front porch in which were stored some articles of clothing which they used. When the Indians had first begun circling the house Mamma had wanted to shoot. But we had only the one gun, a double-barrel shotgun, and none of us knew how to load it. So I advised her to wait until they attempted an entrance. Finally the chief ventured to poke his head in at the broken window. I held the gun up and told Mamma to fire. She pulled the trigger, the report rang out and the room filled with smoke. A scream was heard, then a heavy thud, and silence reigned. Just as the trigger had been pulled the Indian had raised his shield and the full charge struck that, glancing into his abdomen. Soon the other warriors summoned up courage enough to remove their wounded chief, and in this attempt they came in close range again. We fired our second, and last shot, again striking a shield. This time the shots scattered, wounding two or three.

Mamma looked out through the window, and whizz! came a lance, passing close to her temple and sticking in the table nearby. But after making a few more sallies, careful not to expose themselves to the deadly shot-gun fire, they galloped away in despair of murdering us.

When father and Adolph came home they became so enraged they wanted to follow the band all by themselves and Mamma and I had to literally take them off their horses to keep them from doing so.

When we had opened our door, after the Indians disappeared, there stood our faithful old dog, Max. Several lance wounds and torn up turf showed that he had done his part. With an imploring look and a wag of his tail, he tumbled over exhausted.

This fight lasted about two hours. During the greater part of that time I had stood at one window with a cane knife, or dagger, that Papa had sharpened the day before to use in the cane field. Mamma had guarded the other window with the axe. Some Indians had gone into the other rooms, stole all the blankets, broke up the furniture, cut open the feather beds, and made a total wreck of our once happy home.

I have the dagger yet with which I fought the Indians in that horrible battle, and I also have a wardrobe that has scars and indentations made by lances, rocks and other missiles in that fight.

Mrs. Buchmeyer tells just about the same story of the battle, although some of the details differ. She says, for example, there were only eight warriors and that one held the horses while the rest attacked the cabin. She only tells of wounding one Indian, the chief. She adds that the shotgun had been bought after the first raid when the boys had been taken. This thrifty hausfrau noted one other thing, after nearly forty years; the damage done by the Indians, she says, "must have amounted to seven or eight hundred dollars."

Her account, in *A Condensed History*, continues:

WHEN MY HUSBAND RETURNED, the neighbors were called together and followed the Indians but never overtook them. I begged my husband then to move us away from that place and go where we could rest in peace. But now all the movable property was destroyed and we had done a great deal of work on the place and were so poor that we would have to start life over, [so] I could not get him to consent to go until an accident happened that made him willing.

He and a neighbor had to go to Fredericksburg to attend to some business and he advised me to keep the doors locked day and night. That night I heard the dog barking, about ten o'clock. My blood ran cold in my veins; I knew something was wrong. I had securely fastened and locked every door. I got up and listened; I heard the galloping of horses; I felt that my life was again at stake. I took one long, fond look at my children as they lay in "dreamland." Nearer, nearer came the hoofs of the horses and I feared that in just a few more seconds my cabin would be in flames and my children sacrificed to the gods of the savage men.

The equestrians reached the house and for a while the stillness of death reigned. I heard the voice of the neighbor who had gone with my husband; he said: "It is strange there is no light in the house." I opened the door and said: "What do you want with a light this time of night?" At the sound of my voice Mr. Lehmann [*sic*] fell unconscious. We worked with him a long time but at last

he opened his eyes and put his hand on my cheek and said, "Augusta, I am ready to move now; it is just enough."

He then related the following story: "When we got to Fredericksburg the stage driver came to me and said: 'Mr. Lehmann [*sic*], the Indians have attacked your house. Your wife and some of the children were killed and the others taken captive. Your wife was found lying in the door with a hatchet in her hand and it is supposed she fought [to] the very last.'" Now how this report became circulated I never learned, but it served as an incentive to make us move.

We came to Loyal Valley September 20, 1870. Well it was that we had deserted the old home! Mr. Lehmann [*sic*] and Adolph went back on the 3rd of October and found Indian tracks all around. They again had been into everything. Cattle were found with arrows through them. The Indians, no doubt, had come to murder us for wounding their Chief.

We were still notifying soldiers, rangers and making every effort to rescue Herman and thus went all of our hard-earned savings.

This band which attacked the homestead of Augusta and Phillip Buchmier turned out to be the very one which had captured Herman earlier. The chief whom the women had wounded was Carnoviste, Herman's Indian master. Thus, Herman also had a version of the story to tell from his end:

AFTER I had been with the Indians about two months, Carnoviste and eleven of his braves started on another raid down into the settlements, and they visited that region where I was captured.

When they returned they brought back a drove of stolen horses, and Carnoviste and another Indian, named Genava, were carrying gunshot wounds which had been inflicted by my mother when they attacked her home.

The Indians gave me an account of the attack and told me they had killed my mother and all of my people, and showed me clothing and a small pistol which I recognized as my own. They beat me unmercifully, and I am sure if either Carnoviste or Genava had died of their wounds I would certainly have been put to death.

My mother had used a shotgun loaded

23

with No. 4 turkey shot, which had peppered the breast of Carnoviste, while Genava caught a full charge at the lower end of his back which forced him to either lie on his stomach or stand up. He could not sit down. For a long time it was thought he would die.

The process of picking shot from these two occupied much time, and was generally accompanied by grunts and howls of pain. As to a full account of this attack on my mother's home, I had only the Indian's version of it. Only years afterward, when I was restored to my people, did I learn the truth.

This incident seemed to have a profound effect on young Herman. Believing his white family was dead he seems, at this point, to have begun considering himself truly an Indian and his Indian family his only family. Henceforth, when one can pick out the boy's true ideas from the lurid prose of Judge Jones, one senses the rapid swing in Herman's viewpoint from loneliness and thoughts of home to a kind of exuberance in the new life of an Indian warrior. From now on the boy not only grows more proficient in Indian ways, but he gains a self-confidence that he is not only a peer among the warriors, but is in fact their superior. Several individuals he once feared he comes to hold in contempt. In other words, the shy, introverted white captive quickly became a cocky, capable Indian.

THE INDIANS WERE COWARDS in a practical way: whenever there was danger they would send me. The first raid I accompanied them on they stole a bunch of horses near the head of the San Saba River. The first I tried to steal was a large black horse staked near Fort Concho. The Indians were afraid to go up to him, for they thought somebody was watching. Carnoviste told me to go for the horse. I hesitated. He drew his gun on me and commanded me to go, and of course I consented—a boy can't answer such argument.

He gave me a pistol and I moved cautiously toward the horse, crawling part of the way. I saw something bulky near the horse and thought I could see it move. I was within three foot of the bulk. When I cut the rope that held the horse, suddenly the man (for the bulk was indeed a man) rose up and shot at me, the charge passing just over me. The jar knocked me flat, the smoke and fire blinding me. My face was burnt and it made me deaf in one ear for a month.

I was so excited that I dropped my pistol, but I managed to get away. The noise stampeded the horse, and the man must have run, too. I hid in the grass nearby and lay deathly still for a long time. Then I heard something resembling the howls of wolves, and I went to them—not wolves but my companions—for that was our signal when we separated.

I told the Indians that the pistol was shot out of my hand and that it fell in reach of the white man. Had I told the truth I would have had to have gone back for the precious firearm.

We came down the San Saba River to about Voca and then turned south, crossed Mason County and slept awhile near Hedwig's Hill, on the Llano River.

We went down the river to near the town of Llano and there we rushed up on some men who had stopped and stacked arms for dinner. We put them to flight, destroyed their camp, stole their horses, and went on our way rejoicing, but we changed our course and made for House Mountain so we could survey the country and see if we were followed. We killed a fat beef and roasted him on top of the mountain.

We had a feast and rest there, then we went up Hickory Creek. We saw two white men coming toward us. We sat still until they were within 100 yards of us, and then we showed ourselves. One man rode away, the other stayed long enough to send us his compliments with two bullets, then he, too, turned to run. We charged, but our man was not much of a coward, for occasionally he returned a shot. We crowded them and they quit their horses and hid in a thicket. We drove off their horses and I never learned what became of the men.

We came back near my old home and somewhere near Beaver Creek we stole more horses. By that time we had a respectable herd, but the scouts came in and reported a band of white men following us. On Little Devil's River we were overtaken and several shots were exchanged at long range. None of our party was injured, and the whites retreated, so we changed our course and went northwest, and away up on the head of Bear Creek the whites overtook us again and a hot time ensued—a fight at close range. One Indian was severely wounded but afterwards recovered. Again the whites were put to flight and we made our getaway from there. Nothing else eventful happened until we reached our village. We found no Indians there but we did find bones, symbolically arranged, and signs which told the warriors why the village had been deserted and in which direction their wives and children were traveling. Another tribe had driven them northward. The chief easily followed their trail, although I could see no signs.

We hunted on the plains for a while and then came back south. In the summer we wore nothing but a breech-clout; part of a buffalo robe around the hips and loins. The warriors found a bee cave on the side of a bluff that must have been fully 200 feet high. From the amount of signs and the number of bees, the warriors said there must be an abundance of honey in the cave—but how to get it, that was the question.

We had a hide sewed up and lined with the paunch of an old bull. It would hold several gallons. We had a good supply of ropes. We went around and climbed up on top of the bluff from the other side and came up over the bee cave. A consultation was held and they decided to send me down. Ropes were tied together until they would reach the cave below. A stout stick was fastened to the end of this rope, and after tying the bag onto the rope and around my waist also, I was put a-straddle the rope on that stick and lowered down the bluff. I would strike the bank and push myself away from sharp projecting rocks. Down, down, I descended until I came even with the bee cave and there I was stopped.

This was a cloudy, damp day and the bees were out of humor, but I went naked in among them, filled up my bag with nice, new honey and comb, and hooted to be drawn up. The bees were stinging me and had, indeed, already covered me with black, poisonous stings, but still the Indians would not draw me up. An old warrior down in the valley (who had been stationed there to see that I did go into the cave or he would shoot me) finally said it was all right, so up they drew me. They had trouble getting me over the top, for part of the bluff extended outward, but I did all I could by reaching up and climbing (despite the heavy bag), and at last got back up with a fine lot of honey.

They asked me if there was any more and I, fool-like, answered in the affirmative. It was not that I was too honest to tell a lie, but at that time I was afraid to. So down they sent me again. This time I procured all the good honey handy, although there was more further back in the cave for the bees, too. Far back I could see great clusters of comb honey, much of it black with age, and the storage must have been going on for years.

The bee stings were pulled out of my body and a kind of ooze made from the bark of a shrub root they found nearby was poured over me, and that killed the poison of the stings.

This cave reminds me of the bee cave on Squaw Creek near Hedwig's Hill which I have seen in recent years and which has never been robbed. It is situated high up on a bluff overhanging the river. Below it is a deep lake of water, and it sometimes happens that the honey is seen running down the face of the cliff to the water below. I have been told that the bees never swarmed from this cave and old settlers say they have known of its existence for over sixty years.

9

WE WENT OVER to the Rio Grande and I was taught to swim. They placed a rope around my body and threw me in deep water. I sank, came up, made some wild pawing at the water, went down again, came up almost drowned and made a few flounces, while the Indians sat on the bank and laughed, and went down never to come up on my own accord any more. They drew me out, turned me over on my face with my head lower than my body, moved me up and down and got the water out of my lungs and restored respiration.

The next day the ducking process was repeated. Several days they nearly drowned me but still I could not swim. But Carnoviste went in with me, gave me a log to hold to, taught me how to use my legs and arms, and finally I made a good swimmer.

The Indian boys were taught by the same process, only the most of them were more apt. Being a good swimmer several times saved my life and enabled me to save the lives of others.

The craft, or canoe, that a squaw used to carry her young across a stream was a large hoop made of pecan, hickory or some kind of wood that would bend. A buffalo robe was stretched over this, and to each side of the hoop was fastened dry poles that would float. The children were placed on the robe; the squaw, swimming behind, guided the craft. It usually took not more than fifteen minutes to manufacture canoes to carry the young and other perishable property across the river.

When we got back to our village we found three Mexican traders camped with the squaws, and we soon gambled off or traded our horses to those Mexicans for guns, ammunition, blankets and so forth. Sometimes we would give six or seven horses for one gun.

We stayed in camp about a month, killed mustangs, antelope, buffalo and deer enough to run the old warriors, the manikins and the women until we came back. Then we started on another stealing expedition.

Our chief was not elected, but he was the bravest and most powerful and went in front because he could. The next in strength and power of endurance came second and so on down the line. No Indian went on a raid unless he wanted to go, and the weakest was always found in the rear.

We took only the ponies we rode, each of us mounted on a separate pony, our guns primed and ammunition handy, plus a supply of bows and arrows.

If a horse gave out, that Indian had to take it afoot until he could steal another one, but if we got in a tight we took him up behind.

On this raid, which twelve of us made, we came southeast about one hundred fifty miles toward the settlements and camped on a little ravine. We had killed a big, fat buffalo bull and had a big feast. One of our warriors was stationed on a high point to watch for rangers and when another went to relieve him they discovered four buffalo hunters—white men and Mexicans together—coming toward us on foot, their camp being behind a hill some distance away.

The alarm was given, and all of us went to watch these buffalo hunters to see if they were trailing us or what they were up to. We soon became convinced that they were not aware of our presence, so we made a charge on them, running our horses toward them as fast as we could go. When we were within a short distance of them they saw us and turned and ran, three of them going up on a hill where they got behind some rocks, the other man running toward camp. Seeing that the three men who had gone up on the hill and taken refuge behind the rocks were well fortified and bent on putting up a stiff fight, we turned our attention to the man who was headed for camp, and we overtook him in an open place. When we came near he began to talk to us in Spanish. He told the Indians there was nobody at the camp. The Indians left me in charge of the Mexican and told me not to let him get away while they went to rob the camp.

Soon I heard firing in the direction of the camp, and it developed the Mexican had told us a big lie, for when the Indians arrived at the camp there were several men there and they opened fire on the Indians. When the Mexican heard the shooting he began picking up rocks and throwing them at me. I took a shot at him with my bow, but the arrow barely grazed him. He then threw up his hands in token of complete surrender, and I kept him covered until the Indians returned. As the men in camp were making it pretty hot for the Indians, they retreated and came back over the hill to where the Mexican and I were. When I told Carnoviste about the Mexican throwing rocks at me he became enraged and ordered me to kill the man at once.

I shot him through the heart with an arrow and he fell dead instantly. Not satisfied with forcing me to kill this Mexican, Carnoviste ordered me to take his scalp, but I did not want to do it for I had never scalped anybody and I did not relish the task. But my chief threatened me with all kinds of punishment if I did not do as he ordered, so I took my knife, made an incision all around the top of the dead man's head, grasped his hair with my fingers and gave a quick jerk backwards and the scalp came off with a report like a pop-gun. Soon his bloody scalp was dangling at my belt, and I was the proud recipient of Indian flattery.

The Indians gathered around me and made me turn the body face downward. Carnoviste then told me to cut a cross on the arrow and lay it on the dead man's back, which I did. While doing so, the Indians smoked a pipe, blew the smoke on their breasts, and held their hands toward the sun, palms outward, in some kind of worship, beseeching the Great Spirit to let good fortune attend them and give them victory over all enemies.

Why the cross was cut on the arrow I cannot say, unless it was to mark it as a weapon which had shed human blood. An Indian never used an arrow the second time which had killed a man, enemy or friend. It was stained with human blood.

We continued our course and that night we came in contact with a company of men and had a little fight, killing one white man and capturing fifteen horses. I think this must have been near where Ballinger now is. We came on down to Packsaddle Mountain in Llano County and there had a terrible fight with four white men. We were in the roughs and so were the whites, so neither had the advantage, but we routed them in about half an hour. I think I wounded one of the white men severely. I had a good shot at him. But they all got away.

We went from there to House Mountain and captured a nice herd of horses. This increased our drove to fifty. We went our same old route up the Llano River, but the rangers got on our trail and followed us up through Mason County. We made for Kickapoo Springs, but the rangers had changed horses and were giving us close chase. We changed horses often and rode cautiously and made our escape, but we were followed to the edge of the plains. Finally we reached home safely, and with all our horses.

10

IT HAD BEEN SOME TIME since we had killed any of the hated tribe of palefaces, and we were all eagerness to try our hand again. So, from our old village we started on a raid upon the Texas white settlements to get more horses and to kill as many of the palefaces as we could.

The Apaches never carried their squaws or children along on a raid, while the Comanches did. In our party was a brave named Tusciwhoski (Whitewood) who had fallen out with his squaw. He had caught her sleeping with a Mexican trader. He had killed the trader and cut off his wife's nose, which was the custom for such offenses. (While the unmarried Indian girls who got pregnant without a husband did like their civilized sisters—either gave their children away, left them in some married woman's tent, or killed them.)

Apache squaw with her nose cut off for infidelity

But Tusciwhoski could not get over his love for his squaw, no matter how she had done him. When we started on the trail he said: "I will never come back. I am going to die." We knew he would make good his prophecy, even if he had to take his own life. As we traveled on he seemed to be all right. He never said anything, but that is nothing for an Indian for we often rode for miles and miles without anyone speaking.

29

We came in sight of Kickapoo Springs and there, riding, was a white man, nicely dressed. Tusciwhoski said, "I will get that man, the first white man I have seen." It was the Indian custom to turn the painted side of the shield out, but Tusciwhoski had the fur side out on his. The chief called his attention to it and said the Great Spirit would not assist a warrior who would be so unreverential. But Tusciwhoski shrugged and said, "Then the white and I must both die."

And thus saying, he dashed toward the white man who was about 300 yards away. Silence reigned while we watched the maneuvers of our companion. He dashed up to the white man and fired his Winchester, and the white man returned the salute with a .44 calibre Colt's revolver. Several shots were exchanged while the white man beat a dogged retreat. We saw our companion reel and fall to the ground. We hurried to him, but he was dead. The white man too tumbled from his horse and made an effort to rise. We ran toward him and he made several attempts to shoot us, but was too far gone. He rolled over on his face and expired.

We examined him closely and found four bullet holes in his breast made by the Winchester balls. We did not scalp or otherwise disfigure this man because he was brave and fearless. He was riding a large, gray horse, had a fine silver-mounted Mexican saddle, new red blanket, a stout, heavy bridle with shop-made bits, and in his saddle pockets we found a great quantity of silver and a roll of greenbacks. These bills we tore up, not knowing anything about their value.

We took the six-shooter and those other things and went back to the dead Indian. In his breast we found three holes where pistol balls had entered, and in his back we found three torn places where the bullets had come out. These balls readily passed through the hairy side of his shield. We buried Tusciwhoski in a little cave, after wrapping his body in buffalo robes and placing his weapons by his side. His horse and dog we killed and left near him, one of the bravest and best of the Apache tribe.

We went down about Fort Terrett and found some rangers camped there. Their horses were loose and scattered. We rounded up thirty or more and drove them away. Some were hobbled with chains and locked and we could not get these irons off, so we cut off the horses' feet to keep the rangers from using them any more. One fine gray we carried along for a while in hopes of picking the lock, but he, too, had to share the fate of the others.

We came to a road and discovered a wagon in which there were a man, a woman and three children. Before they were aware of our presence we had them surrounded, and it was but the work of a few seconds to kill and scalp the man and woman and a little baby. The other two children we carried with us, a girl about eight and a boy about six years old. The man had been working an ox team. We killed the oxen and burned the wagon with its dead inhabitants.

We went north and just as we were crossing a little ravine, four white men dashed in between us and our herd of horses. This was so sudden and so daring we were thrown into confusion for a moment. We rallied and turned on them, soon putting them to flight. One of the white men lost his pistol and Carnoviste got it. The whites outran us, driving our horses before them, but we held on to the captive children. The poor little things would not eat. We carried them four days and nights and they cried all of the time. We could not slip up and steal anything for the noise. So two big buck Indians rode up, one on each side of the little girl. The one on the left took her left hand and foot, and the Indian on the right side took her right hand and foot. They raised her from the horse on which she sat and drove the horse away and swung her three times, the third time turning her loose. She cut a somersault high in the air, and when she struck the ground she was dead. The boy was served the same way at the same time by two other warriors and every Indian rode over the mangled corpses. The bruised and trampled bodies were picked up and hung on a little tree for the vultures.

I hesitate to recite these revolting crimes, but they were true instances of the savagery in which I was engulfed. I tell of them in order to show the venomous hatred cherished by the Indian against the whites.

We traveled on and just north of Beaver Lake we came to a big, clear hole of water. We killed a buffalo, unsaddled our horses, turned them loose, built up a big fire, roasted some ribs of the bison and had things scattered about. Some of the Indians were in bathing and none of us had our firearms. Just in this condition the rangers charged us. In the first fire two of our men fell. We gathered up our guns and scattered into the chaparral. The rangers got all of our horses and everything else except what we could pick up as we rushed away.

We were pretty well scattered as we made our way from there, and we did not all get back to our village. Those who did, arrived one, two, three or five at a time. Three more of our band were killed and one severely wounded—although he made his way to the village. Twenty-two of us finally straggled in, as poor as we were when we came into this world. When we brought in the news of our bad luck there were such hideous cries, such mournful howls. The squaws cut themselves all to pieces with knives and the wives of the dead ones committed suicide. The wife of the wounded warrior burned her own arm every morning that she might not forget her grief until her master's wounds should heal. For several days straggling warriors came in, and the camp was a spectacle of grief, sorrow, and despair.

To add to the desolation of the scene, another defeated party came in carrying one wounded and reporting one dead. Our horses were all taken, our guns captured, our bows and arrows left behind, our blankets gone, our saddles, bridles and ropes in the hands of the enemies. Another squaw killed herself.

Then the third party which had gone on a raid returned defeated—four dead and one taken captive, brought down the old trail to San Antonio by the soldiers, I learned later. We were sure we had offended the Great Spirit, so our medicine men prayed and howled, went up on a hill and waved cow tails; the witches chanted incantations and we all fasted and four more squaws took their lives.

31

Then the fourth company came in with horses and supplies and better humor prevailed in camp. We rounded up a herd of cattle and traded them to Mexicans for guns and made bows and arrows and prepared buffalo robes.

Some time after this we were stopping at a beautiful watering place when a party of Comanches visited us. Among them was a German boy named Adolph Korn who was captured by the Comanches in Mason County a short time after my capture by the Apaches. We talked over our situation. We both spoke German, so our Indian masters didn't understand us. We had a good time, and would have devised some means of escape had we not been disturbed; but the Comanches left us, taking Korn with them, and I had to go back to my old associates and catch and fry lice for Carnoviste.

11

SOME TIME LATER, we moved four miles from the lake and Boho, a young Indian, and I went hunting one morning. I was on a dun mule that had been beaten over the head a great deal and was subject to the studs, or balkiness. Whenever I wanted him to run he would stop and whirl around and around.

We were then at war with the Comanches. We had gone some distance from the camps when we saw, coming over the hill, a big band of Comanches in full war paint. Boho was riding a swift pony, so he ran off and left me at the mercy of our enemy, even though I yelled loudly, "Toko! Toko!" (Wait! Wait!). The arrows came whizzing around but the dun mule balked. Then I heard one go zip! right close and a small spike embedded itself in the old mule's hip. He was no longer a permanent fixture on the landscape, but suddenly developed into a moving, progressive hybrid. I had no more trouble with the locomotion of that mule. My main thought was to ride. The whizz of the arrows was soon lost, but I could still hear the war whoops of forty infuriated warriors on my track. I was too near out of breath to look back. I hugged my mule and leaned over his neck in order not to accumulate too much wind, and rode like a race rider.

I passed Boho, and heard his entreaty not to leave him, nor depart from following after him. But if I had any intention of waiting it was forlorn; that dun mule was on the go. There was no stopping or holding him. He passed through the camp at a two-forty gait, knocking down squaws and children and demoralizing things in general. He went on a half-mile beyond the camp, right into the midst of a herd of horses that were peacefully grazing on the hillside, and there he checked his speed and began kicking and bucking for dear life. I quit him then, the arrow still in his hip, and caught a pony and hastened back to be in the desperate battle which had begun.

Boho was overtaken and scalped near the village, but the Apaches had surrounded his body and forced the Comanches back. Every foot of ground was contested and I saw that several of our men were killed. The Comanches were nasty fighters, but we greatly outnumbered them. The battle began about ten o'clock and raged all day. At sundown the Comanches withdrew, but forty of their comrades were left on the battlefield. We never tried to follow them, for twenty of our braves had gone to the Happy Hunting Grounds, while eight more were writhing in pain, four of whom died that night in spite of prayers and incantations of our medicine men. One more died the next day, but the other three recovered.

Our dead were given decent burial. We went over the ground held by the Comanches and took possession of all their guns, bows and arrows, shields and what horses there were that were not dead or wounded. We gathered up the Comanche carcasses and threw them in a hole in the ground and left them uncovered.

We then moved our village further north, and the old dun mule was left behind with the rock projectile touching the "nameless" bone. Near here the next day two Comanche spies were seen. One was ambushed and murdered, the other captured and retained for a worse fate. Carnoviste cut a hole through each of his arms, drew a rawhide cord through the openings and hung the poor fellow up in a mesquite tree to die. But an unfaithful squaw—without a nose—slipped back and cut him down.

We moved on about sixty miles to a spring and prepared to camp there permanently—or for a few months, at least. We had been there several days and had grown a bit careless because we had made breastworks and otherwise fortified the place. One night Yellow Cloud dreamed that a large band of Comanches was after us and that we would be overpowered and suffer great losses. The next morning a great war council was held and a difference of opinion prevailed. We had speaking and fasting all day. The second morning the majority were in favor of getting out of the way of the Comanches, so we started on the move again and had gone about twenty miles when we found ourselves surrounded by the Comanches. All of our women and squaws were captured, forty warriors were killed, twenty-five wounded, our horses driven away, our tenting outfits taken and we were left in destitute circumstances. I do not know about the losses of the Comanches, but we had little red rifles which did very effective shooting and I am sure many were killed.

Something like one hundred warriors (including me) and six women made an escape on foot. We turned back and drifted around for about a month, generally going in a southern direction. We met one hundred and fifty Apaches well mounted and equipped with surplus arms and horses. They supplied our needs and we all moved on south together, a little happier than we had been for a month.

We sent out scouts in all directions and called for the scattering bands of the Apache tribe to come together at a certain lake on the plains. Time was allowed for the members who were in Arizona, Utah and Mexico to come together. In the meantime we were gathering up all the guns, ammunition and war equipment we could beg, barter or steal.

Weapons were being manufactured in every wigwam, ponies were trained, even squaws and children were given instruction. We were getting ready for war.

Victorio, the big tribal chief, and his favorite scouts, went out to look for Comanches. In about three moons warriors began to come in from every source, and thousands were ready to help us rescue our women and children. In a few days, before our forces were fully recruited, Victorio returned alone. He and his scouts had had a fight with the Comanches and all were killed except Victorio.

Victorio, Geronimo, Red Wasp and other noted warriors made speeches. Victorio favored peace. He said, "I fear not the Comanches myself, neither am I afraid of their allies, the Kiowas. But these tribes are strong among themselves and greatly outnumber us. Besides, the whites furnish them with guns and powder and lead to help exterminate our tribe. The white man is the Indian's enemy, and the Indians must quit fighting among themselves and all go together to fight the palefaces. While I was gone I saw as many palefaces as there are sprigs of grass on the plains or stars in the sky, and if we continue to fight each other we will all be exterminated by the white man."

Red Wasp said: "We do not fear the cowardly palefaces. They have robbed us of our hunting grounds, they have destroyed our game, they have brought us disease, they have stirred up discord among our own; they have bought out and intimidated our braves; they have made profligates of our children, whores of our wives, and destroyed our traditions. They have wrought despair and desolation to our tribe, and for my part, I am ready to fight for my hunting ground, fight for my former liberties, fight for our wives and children, and F I G H T for the love of gore!

"As to the Comanches, our grievances are great and the cause of the war is just, and I will be glad to kill them when they come, kill them as they kill our companions, kill them as they mount their steeds, and kill them as they attempt to escape. And if we must die let us fight to the bitter end and at all cost retain freedom and honor. Others may do as they think proper, but as for my part, I choose to fight."

Other speeches followed pro and con, but the opinion prevailed that all the Indians should unite in one great effort to exterminate the palefaces, and for the common cause emissaries were sent to the several tribes, with the result that a treaty was finally made which resulted in the return of our women and children.

We moved toward the Comanches and camped within three miles of their village. The Comanches sent out a warrior who galloped around our camp at a safe distance, waving a black shield in the air, which meant fight—death to the vanquished. Had the Apaches sent a warrior in return with a red shield, it would have meant "We accept your challenge and are ready to fight." But we raised a white string and that meant peace.

Victorio, the most effective Apache chief

The Comanches made signs that six of their men would meet a like number of our men on half-way ground. The rest of the warriors were collected and ready for battle at the first signal.

The Comanches agreed to make peace if we would deliver to them the men who split open the Comanche's arms and hanged him to the tree. We promptly disavowed the act and declared that the warriors who did it had been killed in battle. But one of the very men who formed our commission was one of the guilty parties. So the Comanches, trusting to our honor and veracity, agreed to the treaty, and our women and children were returned—all except the woman who cut down the spy from the tree. She was adopted by the Comanches for we did not want her. She had had her nose cut off for unfaithfulness to her husband. Also, some of the maidens had been chosen by the Comanche braves, and these were allowed to stay, and thus the tie of union was more securely bound.

To Victorio belongs the credit of this treaty, and some of his daring experiences would not be out of place here.

Once he was out hunting and killed a buffalo. The weather turned intensely cold. He dressed the buffalo and night overtook him. He had no other protection from the cold except the hide, so he enveloped himself in it. He spent a warm night and morning came, but the norther was still here. Victorio attemped to rise, but to his horror the fresh hide was frozen and he was unable to move hand or foot. He heard the wolves howling and expected to be torn to pieces by their tushes, but he was covered with snow and the wild beasts passed him by. He was thus imprisoned for two days and nights, but the third day the sun shone out and the old warrior managed to get free.

Another time, in Mexico, we were fighting the soldiers when one of Victorio's brothers was captured. I was up on a hill watching the conflict. Victorio rode down a canyon and, under the cover of the smoke, he rode right in among the soldiers, waving his shield, and his brother jumped up behind him and they rode back to our men amid the crossfire of battle. But just as they reached our line a ball struck Victorio's brother in the back, passing through his body, and went into Victorio's back and came out his breast. The brother fell from the horse dead. Victorio turned, and saw his brother was past all earthly aid. He dismounted, placed the dead Indian on his horse, leaped up behind and rode on to our headquarters. When he reached there he was covered with blood and blubbery froth from his chest wound. The Indian surgeon probed the wound, cut away the bruised part, and blew in a solution of careless weed (or some kind of weed) and clear water. Victorio finally recovered, although the ball must have passed through his right lung.

Victorio was a remarkable Indian. He always wore a blue suit, and would allow no other tribesman to dress as he did. He did many daring deeds and the Mexican government offered $1,500 for his scalp. He liked women. He had four wives and several good-looking daughters. One time he offered to trade me a real pretty girl

36

for a saddle I had captured, but I declined. I could have fun enough anyway. Girls were easier to get than saddles.

Once in Mexico, where he did most of his fighting, a warrior was captured and forced to tell where Victorio was hiding. He was alone, under a bluff, but well armed and equipped. He killed every man who tried to approach, then at nightfall made his escape through the enemy lines. Once he decoyed off a party of hunters into the Black Hills and got them separated and killed the whole company. It was said that he stole more white children than any two divisions of the Apache tribe. Unlike most Apache chiefs, he usually moved with all his women and children in camp. He was killed in a drunken row by a treacherous Mexican.

VICTORIO was actually killed in October, 1880, at Tres Castillos, in Chihuahua, Mexico, during a siege of his camp. He is said to have been mounted on a conspicuous white horse. James B. Gillett, in *Six Years With the Texas Rangers*, says that "in making some disposition of his braves to meet the expected onset of the enemy [he] exposed himself unnecessarily. The Mexicans fired a volley at long range and two bullets pierced his body.

He fell from his horse dead—a good Indian at last."

Herman Lehmann may have found out the true nature of Victorio's death later, for the story of the drunken row killing is omitted from the 1927 version of his story. It has been included in the text here mainly as an example of how he revised his account upon discovering the facts of certain episodes.

12

EVENTUALLY we consummated a treaty with the Kiowas as well as the Comanches, and all prepared to annoy the palefaces as much as possible and kill as many as we could. In order to do our work secretly we divided into small squads or bands.

The band to which I belonged went down our old route to Fredericksburg and Mason. One night some of us went into Fredericksburg, walked all over town, and saw the boys drinking beer in a saloon. We let them drink in peace but we took charge of all the horses we could find. We then went up on the hill north of town and I went into a man's lot and got two good horses while my companions captured a nice herd nearby.

We then went north, some traveling the road and the others exploring the country on each side. We got several good mules from one of my old neighbors, Fritz Ellebracht, and somewhere the party captured a boy thirteen years old.

We passed right by my old home and the Indians tried to get me to go to my people. They called me paleface and urged me to quit them. I looked at the old house and saw it was vacant and believed the stories I had been told that my family was all dead. I knew very well that if I tried to rejoin the whites I would be killed on the spot. They rushed on and left me for a short while, but I followed and near there we stole some horses from William Bickenbach, another old neighbor, then hurried out of that section. We reached our camp with about forty good

37

horses and some mules, several saddles, and scalps—two families having been killed in Mason County. We kept the white boy about a year, but as he would not take to our ways, we traded him to some Mexicans. Whether he ever succeeded in getting back to his people, I do not know, nor do I remember who he was.

We had no bad luck on that trip because we had been at war among ourselves so long that the white people had got careless, so we celebrated. We enjoyed camp life and supplied the squaws with game.

Next we moved across the Pecos and met a band of Kiowas. We united and went to steal cattle that some cowboys were driving nearby. We killed and scalped two of the cowboys and left their carcasses for the wild beasts—after scalping them. The others escaped. Each of us killed and barbecued five head of cattle and at one time there were two thousand head of cattle being cooked. We turned the others loose on the plains because we could find no Mexican traders.

The cowboys had sixty choice saddle ponies which we succeeded in corralling, and taking with us. One of our Kiowa companions was wounded and later died.

We went back to camp, then moved southeast. Some of the warriors went on a raid, but I stayed in camp to recuperate. Carnoviste went along and when he returned, two white scalps dangled from his belt and a little white boy was brought in. The warriors claimed to have killed two whole families.

We changed our plans, shortly after this, and went about three hundred miles into the pines of New Mexico and among the mountains we killed bear and elk, and wild sheep and goats.

Our chiefs made a treaty with the whites, and soldiers in gaudy colors came into camp, but another white boy and I were kept hidden in the pine forest. This other white boy would not stay, but would slip back in camp when he thought it was time for the white inspector to come, so Snapping Turtle carried him away out into a thicket and left him tied to a tree, without food and water, and there he died.

The soldiers kept close guard over the Indians for three moons, and I had to stay in the woods among the bear, but from time to time I would slip up to the camp of my old chief and get food. The soldiers eventually became less vigilant and squatters traded us corn. This we soaked in warm water until it fermented and made a kind of sour mash. This malt, or sprouted corn, was taken out and dried and beaten up and then thoroughly boiled. Then it was strained into another vessel and mixed with hops. It was kept in a warm place until it again fermented and then we all would drink. All would get drunk, and even I would get tipsy.

Gambling and fighting would be the next thing on the program. Squatters made this drink and sold it to us after we were too intoxicated to make it ourselves. It was no unusual sight to see braves, squaws and squatters all in a bloody pile, gnashing their teeth and swearing vengeance on each other. It is astonishing how much of the poisonous beverage we could drink. Eventually the supply would give out, or the "wild-catter" would be marched off to answer a charge of violating revenue law, and he would never return, but somebody would always take his place.

After a week's debauchery we would lie around and sleep and grieve over the death—maybe brought about by our own hands—of some loved one. When an Indian is maddened by drink, he is even more brutal than his palefaced brother in the same fix. It is not unusual for an intoxicated warrior to murder his wife or children, or rape his own daughter, or for an infuriated squaw to stick a dagger into the heart of her husband, or dash her innocent babe against a rock and indulge in a maniacal laugh as its brains ooze out. You may talk about your hell holes in cities, and gambling dens, but if you want to see desolation, visit an Indian village during a spree. The misery and destruction, the suffering and deaths are appalling!

We stayed there about a month after the soldiers quit coming around regularly, thinking no doubt we were pretty well in hand. But some of our boys stole some horses and ran away, and we all broke out and followed. I must here state that our band did not comprise all of the Apache tribe, as there were several bands which had not made a treaty with the whites.

We roamed over our old haunts and enjoyed the freedom of the plains. We crossed the Pecos and were preparing for a raid into Mexico when a pestilence broke out among us. A great many died, and among them was Carnoviste's wife. They carried her down the hill to the burying grounds and laid her to rest with her two favorite dogs and all of her other valuables and trinkets. Everything was killed that belonged to her, and I was led up to a rock to be slain also. The bows were strung and guns primed and the ceremony said when suddenly a young Indian maiden rushed forward and threw her arms around me, and I was spared. [Editor's note: the 1899 version says "a young Indian cub threw his arms around me and I was spared."] Carnoviste's squaw left an "indehe" (baby), and I had to take care of it. I hired a kindly squaw to nurse it for me. Its grandmother took it in about six months.

Despite the pestilence, some of our warriors had gone on a raid. In a few days they came back. They had had a fight and Carnoviste had been severely wounded and he had been left, with two warriors to feed and protect him, while the others went on stealing and marauding. They captured a large bunch of horses and came by where their wounded chief was and by that time he was able to travel. Dare-Devil had two white scalps so the whole party proceeded back to camp, but no dance or festival was held on account of the misfortunes.

Our people continued to die from the disease and the medicine man in our camp seemed not to understand it. But a famous medicine man came back with these warriors and he examined the sick ones. He went up on a high mountain and there he offered up his prayers to the Great Spirit to come to his aid in combatting the pestilence. It was wintertime and despite the cold he spent the night unprotected on that mountain.

The next morning when he returned to camp, he commanded a hole to be dug near the river. When this was done he ordered big fires be made and large stones heated. The stones were placed in an airtight wigwam. The sick Indians were stripped and placed in the airtight wigwam and sweated as long as they could stand it; then they were suddenly plunged into almost freezing water and kept there for several minutes, and when they were brought out the cold norther froze icicles on their hair. We then rubbed them with wet grass and rough blankets, wrapped them in warm buffalo robes, and gave them a strong drink of hot, bitter tea made from the root of a plant that is indigenous to the Pecos country, but I do not know the name of it. The well ones had to undergo the same treatment, and then we moved camp, the well carrying the sick. No more Indians died from that plague.

While traveling along we saw some buffalo hunters. We carried our women and children back several miles and stationed a guard around them, and a party of us went out after a man we spied killing buffalo—he had over a hundred killed around him. He had left his pony and had concealed himself behind a bluff near a watering place. We slipped up a little ravine to where his horse was tied, and just as we captured the horse we saw other palefaces coming in a wagon.

The hunter heard the wagon and started for his horse. We wanted to kill them all, so we hid in the grass. These palefaces were approaching us from opposite directions and had come to within fifty yards of us when we arose with a volley and a yell, part of us giving chase to the hunter, the others following the wagon. I went with those after the wagon. We let our ponies out. Those men in the wagon lay down flat, and how those horses did run! Sometimes the wheels of the wagon would all four be off the ground. We kept up a steady fire. The spring seat came unattached and tumbled from the wagon right into the path of one of the warrior's pony so that the horse, in attempting to run over it, stumbled and fell, breaking its neck and demolishing the seat.

These unguided horses made toward a steep bluff over a canyon about forty feet wide and fifteen feet deep. We circled our ponies as the wagon went over the bluff, then hastened to the site. The tongue of the wagon had stuck completely up in the opposite bank, the felloes of the wheels were smashed, and some of the spokes were driven into the bank by the tongue. One horse had his legs and neck broken, but the occupants of the wagon cut the harness off the other horse and made good their escape down the ditch. But they left their fine buffalo guns and ammunition in the wagon. These we confiscated, burned the remains of the wagon and returned to where our comrades had pursued the lone hunter.

When we found them one brave was wounded and all the others were being bluffed. Carnoviste said, "You cowards! All of you cannot kill one paleface." He fixed his shield and charged the hunter. The hunter put his hand to his side like he was getting a cartridge, then he held his gun on a level until the chief was close, then fired. The bullet hit the shield and glanced off, and Carnoviste made a leap and was on the hunter, dispatched him and took his scalp. We examined the mangled body and found four bullet holes that our men had made. Our booty was a horse, saddle, three fine guns, plenty of ammunition, and a white scalp. We returned to camp, smoking our tomahawk pipes and dancing over our success.

The next morning we heard some shooting, and several of us mounted our ponies and set out toward the firing. We had not traveled far until we saw some white men coming toward us. We concealed ourselves and waited until one came very close to us and changed his course. He was scanning the horizon for buffalo and did not see us until we were right at him and had our guns leveled on his heart.

He threw up his hands and dropped his gun. He was of light complexion and had blue eyes and could speak a little Spanish, which most of the Apaches understood. He begged for life, and we took everything he had—clothes, a fine gun, a belt full of cartridges and a nice dirk. After he was stripped of everything, we told him if he would let each one of us strike him one lick apiece we would allow him to go; but first we made him promise to move his camp and use his influence to keep the palefaces out of our territory. We told him furthermore if he or his party killed another buffalo we would follow them and exterminate the whole party. We made ready our quirts and each passed by and spent some of his elbow grease on the man, each stroke bringing blood. The chief would not hit him.

The hunter then started off at a run, but we called him to halt and told him to walk. He obeyed until he passed over a hill and then he burnt the wind. We followed at a distance to see that our orders were obeyed. His comrades met him and escorted him into their camp and, well, they moved on short notice, leaving their buffalo hides stretched—about thirty in number—and we never saw them again.

Just after this episode we heard shooting south of us, so we set out that way to investigate and in a few minutes we came in sight of three men and a boy. We gave chase. They rode toward the roughs and were just ready to forsake their horses and take refuge in a canyon when I roped the boy and took him prisoner.

He proved to be a friendly Mexican and told us where their camp was. We had taken the men's horses when they left them, so we carried the horses back to them and set the boy free. We traded and gambled with these men and one of them said that he could rope the biggest buffalo on the range and hold him on a little grizzly dun pony he had. Two ponies were put up by the principals and heavy betting indulged in on the side.

The Mexican had a four-twist new grass rope and an exquisite Mexican saddle with a horn as big as a hat, and the horse was well trained. We were on a little slant. The Mexican rode up and threw his rope around the neck of the bison and down the hill they went, the buffalo jerking the pony forty feet at a stride. The pony was a good one and very gritty, so he lighted on his feet and kept his head toward the infuriated bull. He rushed to the verge of a precipice and pitched pony and rider down into the abyss but fortunately for the rider the girth was not tight and the saddle came off over the pony's neck. The buffalo joined his millions of companions dragging that precious saddle. The horse was skinned up and the man bruised, but neither was killed. The Indians took the ponies that they had won and went away splitting their sides with laughter.

From there we moved south about sixty miles and some of us started on a raid. We came in sight of some hunters but we just stole their horses and went on our way until we ran up on another camp where the buffalo hides were piled four feet high. A man was hobbling some horses, and just as he stooped down we dashed up. He ran into the chaparral and got away. He was the only one we saw about the camp. We ransacked the camp, burned the hides and destroyed everything except one blanket, one gun and some gunpowder, which we took, along with two ponies.

We had collected a considerable herd of horses and other property, and everything was going well. One morning about sunup we were fired on by about twenty men. We had not got up and were taken entirely by surprise. We were near the Pecos River, in New Mexico, so our enemy must have been buffalo hunters. White men sleep with their guns under their heads, but the Indians place their arms under their feet, so when they rise their weapons are in reach.

For a few moments there was nothing but discord and confusion in our camp. Women and children were crying, warriors scattered, and the whites were playing havoc in general with us. But we soon collected ourselves and hid behind bluffs and rocks. We made a fight in good earnest. (One warrior, in going through a little opening, was shot through the arm and the ball also cut the striffen that held up his bowels. He fell back out of sight of the enemy and our medicine man sewed up the wound, using whit-leather, or sinews, as the thread. He recovered.)

One warrior with a buffalo gun hit the saddle stirrup of one of the horses and stampeded them. Other warriors went around and corralled them, so we had twenty new saddle horses already equipped. This same Indian shot one white man through the leg, then the whites fell back. They were afoot, though. We followed, but the whites were too well armed for us to get very close. One of our number was wounded and a short time later died. One of the palefaces also died and they buried him under a bluff, but we found and scalped him. He must have bled to death.

We never overtook the palefaces, nor were we very anxious to, for those boys were as brave and daring as Indians.

13

AFTER A WHILE we moved north and came in sight of some soldiers, but changed our course and were not observed by them. In a day or two they struck our trail, but we decoyed them over the plains along a route where there was no water, making our trail plain.

After traveling several days they sent out scouts who found a spring and there they camped. We watched them closely and tried to steal their horses but we never could catch them off guard.

Finally they hoisted a white flag and we did the same. They sent out a man and Indehe went out to meet him, but just before they came together Indehe discharged his Winchester at the white man and ran him back to his comrades. We hurriedly struck out for Mexico. The soldiers followed us, but we crossed back into New Mexico and were driven into the [Whites Pines] reservation and promised not to run away any more. Besides, we were ready for another drunken carousal. I always had to keep hid or be killed by the red men. I was afraid of the whites anyway.

Different parties of our tribe would continue to raid, and a brave by the name of Road-Runner and I killed a white ox-driver and stole his oxen. One of us drove the oxen while the other brushed out the tracks. There were so many Indians on the reservation that we were not watched very closely. We killed those oxen and ate them and then all got drunk, and a very bad Indian from another party killed one of our number, and this man's brother killed the bad Indian, and a feud began. A great fight followed. Our party, being the stronger, killed the others and had to run away for we didn't care to be tried by the white men.

We soon came upon a party of movers, but they were in camp and one man was herding the horses. In order to see further he had climbed on a tethered horse. When we shot at him the horse ran to the end of the rope and that stopped him suddenly and the man tumbled off. A brave named Jump-And-Eat-Him rushed at the white man and the paleface tried to use his hat for a shield, but Jump-And-Eat-Him shot and killed him. We unloosed the horses and stampeded them, but we had no truck with the rest of the men. They were too well armed. We always made it a point to avoid well-armed and equipped men.

The soldiers eventually located us, rounded us up and drove us back into the reservation. I still had to be kept hidden. The various bands of our tribe would have their camps as much as fifteen miles apart, so I would always be somewhere between. One day an old Indian brought me out a large quantity of beer. We both drank freely. He began boasting of how he had treated me when I was first captured and made fun of me for being a paleface. We were both tipsy. I drew my six-shooter and ran the impudent old rascal away, shooting as I ran, and when the last chamber was empty I tumbled into a ditch and was too drunk to get up. I lay there until nearly sundown. I don't think I hit that Indian but I was trying to.

The next day, when there were no soldiers around our camp, an Indian and his squaw had a fight. The warrior came out second best in the brawl. He crawled away and picked up an old cap-and-ball rifle and was just ready to shoot the squaw when I wrenched the gun from him, cocked it, and removed the cap. I was

Tonto Apache Scouts

just letting the hammer down when it slipped and fell hard on the tube. The cap was an old "G-D" and left sulphur in the tube, so the gun fired just as a squaw walked directly in front of me with a load of wood in her arms. She tumbled over and I ran away. I thought I had killed her. Accidents are not excusable in Indian life. To kill an Indian, even by accident, means to be killed by the nearest relative of the deceased. I learned that night from my sweetheart—who knew from experience where I had hidden—that the ball struck the wood and knocked the old woman down and that she was not hurt, so I was at liberty to return to camp. I slept in Carnoviste's wigwam that night.

The next morning I went out to drive up the horses. I rode a gentle horse with a rope around his neck and a half-hitch over his nose. I made a loop in the other end of the rope and threw it around the neck of another horse. My horse stopped, but the other horse began to pitch and rear. I jumped off and horse No. 2 broke my horse's neck. I had thought the other horse was gentle. Carnoviste beat me nearly to death for this.

We moved out on the plains, a short time later, and met another party of our tribe. With them was a beautiful Mexican girl. The Indian to whom she belonged wanted us to marry and Carnoviste acquiesced and made me a long argumentative talk to that effect. I would write out his speech but decency forbids. The price of the girl was two horses and these Carnoviste offered to pay. He thought the match was a good one and was bent on leading us to the hymeneal altar together. They dressed this girl in a buckskin dress trimmed with beads and red strings. I thought she was the prettiest girl I ever saw. Then they fastened us up together in the same wigwam to see if that would make us want to marry. But in spite of her beauty and the excitement of the time together in the wigwam, I was mad. She didn't want a husband and I didn't want a wife, and furthermore, I did not intend to have somebody select one for me when I did. So what the Indians had thought was a well-arranged match did not materialize.

The Indian view of marriage was different. Some warriors would buy little girls six or seven years old and train them according to their own fancy.

When springtime came we drifted near Fort Griffin and there stole six head of horses. The soldiers followed us. We went until we struck the trail of some Lipans and Apaches. We followed this trail a ways, then scattered. The soldiers, however, kept on following the trail of those friendly Indians. These had done no harm and therefore were not afraid. They supposed that the most the soldiers would do would be to carry them back to the reservation, so they made no resistance when they saw the soldiers coming. But not so. The soldiers rushed into camp and murdered men, women and children and only a few warriors escaped to tell the tale. Thus the innocent were persecuted while the guilty went free: the vengeance was intended for us.

We quickly left such dangerous quarters and in a day or two came up on some

Mexican traders encamped in a canyon. We made a run at them and they dropped their guns and ammunition, left everything and fled. We overtook them and returned to their camp with their scalps. We took what we wished and destroyed everything else and returned to the dead bodies, cut off their heads and put them up on long poles as a warning to others. We collected all our tribe that could be found and had a big war dance around the heads of those dead Mexicans. The men marched around to the right and the women to the left. Men gesticulated and whooped, the women made signs and gave incantations. When the warriors met their wives they turned back and danced with their squaws. Guns were fired and great fires were kept up all day and night. We then moved.

We came in sight of a yoke of oxen hitched to a wagon and we sent a volley of arrows at the oxen. They reared and bucked around but fell over dead. One white man jumped out of the wagon and made his escape in the chaparral. Another man pulled his gun and stood us at bay. He was a crack shot, and the balls from his gun struck heavily on our shields. He escaped death.

We discovered that the Comanches and Kiowas were fighting the soldiers and we joined them. We surrounded a trading post, killed the keeper, and stole all we could carry. The house and what we didn't take caught on fire and was totally destroyed. I believe it was set by an incendiary.

The soldiers had buried themselves in a great ditch so we could not get to them, but we cut them off from their commissary train and tried to starve them out. Reinforcements came, but our scouts saw them and we escaped before they got to the scene. The Comanches and Kiowas stayed and fought the combined forces and were badly defeated. Many of the Indians were killed or captured and their chief was sent to Florida.

We left in the direction of Mexico, for we knew that the soldiers would not follow us there. At this time we had a great many knives made of flint rock with deer horn as handles. We would heat the flint and break them off to a sharp point. We made a great many arrowheads and strung many bows at this time.

Down near the Sandy Hills we met a party of Comanches and stayed our flight. Food was scarce, but the country abounded in tarantulas. We pulled out their legs and ate them. They are delicacies, and also, we believed that if we ate those things then the bite would not be poisonous. When we killed a beef or buffalo we would cut the gristle out of the nose and eat that raw to enable us to smell game when it was near.

HERMAN LEHMANN seems to have remembered very well his encounters with women. The affair of the beautiful Mexican girl, for instance, is given the same in both of his accounts. We do not have to have prurient interests to read between the lines of many of these sexual ventures and understand that had it not been for the times in which he wrote (he was a happily married father by then, of course) and his collaborators—both of whom seemed to soft-pedal his sexual adventures—Herman would have been much more explicit about the Indian attitudes toward sex.

Herman seems to have had great attraction for the Indian girls as well as vice versa. Part of this was his status as a white man while brother to the red, but part of it may have been the kind-hearted attitude he constantly manifests towards the Indian women, who were misused and abused according to his standards.

At about this section of his story, Herman Lehmann gives some conflicting data as well as doing a little wool-gathering, so to speak. In the 1899 account he suddenly injects this paragraph:

"I may not narrate these events in chronological order nor get the right names to the rivers and towns, but in the main my story is true history."

Readers who compare the texts of the two accounts will find them utterly confusing during this period. It is evident that the Indians wandered about the Texas and New Mexico plains, encountering Mexican traders, lonely travelers, soldiers, other Indians and other adventures without any ready reference points geographically or chronologically. This wandering could have been done over a period of a few months or a couple of years. It is hard to say.

Readers may also notice that some of the events related bear a similarity which might come from the same event being related twice. Judge Jones was no help. He apparently stuck in a story at whatever point he heard it or thought about it. J. Marvin Hunter, through this section, does not record several of the eposides. I suspect this stemmed from the fact that Herman may have repented him of his white-hating ways somewhat during the twenty-eight years which intervened between editions, or more likely, he had grown older, a respected citizen in his Mason County community, and less inclined to tell tales which would make him villainous in the eyes of the citizens. By 1927 few of his red brothers survived to count him heroic. Also, Mr. Hunter, possibly at Herman's insistence, gives fewer episodes which might cast a shadow on Herman's moral standing—or tones down the ones he uses.

However, I have used every event and every fact given about an event which I could obtain from a comparative reading of both versions. I think it is better, in this case, to err in favor of surplus than by selective neglect. Now and then the reader is simply left to flip a coin, as has already been noted in a case or two. For instance, in the upcoming chapter, Herman is pitted against a Mexican boy who is also a captive of the Apaches. In the 1899 book Herman makes a great deal more of their friendship, gives the boy a name, and describes several adventures involving the two of them, including a target shooting event which turned into a battle with two other Indian cubs, as Herman (or Judge Jones) called them. In the 1927 book there are two Mexican boy captives, one named, the other nameless, and Herman says of the first one that after a given fight he never saw him again. He also blames the Mexican boy for shooting him in the lip with an arrow—the act he blames on the "cubs" in the 1899 book.

I have taken this bull by the horns and opted for the 1899 version. It makes more sense, to me, and is much more interesting. I believe a reading of the two stories will, in the eyes of most readers, bear me out in this decision. As is the case in so many of the conflicting and confused details, how we wish that Judge Jones, Mr. Hunter and Herman were here to tell us how, or why, the stories were changed.

14

WHILE OUT ON THE PLAINS we met another part of our tribe who had been for a long time in Mexico. A Mexican boy was along, with whom I often fought, and he always whipped me. He and I were placed on fast horses and made to run a horse race. My horse came out ahead and my Indian won his bets. He was bragging on me and said that I was the better rider. The Mexicano's master said that

47

I might beat his boy riding, but Mexicano could whip me as a fighter. A wager was laid and I entered the arena. I knew that if I didn't whip him I would get a terrible beating from my master.

We hitched. Mexicano was stouter than I, so he downed me quickly and was giving me a terrible flogging when my arms stole up and my fingers became entangled in his long black hair. I gave a few jerks, made a quick twist of my body, and found myself on top. I took new courage and did some hard pounding myself. We were cheered and hissed the same as the combatants of civilized sportsmen, and we both rose and went to kicking each other. I got in a good lick below the belt and cut off his wind and won the prize. Nothing was said about a foul.

We rested a bit and then went at it anew. This time we clawed, bit, scratched and kicked. By accident my fingers strayed into his mouth and he nailed them—but by a sudden stroke I downed him and he let go. I was in a good way to win again when his master rushed in and kicked me in the head, knocking me loose.

Carnoviste instantly drew his pistol and knocked the Indian down. Our men drew their weapons and the whole crowd prepared to fight. Times looked squally. Some friendly onlookers brought about a compromise and nobody was killed, but Mexicano was not able to get up. He was carried into camp and washed and dressed. I was scrubbed and painted. I was very sore, but I had to ride races that evening. My party had the best horses, so we always won and soon the other party had nothing.

That Mexican never did whip me any more, although he tried it several times. We made friends and gave up the fight. But fighting one Mexican was nothing. I have fought three Indians at one time.

This Mexican and I were herding the horses one day and we got up a game of craps. We had no dice but we used cactus with different numbers of specks on it. Two Indian boys came along and challenged us to shoot at a mark with them. We used cactus as a target. Mexicano and I shot there until we won nearly all of the arrows that the Indians had, so they got mad. The Mexican ran them off and they had gone some ways when one of the cubs shot Mexicano through the thigh with an arrow. I ran down that way and the cub stuck an arrow in my lower lip. I shot a poisonous arrow into one of the Indians and they ran away for they had no more arrows. I pulled the spike out of my lower jaw and carried my partner back to camp where he could get attention. The Mexican soon recovered from the wound, but the poisoned Indian was sick a long time. The Indians would not allow us to eat for a long time but we killed a civet cat or two and ate them raw while herding horses.

We journeyed southeast for three or four days and met a large company of friendly Mexicans with pack-jennets, or what they call "burros," well laden with flour, meal, coffee, sugar and little trinkets to trade to the Indians for cattle, horses and mules. We had no cattle near us, so many of our saddle ponies went for these articles of civilization.

But the Indian boys and I would steal these burros and drive them twenty-five or thirty miles during one night and leave them near water. Then we would go back and the warriors would give us a plume or a red string, and we would feel well paid for our night's work. When the burros got fat we would kill them and eat them. Sometimes the Mexicans would hire us to look for their burros, and they would give us blankets and trinkets for finding them. If we worked by the day we would be out a long time; if by the job we would go straight and get them.

When the Mexican traders left us we were what you would call nowadays "busted"; that is, we had nothing left but the bitter end of a guilty conscience, so we had to go immediately on a stealing expedition.

We came down a river, I think it must have been the San Saba, but of course I do not know. I can only tell by the looks of the country since I came back to the whites. We stole a small bunch of horses. We had come in afoot and had secured enough horses to mount each Indian. There were thirteen Indians in our party and we were traveling at night, going up the river. We had taken forty or fifty horses and killed two men when the soldiers got after us. We had ridden a day and night without saying a word or eating or drinking. We were in terribly rough country. Suddenly somebody opened fire on us from the front. We were in a narrow canyon with the river on one side of us and a high bluff on the other and our enemies were hiding under the bluff. The night was dark and the fire from the white men's guns blinded us. There was a gulley just in front of us and some of the warriors saw the danger and ran back by the palefaces but the herd of horses —and most of us—dashed blindly into the ditch. My horse was killed in the fall but I caught another in the confusion. We scattered and some of us rode right through the attacking party and made our getaway. Not an Indian was killed or wounded; but one of our party, Chinava [Genava?] had his knee badly sprained when his horse fell on him. We were separated, but the horse on which I sat was young and stayed with the herd. Presently I heard the hoot of an owl and several wolves howling and I knew the signal. In a very short time we were all together again and hastened along on our journey.

Next day, just before sundown, as we were nearing the Kickapoo Springs, we discovered two men in camp with a large herd of horses. We concealed ourselves and watched them until nightfall. We saw them round up the herd and prepare to spend the night there. Just as the moon rose we rushed into the camp, stampeded the horses, and started them on a run in the direction we were traveling. The two men were asleep, and as we rushed by their pallets we shot at them, but I do not think we hit either of them. We wanted their horses, and we got them.

We kept those horses in a run all night, changing mounts frequently, and when the sun came up the next morning we were many miles from there and still going strong. But in the late afternoon of that day we discovered a party of rangers on our trail and we whipped up the herd and kept going. For four days and nights we rode without food or water. I got so tired and sleepy that I fell off my horse

Texas Rangers—the fighters Herman feared most

exhausted. The Indians picked me up and lashed me to a new horse, and on we went.

We gained a little on the rangers and watered at a spring. We went up on a hill and alighted to rest. We saw the rangers dismount at the same spring. We saw them put up ropes for their horses and prepare for camping. We were so tired we soon fell asleep.

During the night we heard shooting. We didn't realize it but a band of Kiowas had been just behind the rangers and had routed our enemies. The next morning we got up early and wearily mounted our broken-down horses and made it across the country to a spring. We were approaching the water when we saw heavily mounted men riding toward us. They had the uniforms, horses and equipment of soldiers. We thought some soldiers had passed us in the night and beat us to water. We were just about ready to give up and fight it out when one of our party, with a small mirror, flashed a ray which caught the eyes of the other group and they signaled across to us that they were friendly Kiowas.

What we had not known was that during our rest, off to our right, General Mackenzie and a large body of soldiers were encamped and sound asleep. The Kiowas had been right behind the rangers, hoping to steal their horses, and when they discovered the soldiers' camp they charged it and succeeded in driving off fifty-six head of cavalry horses. We joined forces with them and went on across the plains together before separating, the Kiowas going west to their headquarters in the Yellow House Canyon, and we to our village higher up on the plains beside a great lake of water.

50

Some time after this a party of about fifteen warriors, myself included, went down on the Pecos on a stealing expedition. We moved across the Big Devil's River and met some Mexican traders who were coming up a draw with their burros loaded with their wares. We talked with them awhile and they prepared for camping. Some of us boys cut off their pack burros and stampeded them. The Mexicans drew their short rim-fire Winchesters and demanded an explanation. We informed them that taking was less expensive than trading. We saw that most of their guns and ammunition were on the mules, so we felt safe. We displayed our firearms in a boisterous and vociferous manner and our friends the traders fled to the mountains.

We were elated over our easy victory when we were greeted by a shower of rocks and missiles from above. One warrior was struck on the shoulder and knocked from his horse. The Mexicans had slingshots with which they were hurling rocks at us with great expertness. We fired at them as they would show themselves and pretty soon they let us alone and disappeared. We took all their possessions and left them among the roughs to starve. If we killed any of these Mexicans I do not know it.

Just before we reached the Rio Grande we overtook another party of Apaches going to Mexico and among them was the Mexican boy I used to fight. His name was Salito. We crossed the river and this boy got a terrible beating from his masters—for what he never knew, unless it was because we had come into his country.

Carnoviste was not along. He had gone up into the extreme northwestern part of Texas to look for another bunch of our tribe. We had decided to spend the winter in Mexico because it did not get so cold in that region and there was an abundance of wild game to sustain us. However, he came into Mexico and joined us before the middle of the winter, bringing with him some more Apaches.

While we were down there Salito and I were often together and became great friends. As I had no boss at the time, we decided to steal away from the Indians and make a raid on our own hook. We slipped off afoot and soon got lost in the mountains, away from food and water. One day we looked down in a canyon and saw a colt grazing. I went down and drove the colt up the canyon and Salito got right over him and shot him with an arrow. He was so weak from starvation that it took several shafts to kill the colt. We lay around there and ate colt for several days and recruited. We skinned the colt and made us a canteen each out of the hide. After filling the canteens with water we cut what flesh off the carcass we could carry and journeyed on down the Rio Grande.

Somewhere near Laredo we undertook to swim the river, but it was swift and full of suck-holes and Salito came near drowning. He gave out before we got across and I had a time getting him to shore. Just as we landed we saw two men approaching and started to hide, but by their signs and maneuvers we saw they were Indians—and, indeed, proved to be from our own band. That night we went into a town on the Texas side of the river and stole thirty head of horses, Salito and I getting sixteen of that number. We reswam the river and, with the guidance of the two Indians, reached camp in about ten days.

Some time after this a party of our warriors made a raid into the interior of Mexico. I went along with this party and so did Salito. We went into town one night to steal horses and discovered five horses tied in a stable. The Indians were afraid to undertake to get them, so they sent Salito and me in to bring them out. We roped and led two out and went back for more. We struck wild ones, and they snorted and kicked. The Mexicans must have been watching, because somebody shut the stable door and fastened us up with those kicking horses. They thought they had us trapped, but I jumped out a feeding window. I made no noise, and a man passed right close to me. I sneaked away. The Indians had also slipped away when they saw the whites close in on the stable, thinking Salito and I had been captured. I waited, howled, hooted and whistled, but no Salito. I went, then, knowing he had been captured. My Indian companions had departed hurriedly, so I headed for our campsite on foot and only after traveling four days without anything to eat did I accidently find them. I had stopped at a spring to rest when these Indians came in, driving a bunch of Spanish ponies which they had stolen. They were surprised to find me there, having believed both Salito and I were captured in the stable.

We went into another town at night and divided into two parties. After prowling around for a while separately, we unexpectedly came together and each took the other for a bunch of palefaces. Several arrows were exchanged, but being saluted by no powder we discovered our mistake, and no damage was done. However, we each blamed the other for the encounter and a quarrel, or rather a debate, followed. We smoked the pipe of peace, then stole twenty or thirty head of horses and two good mules in that town and went our way.

We met a wagon, killed a Mexican man, woman and two children, scalped them, burned the wagon and carried off the horses. We proceeded to our village. Salito finally managed to escape his own people and returned to our Indian village several weeks later.

The Mexican soldiers, meanwhile, had begun to make it hot for us down there and we decided to drift back to our old hunting grounds in the United States. One day a large party of those soldiers was reported to be advancing on our camp, so we hurriedly gathered our belongings and started on our return. It took us four days and nights to reach the Rio Grande and when we did it was on a big rise and we had to swim across. We made buffalo hide boats for the children and our supplies and with several Indians on each side, ferried them across with the live cargo in safety. It took us all day to get across and we lost one man to the river. We stopped in the roughs and rested, hoping the Mexicans would not cross over into the soil of Uncle Sam to attack us, however, we made breastworks and prepared to fight, for we knew they were determined to punish us. Sure enough, the Mexicans did come on, and in a force outnumbering us five to one. They stormed our fort the next morning after they crossed the river, but we met them bravely and drove them back. They drew up a line of battle that completely surrounded us but parleyed awhile and in this cessation, Carnoviste made a speech:

"If there be any warrior here who will forsake his comrades, quit his wife and children and leave his hunting ground in the hands of the enemy, let him go now. The enemy is well armed, but we are, too, and we are protected by the nature of this place and our own fortifications. Just under this sand flows plenty of water, as you can see from that hole; our stores are plentiful and we have food enough to last us a moon. Our horses are given out and to escape by flight is impossible. Let us fight together and be assured that no force the Mexicans can raise can rout us from here. But if our fortifications protect cowards, let them now go."

Not an Indian attempted to escape. All resolved to live together, fight together and conquer together.

The Mexicans made another furious charge but were repulsed; up they came again, but fell back before our deadly fire. This time they seemed determined to take our camp at all costs, and scores of brave warriors succumbed to their bullets, but each one let his strength be felt in the line of the enemy. Carnoviste ordered his Indians to shoot deliberately, picking out a man. Night came on and the Mexicans withdrew. We had sixty-two killed and about twenty wounded. Under cover of darkness, we buried our dead in a cave nearby, killed their horses and dragged them in too, then filled the mouth of the cave with rocks. One warrior, Wollolloomoomo, who was killed had a Mexican boy. We killed him and buried him beside his master.

The Mexican attackers did not renew the battle next morning. I do not know whether it was on account of their losses or because we were in the United States. It was not often the Apaches would fight hemmed up, but we knew from tradition how merciless the Mexicans were. Had these been United States soldiers we would have surrendered without firing a gun.

Our whole camp was in grief. The squaws would beat their breasts and cut great gashes in their arms. These were sad scenes, and civilization cannot comprehend the suffering, woe and misery of them. All was one continuous wail and lamentation. There was neither sleep nor rest that night.

We carried our wounded on a litter made of two poles fastened on each side of a horse's shoulder and the other ends on the ground. The poles were long enough to be springy. Withes were tied between the poles behind the horse, blankets spread over them and the wounded Indians laid on and closely bound. There was a horse and litter for each wounded Indian. We were very careful in driving the horse with a wounded comrade, although at times we would have to make him run to keep from being captured. We came on north far enough to be out of the way of the Mexicans and joined another party of the Apaches.

15

WE EVENTUALLY RETURNED to the Llano Estacado and camped near a watering place which was a large natural lake. Bohoha and I twisted a rope of buffalo hide and made it so large and strong that we thought it could not be broken. We saw a cloud of dust rising in the distance, and we knew the buffalo were coming to the lake to water. We climbed a tree nearby, fastened our rope to the trunk of the tree some twenty feet high, and made a loop in the other end. We selected a big buffalo bull and dropped the noose right in front of him. He stepped right in and we tightened the rope, then gave him slack enough to drink.

The herd became frightened at our teepee on the other side of the lake and started to run. This bull, being in the middle of the herd, could not have stopped if he had wanted to. On they went with a dash, and our tree began to bend very rapidly. But all at once the rope gave way and the trap sprang back upright and something went "Splash!" Bohoha and I swam out of the lake and laughed over the episode.

That night Millalamo, an Indian squaw, with a tomahawk, killed a Mexican lion under that very tree. The next day she went into a nearby cave and killed a panther, carried it out, put it on her horse and brought it into camp and took a quirt and made her husband skin it. We all stood by and enjoyed this domestic felicity. On another occasion Millalamo roped a bear, hog-tied him, and brought him into camp alive. She said she wanted the bear alive to train her dogs on.

When we were in the pine country of New Mexico there were many encounters with bears. One day I was out hunting afoot when I came in sight of two big cinnamon bears, but they were running and out of range. I had a rim-fire Winchester and a cap-and-ball six-shooter. I went on a little farther and heard a rustling. I stooped and looked under the limbs of the trees and saw a big grizzly bear watching some deer. I slipped up cautiously in close range and aimed at the heart of his bearship and pulled the trigger. Instead of tumbling over dead, the bear growled fiercely and came at me.

I threw my Winchester down and ran. I dodged him and climbed a small pine tree. The bear trailed me there. He walked around my tree and then up to it. He smelled up it, then sat down on his haunches with his paws around the tree. He looked straight up at me as if to say, "I can stay here as long as you can."

I took out my pistol and fired. Bruin didn't move. I tried him with another shot, and another, and another, and I continued shooting at him at intervals for several hours. I would climb nearly down and I would see the long hair waving on his neck and up the sapling I would go. I shot away all my ammunition and shouted myself hoarse, but no help came. I climbed out on a limb something like twenty feet from the ground, but I was afraid to drop, so back to the trunk of the tree I went, and then I would try the limb again, but it looked a long ways to the ground and I was afraid the bear would hear me when I jumped—even though his back was turned—and catch me.

The day waned and I was desperate. I hung down by my hands. Still I was a long ways from the ground. I held there and debated whether to get back up on the limb or turn loose and finally I decided to climb back and wait for help, however long it took, but when I attempted it I found that I was too weak. I held on as long as I could but my muscles relaxed, I lost my hold and fell to earth.

I felt a shock and fire flew from my eyes. I rushed away, stumbling over logs and becoming entangled in briers and vines, but at last I breathlessly reached camp, all torn and bruised. I rested awhile and recovered somewhat from my fright, recovered my wits, and told my story to the excited group which gathered around me.

Several braves and I mounted fast horses and made our way to the tree and there sat the old grizzly in the same, silent, unconcerned posture. We reluctantly approached and cocked our Winchesters. One warrior went nearer to lance him, keeping the tree between himself and bruin. Suddenly he gave bruin a stab with the spear, but the old fellow never moved. He was dead—cold and stiff. The first shot from the Winchester had done it. My pistol shots had not even broken the hide, but were all rolled up in the wool. We dressed him and barbecued him and he was fine eating.

We stayed in those parts all one autumn, hunting bear. We were not afraid of black bear but grizzlies were dreaded, and more than one of our braves went out and never returned from a grizzly chase. Even while we were feasting on my fellow, three of our boys met their doom from his family.

We had our camp at a spring, the only water for miles, and one evening we were all sitting around, lazily smoking cigarettes when, to our astonishment and awe, a huge grizzly bear came stumping into camp uninvited. His paws were simply immense. He brought terror to our hearts. He sat down and quietly surveyed the teepee with an inquiring glance.

Confusion, no, consternation, reigned, but gentle bruin didn't seem the least excited. Such skipping, scampering and squalling of the squaws and the little squallers. What was to be done? To pour a volley of Winchester balls at him might only infuriate him, besides maybe killing half a dozen Indians.

A council of war was held and all formalities disposed of. The chief picked out two fine spears and offered them as a prize to the man who would kill bruin. A young Indian named Yumana and I took the implements and started at the grizzly from opposite directions. He growled and started at me and Yumana made a lunge at him but missed. I attracted the bear's attention so that Yumana escaped, but eventually we retreated and left bruin the master of the situation.

Several other Indians tried to kill him but bruin bluffed them. We were all mounted, by this time, on fleet horses. Then the chief and the sachem became furious at our mishandling of things. Both made a dash at bruin and left two spears in his heart. He soon expired and we young braves had all lost our chance to become chiefs and the old heroes retained their former places.

Only one thing we found that these bears were afraid of and that was a mule. The braying of a donkey would frighten them away, so we learned to ride mules. One day Carnoviste and I were out hunting and a grizzly tackled us. Carnoviste was riding a mule, and just as the bear reached out to seize him the mule brayed. Bruin turned and covered my master with heel dust. As the bear passed me I sent a ball through his heart. He ran about one hundred yards and gave up the ghost.

One day late in the fall I was out horse hunting and saw a great quantity of brush and debris piled up near a large pine tree. I saw in this heap a large grizzly sucking his forepaw. He was in winter quarters. I went back to camp and reported. A war party went out with me to butcher him. He was easily slain, and he was a monster. Every Indian family had a separate campsite, but all were liberal in times of plenty, so that night we all had roast bear. When food was scarce the squaws became very saving, so economical that we were not allowed enough to eat, and then we would be dead sure to visit the whites and see what we could steal.

One day a stout, agile young warrior by the name of Eatquick rode a young horse out hunting and found and shot a bear. The horse became frightened and threw Eatquick off and he landed in a thicket right between two young cubs. The little bears nailed Eatquick. It was first the cubs, then the Indian on top. At last the Indian got his knife from his belt and ended the little bruins' days on earth, but when Eatquick came into camp he was all bruised, clawed, cut, torn and bleeding.

One warrior had been missing for several days and we were searching for him. We found him and his horse, both dead. His arms were torn from his body and he was otherwise terribly mangled. A grizzly had been there. Our men buried him and went home mourning and lamenting.

Another red man we found dead under the paws of a dead bear. Both were conquerors and conquered. The victor and the victim were buried in the same grave, but we ate the bear. Over the grave we smoked the pipe of peace. With uplifted eyes and lowly spirits we sent smoke curling to the sun, apologizing to the Great Spirit for destroying the grass where we dug the grave and also for the weeds we burned in our pipes.

The Apache was ever mindful of the great Creator and stood in awe and reverence before all nature and the handiwork of the Great Spirit. He had no idea of Christianity but he bowed to every weed he bent, every stream he crossed, and begged the pardon of every animal that he killed, and he always praised or implored the Great Spirit after each chase, engagement or war.

16

ONE YEAR we had a brush with the soldiers on the plains and we again made for Mexico, where we knew they would not follow. We reached the Pecos River and in crossing that turbulent stream one Indian girl's horse gave out and she went down the river. I jumped in to catch her but she caught me around the neck and I could not get loose. In desperation I struck her and knocked her almost senseless. I caught her by the hair and an Indian on the bank pitched me a rope. I caught it and gave it to the girl, and the fright and excitement made me so weak that I could not swim. I caught and held to some reeds until help came and pulled me out. I was strangled and exhausted and more dead than alive when I was taken out.

Here we prepared a camp for the women and children, on the west bank of the Pecos. Then some Comanches came up and we all left our families there, recrossed the river and started to make a run on the palefaces.

We came to near the head of the Llano River, where we separated; the Comanches going farther north while we went downriver. We saw two men with an ox team and made a run at them, but they fought us off until they had a chance to dash to a house nearby. We prowled around and waited for them to come out but they did not show themselves.

A night or two later we slipped into a small town where we watched from the streets and saw men drinking. We peeped in the windows and saw a great many pretty things. We came out north of the town and discovered two men camped under some live oak trees. We killed and scalped them and stole six horses. I think these men must have been freighters because the horses had harnesses on.

Out northwest of there we burned a house and killed a man, his wife and four or five children. We tortured them before we killed them.

We went on and found a spring. We stopped to water and rest. An Indian named Rover was lying down drinking when we heard the report of a gun close to us. The Indian drinking howled with pain. We thought the rangers were on us so we stampeded and hid behind rocks and trees, prepared to fight. All was quiet for a time and Rover, at the spring, remained there. Carnoviste cautiously stole back and found that this Indian's pistol had struck a rock and accidentally discharged, striking him in the knee and inflicting a painful wound. This Indian became a cripple for life.

We traveled leisurely along going back to camp, for we were not followed. We came in sight of four men, two on horseback, two in a buggy and leading a pack mule. We rode down toward them Comanche style, and they separated. We followed the buggy but some of the boys pursued the horsemen. The buggy headed for a mesquite flat, the lines broke, and the horses ran headlong into a deep ditch.

We overtook them, killed and scalped the men, grabbed the horses and got their pack animal. In the pack was a large quantity of greenbacks, silver, and gold. The greenbacks we tore up, but made ornaments of the silver and gold. We burned the buggy and by that time the others came up with the scalps, horses and money of the two horseback riders. Those men had, however, killed one of the Indian's horses from under him.

This time we went into camp fat and full. We procured several long poles and placed the scalps we had on them, and had a big feast and dance. We had an oversupply of silver and gold. We would throw this money and whoever got it when it fell kept it. We beat out gold and mounted our pipes, decorated our tomahawks, put strips around our knife handles and fancied up all kinds of personal items.

Shortly after this we moved camp and prepared for a great festival, the significance of which was not clear to me. We first had to undergo seven days of hunger, then the seven strongest and most robust Indians were selected to dance continuously for seven days and nights without partaking of any food except a moist root prepared especially for this ordinance.

The medicine men who prepared this food performed many tricks that I don't understand even yet and no others could do, such as sticking knives in their bodies without bringing blood. Why, I have seen them cut great gashes in their legs and no blood would flow. Then they would eat small apples that grew on a cactus found only in certain mountains of Mexico, and were of great commercial value among the Indians.

They made a preparation from these apples called "hooshe." We ate nothing but hooshe for four days and we felt so light and happy that we loved everybody and wanted to fly away. There is a plant which grows in Mexico which is called peyote, and is held in great veneration by the Indians, and it is quite possible that the medicine men used this in the preparation of the hooshe, also. The medicine men charged us enormous prices for hooshe and by the time we got over one of these dances they owned all the property.

Some medicine men claimed to control the atmosphere and command the rains to come. I have seen them go out on a high point and wave a cow's tail and chant and pray to the Great Spirit for rain, and if it doesn't come they draw the conclusion that some of their people have provoked the Great Spirit. So they go back to camp and assemble all the people to see who the guilty party might be, and when they find a devil, it is banished, exiled, or put to death.

Once I knew them to be trying very hard, but the drouth continued, so the medicine men came into camp and put the blame on a Mexican man who was staying with us. This man was then firmly bound, hand and foot, with rawhide, carried away up on the mountain and bound to a flat rock. Near him was staked a large rattlesnake, placed just near enough to strike the Mexican whenever he moved.

58

Apache Devil Dance, which Herman witnessed

We returned to camp and the incantations were repeated, and there came up a funnel-shaped cloud and a regular waterspout followed. Our wigwams were washed away, one squaw and one white child captive were drowned, several horses went down in the mighty waters and also many weapons disappeared. We had to flee to the mountains for safety. (The Indian that was drowned had an illicit child.)

Indians could forecast the weather by the webs of spiders. In dry weather the web is thin, long and high, but in rainy weather, or just before a rain, the web is low, short and thick.

After our religious festival something happened to one of the braves. One morning a warrior named Rip-It-Out put on an antelope skin and went on his all-fours to surprise and kill antelope. He crawled out to within a hundred yards of where the animals were grazing. Another brave, Blue Cloud, saw this animal away off by itself and not knowing it was an Indian, he took aim and brought it down. Blue Cloud crawled up to skin his antelope and found the dead Indian wrapped in an antelope hide. He went back to the camp in grief and told his pathetic story. Rip-It-Out was a relative of Carnoviste so, under the tribal code, he started to kill Blue Cloud, but the squaw of Rip-It-Out stepped between them and saved Blue Cloud's life.

We hunted buffalo frequently at this location. We would mount our best horses and rush out when the herds passed near. The one who got the first shot usually brought down the biggest and fastest, so we raced to be first. We would ride right in among the animals and that would stampede them. After we had emptied our guns, we would work our way out of the herd, but if it proved to be too large and the pack too thick, we might be carried in the mad rush of the infuriated herd for miles. Nothing would turn buffalo when stampeded. They would go right off a bluff, into a river, or anywhere. I once knew two Indians carried over a bluff into a great hole of water who perished among thousands of buffalo.

In one of these stampedes you could not see the source of danger, even if you might have been able to avoid it, for there was so much dust it was blinding, and those behind you would press you on. I was once caught in a stampeding herd. My horse ran against a mesquite and fell. I fell under him, but up near a large log. The herd trampled my horse into sausage meat. I was stunned, bruised and skinned, but I got over it. You lovers of excitement, how would you enjoy being among millions of buffalo, enveloped in dust, and traveling at the rate of thirty miles an hour and not permitted to select the ground over which you ran?

We were always fed on body lice after a race of this kind. Sometimes we would fry the lice and consider them a dainty and this gravy was a favorite flavoring.

A kind of snake infested the plains in that region, something like an asp. Its bite was almost sure death. These snakes nearly always went in pairs, and if you killed one, its mate would trail you up and bite you, even though you were fifty miles from the dead mate. Ai-Ai, a young fellow, had just married and one day,

60

I was told, he killed one of these snakes, then traveled twenty miles and camped that night with his young bride. This snake's mate trailed him up, and just as the moon was straight overhead this serpent pierced its fangs into the throat of Ai-Ai's new wife, and she died immediately. From that night on Ai-Ai quit us and I saw him often, later, roaming over the plains; at his belt bundles of the "scalps" of these snakes.

Once we were camped on a little sandy creek where the grass was high and dry. Suddenly we smelled fire and, looking up, saw a cloud of smoke. We all went to work trying to clear an area around the camp, pulling the grass or burning it to check the fire and prevent it from reaching us. Soon the fire came as fast as a horse could run. The blaze reached out fifty feet with its great, fiery tongue, and the smoke stifled us. Some of the Indians got in water, others buried themselves in the sand, and all sought cool places. Snakes, deer, antelope, buffalo, smaller animals rushed to our places of refuge. Thousands of animals and reptiles perished in the flames. We lost several members and twenty horses. Some squaws rushed on ahead of the flames, leaving their children behind them to a horrible death; others buried themselves in buffalo hides and were saved. One old woman's eyes were literally burned out, and several children succumbed to the heat alone.

17

ONE DAY I was out hunting with an Indian who was afterwards killed by the Comanches, whom we called Totoabacona—which means "come when you get ready." I was riding that noted dun mule and he a swift, manageable pony. A buffalo made fight and took after old dun and me. I spurred and whipped, but old dun was an established mule, and would not go until he got ready.

The Indian, like a martin, would dart in and goad the buffalo with a spear, or pierce him with an arrow, and thus for an instant distract his attention from old dun and me. Totoabacona made one good shot, but the furious buffalo wanted dun and me and kept coming. But Totoabacona rode between us and shot the buffalo again, but he rode so close the buffalo gored his horse. The buffalo staggered and fell right under old dun. The Indian's pony ran a little way and fell dead. I hitched the mule and went up to skin the buffalo, but the beast was not dead. It jumped up and charged Totoabacona, but the red man was too quick, and the shaggy animal tumbled over a low bluff, breaking his neck in the fall.

This little episode took place in the hills not far from where the mountains made a circle, enclosing a level prairie of two or three hundred acres and coming within sixty yards of each other at the foot on the south side. The slope was almost perpendicular, at least the ascent was impossible on that side.

It was a common pastime of ours to head a drove of antelope for that natural amphitheatre and when they went in we would form a phalanx of warriors at the mouth, then put some of our boys on fleet horses to give chase to the animals. When the antelope came near the mouth, we would set up a yell and close in, and thus the poor beasts would be compelled to circle and run themselves down and collapse in utter exhaustion. This was sport for the whole tribe; squaws, children and all. Much and heavy was the betting, each warrior selecting his pony and his rider, each participant straining every muscle to catch the first antelope. Often horse and rider would fall exhausted at the feet of their dying game, and thus ponies, saddles, blankets and guns changed hands. (An Indian considered it his religious duty to pay his gambling debts.) Not a few times I was selected to run these races and I became a favorite rider.

Remembering these exciting rides makes me think of another time that I fairly flew over this very rough country—this occurring some seven or eight months after I was stolen.

The braves ran a large, fat mustang stallion into this amphitheatre, roped him and tied him down, then blindfolded him. They bound me securely on that charger, then several braves mounted swift horses. The stallion was released. He turned his head around, saw me, and bit me on the arm, taking out a great plug. I forgot that I was a stoic, and gave out a loud yell. That yell, or something, frightened the mustang. He took off across the plains and over the roughs, jumping canyons and running for dear life. The Indians followed, but could not even keep in sight of us.

The black stallion made railroad time for about ten miles, then, in leaping another ditch, stumbled, fell to his knees and threw me off. But up came the horse with a mighty bound and flew away as lightly as he did the first mile, and I have never seen nor heard of him to this day.

I lay there, suffering with my arm and chewing the bitter end of reflection until one of the pursuing party came up to me.

His horse was run down. It was not long then until the other parties came up, one by one, according to the speed and power of endurance of their steeds. They laughed and cheered me, and bound up my arm. One of the riders took me up behind him and I felt as though I was about to be crowned chief. In an hour or two we merrily reached camp.

We had horse flesh to eat that night in honor of that ride. It was getting to be cold weather again. We killed a mustang, cut the fat off his back, roasted that in ashes, cut it up in thin slices and put it out to freeze. Then we would serve it and it was a fit dish for a king.

Calves, snails, whippoorwills and land terrapins thus served are all right, although some of the above are hard to keep until cold weather. We had caverns in the rocks where we would store them away for winter eating. Terrapins make fine soup, when parboiled, at any season of the year.

When I had been with the Apaches for quite a while, Carnoviste decided to seek a new country. We were at that time in the mountains of New Mexico, the Guadalupe Range, it must have been. That region was getting pretty well crowded with Indians because so many of the Apaches had been pushed back by civilization. Carnoviste sent me and two Indians, Esacona and Pinero, to seek new country far to the northwest.

Just after we left camp a little two-year-old girl that I had petted tried to follow. It was away up in the day that she was missed. A search party scoured the country and found her asleep in a dense thicket. Near her lay the carcasses of four monster loboes, and over her stood my favorite dog, a big Newfoundland. He had faithfully guarded and protected the little girl, but the venom of the wolves, from their bites, was in his blood and in an hour or two after the child was found the dog died. The Indians held a funeral dance over him, buried him nicely and erected a stone over him.

We had a pack horse and an abundance of provisions, but the grass was short and our horses got poor and lame. We started out in a southwesterly direction at first and went into old Mexico, where we did not find anything to suit us. There had been a great drought in that country. After traveling many days our horses gave out and we stole fresh horses from some Mexicans and took a course toward what I suppose is Arizona.

We came into a mountainous district that showed signs of habitation, and that night we saw a mining camp. They had a great many burros loaded with mining tools. We stole six of these burros—we had no use for mining implements but picks, crowbars and shovels are hard to destroy, so we left them. We rode these donkeys and drove our horses for about one hundred miles until we came to a spring that we expected to revisit, so we camped there for several days. Our horses had become jaded and tender-footed and we decided to leave them there until we returned. Game was plentiful and the deer almost tame, so we had plenty to eat. After we left the spring, water became scarce. We were not acquainted with the country and didn't know where to find water. The dew was heavy at night and we managed on that, but for nine days our burros did without water.

We traveled along leisurely for several days, going due west until we came to a barren desert region, wholly devoid of vegetation and water; just a stretch of white sand for miles and miles. We must have traveled twenty miles that first day and we seemed no nearer to anything. That night we lay down in the sand to sleep. It grew cold and the wind rose. The next morning we found ourselves buried in a sand bank. Our mules were staked nearby and were submerged in the sand. We had a time digging them out. They had laid down when the wind began to blow.

We plodded along for days, the only thing to break the monotony being the fierce sand storms which would occasionally sweep along, blinding us and impeding our travel. On the sixth day, far in the distance, we discerned a chain of blue mountains, which at first we took to be a low-lying cloud. We pushed on, and as we went forward the mountains began to take form and shape, and we knew that if we could hold out we could reach them within another week at the rate we were traveling, our speed being necessarily slow because our pack burros (we were down to two) were beginning to suffer for forage and water. Our water supply was just about exhausted and we realized that if we did not reach the mountains we would perish there on that desert with our faithful burros.

At last we reached the foot of those mountains on the fifteenth day after starting across that desert, and so near exhausted were we that I believe if we had not reached there when we did we could not have held out another day.

Going up a canyon a short distance we found a fine spring and an abundance of grass, and right there we stopped to rest for several days before penetrating those mountains. When we had rested for a reasonable time we pushed on and traveled leisurely into the very heart of one of the most beautiful regions I have ever seen. Game was in superabundance; black-tailed deer, bear, lions, panthers, and other wild animals were to be seen everywhere and would not run when we approached. While we were prospecting in those mountains and happy in their solitude, we found a most peculiar formation, which arrested our attention and we wondered at its grandeur.

Near the top of a high mountain a kind of tableland had been formed and from this tableland there was a sheer bluff or wall over which water poured, when it rained, forming a basin many feet below. The wall over which this water flowed was worn smooth by the water's fall, and was of a peculiar blue rock formation. In the basin below we found a storage of clear water which had a mineral taste, and which we were afraid to use, for Pinero said it might be poison. In this basin we found the same kind of blue formation, and throughout the whole formation were outcroppings of a bright yellow ore which was in layers an inch or two in thickness and easily removed. Pinero and Esacona suggested that we get some of the pretty yellow and blue rocks to take to the squaws, and with our scalping knives we dug out a number of large pieces of the yellow stuff and put it in our packs and carried it away with us. I had several pieces of it four or five inches long and two or three inches in thickness. We noticed it was very heavy, while the blue rocks were rather light and full of pores.

We had no idea what the stuff was, as we were all three just young Indian cubs and not versed in mineralogy.

After spending one moon (a month) in those mountains, killing game and selecting a location for our villages when the tribe was brought there, we took up the weary march across the wide desert and finally reached the former camping ground by the spring where we had left our sore-footed horses. We found them fat and in good condition, and after resting there a few days, we set out for our headquarters, reaching there in due time and reporting to Carnoviste that we had found an earthly Happy Hunting Grounds where the Great Spirit dwelt in every

64

canyon and where His smile kissed every mountaintop at sunrise each morning.

Carnoviste grunted his satisfaction and delight, but when we showed him the pretty rocks we had brought back with us he sorrowfully shook his head and said that inviting region was not for the Indian, that it would prove a delusion and a snare and if we went there it would only increase our troubles. He said the rocks were gold, and that very thing kept our people from going into those mountains to establish our headquarters. Carnoviste said we would not be safe there, for where there was gold to be found the white man would hunt for it. We gave up all hope of ever finding a land where the white man would not come.

I DON'T KNOW WHAT TO MAKE of this story, particularly the part about the gold deposits. One of the fondest beliefs of the white world was (and continues to be) that the red men knew of fabulous treasures—of raw gold layers in the mysterious hills; of caves stacked with gold and silver bars, of jewels the size of dove eggs or a diamond as big as a mountain. Coronado, Estevanico, Fray Marcos, all went looking for the cities of gold where the savages dwelt in haughty ignorance of its true nature. Perhaps Herman was merely performing as he thought an Indian would be expected to perform with this story.

The implication has always been that the Indians, in not realizing its wealth, were stupider than the white men, who lusted for the gold, the silver, and the jewels the size of dove eggs. Yet there has also been the hint that it is the white man who, in being willing to sacrifice anything and everything to find this wealth, has set a false value on life.

It may be dealing too much in symbolism to hope that Herman Lehmann was attempting to put in parable form some deeper understanding of true freedom he brought out with him from the Indian years. But at any rate, the beautiful tale of the pieces of raw gold and of Carnoviste's dignified denial of the earthly paradise, is not to be found in *A Condensed History*. There the journey is treated in much shorter terms and the reasons for not going to the lost valley are more mundane—primarily that the Indians were afraid to cross the desert. Gold and precious ores are not mentioned.

We might suppose that in 1899 Herman felt constrained not to mention the gold rock and the turquoise (or manganese ore or whatever precious substance we are supposed to take it for) because he hoped to reclaim it someday for himself. Or could the fact that he hadn't mentioned it mean that it was something which came back to him after the 1899 book had been published? Memory does strange things, of course, although it is hard to believe that Herman could have remembered the hard journey and the wonderful country and not have remembered the gold.

There is the final possibility that Herman simply made up the part about the gold, feeling it was required of any western storyteller. By 1927, when the second book—the one with the gold tale—was written, the treasure hunters had already accumulated quite a literature of lost mines and lost hoards of gold and minerals. Herman and his editor, in incorporating a lost-gold story, would have been playing to a guaranteed audience.

Everybody is inaccurate to a greater or lesser degree when recalling experiences. But there is a classic breed of western writers who lie from compulsion, not to mention another school who lie for profit. But J. Marvin Hunter, while he was not always accurate and might accept some highly illogical suppositions as truth, was no liar. He swallowed a lot of bad history and passed it on, but I don't think he ever created it out of whole cloth.

I have said that a lie was the final possibility, but like Herman does a time or two, I will pause and say no, there is another. There is the possibility that after nearly fifty years Herman had become convinced that he had seen gold and sincerely believed it whether he had or not.

Someone might also say there exists still another possibility: that the gold was later discovered by white prospectors and was as rich a find as it sounds. True enough. But the size of those nuggets Herman describes is big enough to have created its own legends. Herman makes it sound as if he could have found some gold rocks the size of the world's biggest recorded nugget, which is about 2,500 ounces. A latter-day find of this mother lode would have remained on the record books.

Whatever the real nature of the gold story, Herman tells it in an almost poetic way and we can be thankful for getting it. As for how much of Herman's illogic and inaccuracy is intentional, how much from ignorance and how much intruded into his story by other hands, we can't know. The earlier little story about the snake (the asp) that pursues you for twenty miles in order to take revenge is pure malarkey, although the Indians may have believed it. A lot of the detail about eating raw meat, civet cats, tarantulas, tortoises, is for shock value. Remember, Herman liked to scare the kids even after he was an old man. It was part of his charm.

18

IN 1875 one of the largest parties of Mexican traders came to our camp on the plains. They had plenty of mescal and corn whiskey and tobacco, and most of the tribe got drunk. A party of one hundred forty Indians and sixty of the Mexicans went on a cattle raid.

West of Fort Griffin, on the old trail, we ran into a big herd being driven to Kansas. There were about twenty hands with the cattle. We rushed up and opened fire. The cattle stampeded and the cowboys rode in an opposite direction. There were enough of us to surround the cattle and chase the boys. We soon gave the boys up and started for Mexico with the herd, but the second day we were overtaken by about forty white men, who tried to retake the cattle. In the attempt two Mexicans and one Indian were killed—the Indian was shot through the neck —and we had four horses killed. We repulsed them and got possession of two of their dead, who were promptly scalped. I don't know what other losses they sustained. We went on southwest with the herd and had about three thousand head when we reached the village. These we traded to the Mexicans and immediately stampeded them. Some of these cattle were branded HEY.

We put the scalps of the two cowboys on high poles and had a big feast and war dance. We slew forty beeves and roasted them all at once. We kept up a chant and dance around those scalps day and night. More Mexicans had come and replenished our stock of whiskey. We had a little disagreement—a debate— and in order to settle the ruckus satisfactorily to all concerned, we killed two Mexicans and raised their scalps on poles.

We drank all the whiskey, sobered up, ran off the Mexicans and kept all their trinkets, guns, ammunition and so forth. But they got most of the cattle, which was more than enough pay. Then we repented over the Mexican affair and hired them to make friends with us again. We moved our village away out to the Sandy Hills and spent some time hunting. There we found deer, antelope, musk-hogs and a few buffalos.

66

A cattle drive coming up from Mexico, choice Apache target

I have often been asked how we made the flint stone arrow spikes, and I will here endeavor to explain the process: We threw a large flint stone, from two to six feet in circumference, into the fire. After the stone became very hot, small, thin pieces would pop off. We selected those pieces which would require the least work to put into shape and picked those hot pieces up with a stick split at the end. While these pieces were very hot we dropped cold water on those places we wished to thin down. The cold water caused the spot touched to chip off, and in this way we made some of the keenest pointed and sharpest arrows that could be fashioned out of stone. Many of these arrows [arrowheads] in perfect shape can still be picked up in certain places all over Texas.

Our arrows were made of a straight dogwood withe, with a feather grooved in one end and a flint rock or steel spike on the other. We first used flint rock for spikes, also flint rock knives, which were used to skin buffalo and other animals. Later, when the soldiers began to come onto the plains, we found old barrel hoops and other steel around their camps, and from this steel we made arrow spikes and discarded our old flint rock spikes. The Mexicans furnished us with files with which to fashion and sharpen our [steel] arrows. For bowstrings we used whitleather (or sinews) taken from the tenderloin of a beef or deer. The Indians corrupted the name to "singers." In a separate quiver we carried a few poisoned arrows to use in battle. The venom of the rattlesnake was used on these spikes.

67

We started south that summer, to make another run on the whites, and the first thing that broke the monotony of the raid and stirred up a little local interest was an affray with several men near the Concho River. The battle was fierce, and both forces were drawn off to care for their dead and wounded. We lost three of the bravest Indians that ever smoked a cigarette. We put some sticks up in a big live oak tree, lay the dead up there (so the wolves would not eat them) and covered them with blankets. All their guns, arrows and trinkets were wrapped up with them and their horses led under the tree and shot, so the Indians would be mounted and equipped when they reached the Happy Hunting Ground.

I do not know what losses the white men sustained, but it must have been great, for the fight was long and fierce and we saw nothing more of our foes.

We came southeast to another river and spied a man who was walking 'round and around. The Indians crawled up, waylaid him, and sent an arrow right through his breast. He stood there and spat blood. The Indians let him suffer for a while, then dispatched him and carried along his scalp. This man must have been lost, for he had nothing with which to fight and carried only some old rusty knives and bundles that looked somewhat worsted by the weather.

Keeping our course, we came upon some men working in a rock quarry. One man had been left to guard their camp. We surrounded them and fired twice at the camp guard and he ran and hid in the chaparral. The quarry workmen made their escape through the thick undergrowth. We took possession of their camp, where we found only one horse, five .44 caliber rim-fire Winchesters with belts full of cartridges, sugar, flour, salt and other necessities of camp life. We strewed the ground with sugar, flour, meal and salt, destroyed the meat, and demolished the men's wagon and everything else we could find that we could not carry along.

We went south, as I well remember, and saw some children playing in a field near a house. We slipped up close and made a run at the children and Snapping Turtle, a Kiowa, grabbed at one child as he ran through the fence. A white man came out with a Winchester and shot Snapping Turtle through the knee. We fought there for about two hours and tried to get revenge, but the man was brave and cautious and we never got a fair shot at him. There were cattle near the house which bore a brand resembling a broadaxe or hatchet, but we did not want cattle, we wanted blood and horses. We would not have fought if it had not been that the man crippled one of our warriors. We went on a little farther and rounded up nine good horses. We sent these, the cattle and the crippled Indian and two companions back to our village.

Farther on we discovered a man making rails. When we rushed at him he threw down his axe and lit out for his horse, which was tied to a tree. He hastily mounted the animal and forgot to untie him. He spurred the horse into a run and when he reached the end of the stake rope the sudden stop caused horse and rider to turn a flip. The man got up running and made his escape, while we got the horse, a little sorrel pony.

We rode up the hill and captured twelve head of horses, a big bay mule and a light sorrel mule. We then started for home by way of Kickapoo Springs, and there we made ourselves the present of a nice drove of fat ponies. But our scouts informed us that the hated rangers were on our trail. We dreaded them, so we made for the plains, although this was not according to our plans, for we had anticipated a fortnight's hunting. We traveled three days and nights without stopping to sleep or eat. We well knew how sleepless and restless those rangers were and how unerring their aim when they got in a shot, so we outrode them.

The fourth day we came up on a big old fat jackass some Mexican had set free, so we butchered, roasted and ate him. He was very palatable after our three day fast. We rested there and grazed our horses. Two days later we killed and ate a mustang. We thought we were entirely out of danger, so we turned our fast horses loose in the herd and most of the Indians rode mules. I happened to be on a fast pony but we were traveling leisurely along.

We had started at daylight that morning, and about half an hour by sun the rangers unexpectedly came at us from the east. They had cautiously kept between us and the sun so they could not be seen. They were right at us before we knew they were near. The chief ordered us to stand and fight, saying there was no hope in flight, but the warriors obeyed no orders but their own wills, and leaping onto their ponies, soon scattered.

19

I LEARNED, after my return to civilization, that this party of rangers was commanded by the famous scout and Indian fighter, Captain Dan W. Roberts, who at this writing (May 27, 1927) is still living at Austin, Texas.

In spite of the orders of our chief, when the fight started our men scattered and only four of us remained to fight the trained rangers. Some of the ranger force followed the retreating Indians. One Indian's horse had a leg broken by a shot, so the rider jumped up behind Mockoash, a Lipan who was with our party, and they rode away. The Indians who had fled carried our rim-fire Winchesters with them.

Another Indian, a brother to our chief, was unhorsed and he ran west. I rode up beside him and he jumped up behind me, and we made for our comrades. I was shooting all the time and I put several arrows in the nearest ranger's saddle. But the rangers were too quick for us and a group cut us off while those who had been after Mockoash and his companion turned on us—and there we were between two fires.

Nusticeno (Old-Trot-Slow) was the name of the warrior behind me. He protected us on one side with his shield and I held my shield up on the other. I directed my arrows to those in front and he shot backwards. Several bullets hit my

Dan W. Roberts, Captain of the Rangers
at "The Fight on the Concho Plains"

shield and knocked it against my forehead, each stroke raising a bump. I could hear the bullets also fairly raining on Nusticeno's shield.

In a few seconds my horse was shot down and fell on me. Nusticeno's bow had broken in the fall, so he seized mine and ran for life. I implored him not to leave me, but he heeded not my entreaties in his mad scramble for life. I was pinned underneath the dead horse so that I could not get up and run before two or three rangers dashed up. I lay perfectly still, accepting my fate whatever it might be. One of the rangers pointed his gun at me and I thought my time had come. I closed my eyes, there was a loud report, and it seemed to me I felt a bullet graze my temple. Two of the rangers began talking, and opening my eyes, I saw they were looking at me and from their actions they must have discovered I was not an Indian.

70

They both ran on after Nusticeno, and I could hear them firing at him. I listened to the firing until I thought they were out of sight, and then I scrambled out from under my fallen horse and crawled some distance on my belly and hid in the grass near a little mesquite tree.

After a little while the rangers came back to look for me. I could hear them ride and talk. They passed within a few feet of me twice. I lay still in a slight depression with the high grass pretty well covering me, hardly daring to breathe for fear they would find me there. They stayed around there and searched for me for an hour or more. Then they went to my horse, stripped him of bridle, saddle and all other equipment, and finally left, going east.

I lay in my hiding place until they were entirely out of sight. Finally I moved a little, then raised up, got to my feet and cautiously surveyed my environment. I went to my dead horse, but all of my weapons had been taken, and I had nothing with which to supply myself with game for food. My comrades were all gone, either killed or flown.

I went to where Nusticeno had been killed and came upon his corpse, or part of it, about six hundred yards from where we had been dismounted. He had been scalped and I thought skinned, from all appearances. All of his weapons had been taken. I viewed this weird spectacle a few seconds, then turned and ran until I fell, breathless and exhausted, to the ground.

We had with us, at the beginning of this battle, a little Mexican boy who had been recently captured. He quit the Indians and ran toward the rangers with uplifted arms, when they came near. The commanding officer ordered firing to cease for a few seconds until the boy could be secured. The rangers carried him back with them.

THIS ENCOUNTER gives us a rare opportunity to check dates and facts on Herman. "The Fight on the Concho Plains," as he called it, was also recorded by three of the rangers who participated, Captain Roberts, Thomas P. Gillespie, and James B. Gillett.

Herman, of course, seldom is able to give the year for his adventures, much less pinning down a month or a day. As to the facts, in this episode at least it is satisfying to be able to note that Herman's account (taking into consideration their opposite points of view) agrees almost precisely with those of the Texas Rangers.

Herman's 1899 and 1927 versions have been combined in the story above. In the 1899 edition he mentions that Nusticeno (or Old-Trot-Slow, as he refers to him) had been decapitated: "There lay his headless body; I saw nothing of his head. . . ." He

also says that immediately after his horse had been downed ". . . I lay perfectly still and the rangers passed me and gave chase to Old-Trot-Slow" leaving out the business of feeling a shot graze his temple and hearing the rangers talk. This last we can understand. Herman, remember, spoke no English and by this time had forgotten most of the German his family had spoken. It is natural that the hearing of meaningless syllables would be forgotten until someone reminded him of them later.

Captain Roberts tells of the fight in his very scarce work, *Rangers and Sovereignty.* Gillett's account forms a chapter ("My First Brush with Indians") in his classic volume, *Six Years with the Texas Rangers.* (Although Gillett is often called "Captain" he was actually a sergeant. Gillett was not responsible for the prevalent error.) Gillespie's story ap-

71

Jim Gillett and Herman Lehmann 49 years after their fight

peared first in 1911 in *Hunter's Magazine*, a predecessor publication to *Frontier Times*, both of which were edited by J. Marvin Hunter.

Herman, in the 1927 edition of his story, says: "In telling of this fight [in the first edition of his book], Captain Gillett mentions a white boy with the Indians whom he calls Fischer. I am the boy he referred to but he evidently had in mind Rudolph Fischer, a German boy, who was captured in Gillespie County near Fredericksburg in 1869, I think —about a year before the Indians got me. As Captain Roberts in his [earlier] book also calls me Fischer, it is natural that Captain Gillett would make the same mistake.

"Fischer was captured by the Comanches, is still a member of that tribe, and now [1927] lives near Apache, Oklahoma. . . . Captain Roberts and Captain Gillett both say the Indians they fought were Lipans, but I know they were Apaches, for I was with them. If they were Lipans, how came Fischer

72

with them? These mistakes often occur in recording history and cannot be avoided."

In later editions of *Six Years with the Texas Rangers*, Gillett corrected the Fischer name: "Forty-nine years later I met this boy, now an old man, at a reunion of the Old Time Trail Drivers' Association in San Antonio and learned that his name was F. H. Lehman [*sic*]."

Gillett, who was himself only 18 years old, tells of chasing Herman and Nusticeno and of a ruse the older Indian tried to pull:

"The Indians had a good animal, but I gradually closed on them. The redskin riding behind would point his Winchester back and fire at me, holding it in one hand. . . . Finally, the old brave ceased shooting, and as I drew a little closer he held out his gun at arm's length and let it drop, probably thinking I would stop to get it. I gave it but a passing glance as I galloped by. He then held out what looked to be a fine rawhide rope and dropped that, but I never took the bait. I just kept closing in on him. . . . [After the Indian was killed] We found the redskin had no Winchester cartridges, and this was why he dropped the gun—he could not carry it and use his bow."

Gillett also makes the interesting statement that the downed rider under the horse "was a white boy . . . with long, bright red hair." This seems to be the only time Herman's features, in his captive period, were recorded.

Herman adds, in the 1927 edition, some other notes on the battle:

"Captain Gillett mentions a Mexican boy the Rangers recaptured in this fight who was stolen in Uvalde County. The boy had been with the Indians only a short time when the Rangers got him and had not learned to speak the Apache language very well. I was present in camp when the Apaches returned from a raid down into Southwest Texas and brought him in. He was taken along with our raiding party to wait on old Chinava [Genava], a brave Apache warrior."

Gillett, describing the Mexican boy captive as having long, plaited hair down his back and wearing moccasins and a breechclout, says, "Had he been in front of me I would surely have killed him for a redskin." Gillett says that after he was rescued by the rangers an uncle of the boy came and took him home to Fort Clark where the boy had been captured while herding oxen with an older brother, who was killed in the raid.

Herman says, concerning the real Rudolph Fischer: "After being with the Comanches for about ten years he was brought back to his people near Fredericksburg, but he had become so thoroughly Indianized that he was not content to remain and resume the white man's ways, and after spending about a year with his parents, he returned to the Comanches, where he had a squaw and a child, and now [1927] lives on his headright in Oklahoma. Fischer became a very brave warrior and is held in high esteem by the tribe. I talked with Captain Roberts at my home in Loyal Valley in 1881, after I was brought back from captivity, and we talked about the fight. He evidently forgot my name and having Fischer in mind, he wrote it that way in his book."

In *Nine Years* the account by Thomas Gillespie (who is also given the honorary "Captain" title) from *Hunter's Magazine* is re-

printed in full. At the time it was written, in 1911, Captain Gillespie was living at or near San Angelo, Texas. As it gives several additional details from the rangers' side of the Concho fight, here is offered a slightly edited version of the 1911 magazine piece:

IN AUGUST, 1875, while scouting in the upper San Saba Valley, we discovered an Indian trail on Scalp Creek, a tributary of the San Saba, in Menard County. . . . Our command consisted of Captain Roberts, Mike Lynch, Jim Trout, Jim Hawkins, Ed Seiker, Jim Gillette [sic], Andy Wilson, Henry Matamore, myself, and a man by the name of Crump. There may have been one or two others whose names I have forgotten, but I think those mentioned were all that were present on this chase. [Note: Gillett's list of the troop also includes Sergeant Plunk Murray, Paul Durham, Nick Donnelly, William Kimbrough, L. P. (Lam) Seiker—apparently a second Seiker—Jim Day, and John Cupps. Gillett gives Crump's name as Silas B., and spells Henry's last name Maltimore. Day and Cupps were sent back to camp with snake-bitten horses before the fight, Gillett says.]

Our horses were in bad condition for a long pursuit, but there was no alternative and we began the chase without delay. The trail led out across . . . the north part of Menard County and on in the direction of Kickapoo Springs, crossing the Fort McKavett and Fort Concho road about nine miles south of Kickapoo Springs. Next morning, some twelve or fifteen miles above the head of South Concho, we again came upon the trail and followed it to the top of a mountain where the Indians had halted and had removed the shoes from their stolen horses. Just why they should want to pull off the shoes from their stock has always been a mystery. [Note: Herman never mentions it.] Several theories have been advanced by Rangers and frontiersmen, but none hold good.

These horse shoes were left where they had been pulled off, and in addition the Indians had torn two long strips from a blanket and had placed these strips in the form of a cross on the ground, and in this condition we found them. It was about 2 P.M. when we discovered this sign on the mountain, the weather was dreadfully hot, but we took up the trail and pushed on as fast as our jaded horses could carry us. We knew from those signs so familiar to a Ranger that the Indians could not be far away and that they were moving leisurely along, and we hoped to overhaul them before nightfall.

We followed the trail all day . . . until we came out on the plains. About half an hour by sun [before sundown] we came to a pond where the Indians had watered their stock. The water in the horses' tracks was yet muddy and the grass along the margin where the horses had come out of the water was still wet, showing that we were close at their heels. . . . It becoming too dark to distinguish the trail, we lay by until dawn, giving our horses a good rest, which they sorely needed. By the time it was light enough to see, we were in the saddle, expecting every minute to come in sight of the enemy.

We rode at a moderately brisk gait until about 7 o'clock, when Captain Roberts suddenly halted, used his field glasses, and said: "Boys, I believe I see them. . . . They have not discovered us yet. Now you fellows follow close up behind me in single file. The sun is at our backs and by following my directions we can get close in on them before they see us."

We rode in the manner indicated and were within 600 yards of the Indians before they discovered us. There were eleven of them and as to numbers we were about equally matched. Besides the eleven, there were two riding along at a considerable distance to the left, and these two were the first to see us and gave the alarm.

We broke ranks and raised the yell, every man for himself, making full tilt for the savages. The Indians began rounding up the herd and mounting fresh horses, and when we got near enough to do execution, they scattered and each sought safety in tall running. However, when we got in about 150 yards of them they rallied on a small elevation and opened fire on us. We killed three or four horses and probably killed or wounded an Indian or two before this crowd broke and ran. We carried Winchesters and needle guns, and every man in the company was a crack shot.

A running fight followed and our men, singly or in pairs, selected their game and put in after them . . . Ed Sieker [sic] and Jim Gillette took in after two well mounted

Indians who, with their shields on their backs, were "burning the wind." After a run of 500 or 600 yards they brought down one of the horses, and as quick as a flash the Indian was up behind his mate and the race continued, until the horse ridden by the two Indians began to lose his wind and began to circle—a maneuver often practiced by the Indians when cornered under like circumstances. The boys had fired at least a dozen shots at these two Indians during this run, but on account of their shields, had failed to bring them down. Seeing this circling ruse, Jim Gillette dismounted, and with his needle gun took deliberate aim and broke the [Indian's] horse's neck, and then sprang back into his saddle and dashed forward alongside with Ed Sieker. When the horse fell the Indian mounted on behind hit the ground a-running, still holding the shield over his back, while the horse, in his fall, had pinned the other Indian to the ground. The boys dashed up to the fallen horse and Gillette threw his pistol on the Indian lying pinioned under the horse and was in the act of shooting him when Ed Sieker shouted: "Don't shoot him! Don't you see he is a white boy?"

Gillette lowered his pistol, and as a bare glance showed that the boy was closely held by the body of the horse, and, even if footloose, he could not escape, they hurried on after the fleeing Indian, whom they overtook and killed after a race of about 300 yards. After having killed this Indian they tarried a short while to get his scalp and to gather up his bow, quiver, shield and other accoutrements worth carrying away as trophies, and when they returned to where they had left the boy under the dead horse, he was gone! At this they were puzzled beyond expression. The scene of the fight and the chase was an open plain with nothing to obstruct the view for miles, and from the moment the horse was killed until their return to the spot they had been in full view of the surroundings and the boy could not have gotten away without their having seen him make the start.

There were a few scattering mesquites but none large enough to offer concealment. The grass was green and seven or eight inches high, and into this he must have crawled off and secreted himself. The search began, and in a short time the entire company came up and joined in the hunt. Every square rod for

74

a mile around was gone over and every bush and tuft of grass was examined, but the boy was nowhere to be found and we gave up the search as hopeless and went away completely mystified as to what had become of him. Some years later I learned that this boy was the captive, Herman Lehmann.

Before we get too far from where he mentions it perhaps something should be said concerning the making of flint implements as Herman described it. Most anthropologists would argue with him. While fire might be used to break up a large flint rock (although even this is held to be unlikely), the use of water to flake or chip a flint edge, particularly as Herman said it was done, is impractical, being almost impossible to control. To put it more positively, the use of pressure, either from another stone or from a wood or bone hammer, is so much quicker, easier and preferable in terms of the results obtained that stone tool-makers overwhelmingly resorted to it. One anthropologist suggests that what might have caused Herman to believe this fire and water method was the way Indians made their "spikes" (as he calls them) was the fact that he never actually saw anyone making flint tools, coming so late in history as he did. Some Indian might have told him this was the way flint pieces were edged and Herman accepted it. It seems quite probable that the little band Herman was with had never actually had to make flint points, barrel hoop iron, which he mentions, being easier and better to use. Whatever the cause, most anthropologists flatly declare the Indians did not use fire and water regularly in edging flint.

20

AFTER RESTING and collecting my wits from the battle and my narrow escape, I realized that I was all alone and quite a long distance from my Indian village— some three hundred miles. There I was with nothing on but a buckskin jacket and no way of providing myself with food. I started on the trail of my comrades who had flown from the attack, walking day and night, subsisting on roots and weeds, grasshoppers, lizards and bugs—anything that I could find. I nearly died of thirst. I knew where there was a small cave, on the route ahead, that contained water, but without some kind of a container or rope to let it down into the water with, I knew that getting it would be a problem. The water was at the bottom of a narrow, steep crevice. But when I reached the cave, I was so near starvation I did not consider the danger. I crowded down into that cave head foremost and, by desperate effort, squeezed myself between the rocks until I reached the water. After drinking my fill I found I was fastened between the rocks, my head and face forced into the water and my body lying uphill so that I could not withdraw. I came very near drowning before I got out. I kept kicking and scrambling backwards until I succeeded in reaching the top.

I tramped wearily on, following the Indians' trail, until I came to where they had killed and eaten an antelope. The wolves had cleaned up whatever meat the Indians had left, but I sucked the bones and gnawed the hide for nourishment. I also ate prickly pear—which is dangerous because of the tiny spines which can stick in the tongue and cannot be got out—because even the roots and weeds I had been eating became scarce. One time I was so nearly done for for water that I ate the dirt where a mudhole was still damp. I became in a measure delirious, wandering unconscious, and when I came to my senses I was at a spring. I drank, but the water would not stay on my stomach, I had starved so long. I lay around the spring bathing my parched tongue until I could keep water down. I stayed there that day and night. I was too weak and sore and fatigued to feel much pain. My sensibilities were dulled, and the anguish of being alone never bothered me.

I recruited and recuperated there, catching a few frogs, which I ate raw and considered them dainty morsels. I was loath to leave because I had nothing in which to carry water. My feet were sore and I felt clumsy and awkward. I would climb the hill back of the spring and look far to the northwest, where the village was, but then, facing the distance, I would go back and get a fresh drink of water. Finally I left, and after several more days terrible travel under the scorching sun, I reached the village. By the time I arrived my toenails had come off and I was sick for a long, long time.

Those Indians who ran when the rangers came up had reached the village some time before I arrived, and had told that we were all killed and that they had killed our horses and buried them and all our other property with us. They told the chief of how I had turned back and taken his brother, Nusticeno, up behind me in an attempt to aid his escape, and great was the lamentation over our reported deaths.

When I reached the village the people were overjoyed to see me, and when I told how my three companions and myself had been forsaken by those cowards, the chief's anger knew no bounds. He made me chief over all those who had deserted me, and I felt doubly paid for all my sufferings. The Indians treated me kindly, made me a nice pallet, and cooked my food tenderly, but for several days I could not eat.

In order to make my honor complete, I told the tribe that I followed the rangers and buried Nusticeno with his face downward and covered his resting place with a rock so that the wolves and other wild varmints could not get to him. (Golly! how they had shot that Indian. He was butchered terribly. There was no face on which to turn him. I can see that headless, bloody form yet when I close my eyes.)

After I got well I could be the leader for a good many grown Indians. I could wear red strings and beads and lead the fight. I was anxious to try my skill and bravery, but I was compelled to stay in camp nearly two months. We moved every few days to better hunting grounds and killed much game. Antelope were plentiful. The first thing we did when we killed one was to go into the paunch and eat what we found there, then his heart and liver. We often feasted on wood rats, polecats, dogs and opossums. We moved across the Rio Grande into the mountains of Mexico and there we killed bear, black-tailed deer and musk-hogs (javelinas).

The Indians have a system of enumeration of their own of which the human hand is the basis. They count upon the fingers until five is reached, when they

76

denote the number by a hand or, if drawing, the picture of a hand. Six is a hand and a finger, and ten becomes two hands. But when twenty is reached a new name is used; twenty is denoted by a man, and forty by two men. For example, forty-five would thus be two men and a hand and forty-six, two men, a hand and first finger. The Indian seldom had use for numbers much larger than could be named by these designations.

21

WHEN WINTER SET IN we stayed in camp and recruited, fattening our horses, and spent much time hunting. Members of our tribe had come from far and near to hear of our terrible fight, and many warriors collected. One cold day I was sent out to bring in the saddle horses. It was cloudy and began to snow. I kept going and lost my way. The snow came down thicker, and as I was riding, my horse fell into a sinkhole and broke his neck. I worked with him for some time, thinking he would be all right, but he died. By then his tracks had been obliterated.

I wandered around through the snow until night, and continued to walk after dark for a long time. At last I gave up and lay down to die. I remember suffering so much with cold as I lay there. Then I seemed to get warm, and I thought it was all a dream. Some nice deer, buffalo, antelope and other game appeared before me, and a good old squaw brought me some food, warm roasted bear— then all went blank. The next thing I knew I was in camp, wrapped up in buffalo meat. I then began to thaw; my fingers, toes, ears and nose were badly frozen. I was rubbed with meat until circulation started. Then I was placed on a bucking horse and he would pitch me off; they would catch the horse and replace me bareback on the wild animal. This was kept up until I caught several hard falls and became able to ride him. Then they dipped me in cold water and rubbed me thoroughly, placed me between warm blankets and gave me some nice fat meat. I was then allowed to sleep for a while. When I awakened I was given a good meal of roasted buffalo hump and after that, how sweetly I did sleep. I soon recovered entirely.

Springtime came apace, and when the weather got warm we made a raid down into the settlements for horses. The soldiers drove us back and pressed us so closely that many of our horses gave out and were turned loose on the way. My horse died and I had to keep up for a while with the horsemen on foot but eventually they all had to leave their horses in a chaparral thicket where we were so closely pursued, and we all came back on foot. We left camp three weeks before well mounted and equipped, and returned destitute. A Comanche joined us on that perilous trip and afterwards married into our tribe.

We made another raid almost immediately (we had to have horses), and on that raid I was left three weeks in the cedars alone, but easily supplied myself with honey and small game. A horse fell down on a warrior and sprained his leg so I took care of him while the other braves went east on a raid. When they came back they rewarded me with a pair of fine horses, a saddle, and several ropes. We returned to our camp well supplied.

We lingered around camp awhile and then went down the San Saba River on a raid. We crossed into Mason County, my old home, where we came up on a herd of horses. A man was pretending to guard them but was fast asleep. We drove an arrow through him and this aroused him for a few minutes, then he turned over into a sleep from which no man can stir. We scalped him and drove off the horses. We had just started when a man in a wagon drove up. We had a little fight with him, scalped him and left him in a dying condition, and took charge of his team, burning his wagon and other gear. Then we got out quickly.

The next sport we had was slaughtering a man who was driving an ox team. We killed the oxen, sucked the paunch and lower intestines, stripped the colon with our hands, tied up one end and filled it with water to carry with us. We ate the hearts, livers, lights, melts and kidneys raw, while warm, and sucked up all the blood we could get. We made a fire, roasted the ribs and neck, and had a feast off those old oxen, while our scouts kept watch to see that we were not found by the whites. We were very careful what kind of wood we burned and watched the smoke to keep it scattered, lest we be located and destroyed. Several scouts were sent out in every direction. One would eat at a time and then go watch as another came in.

After resting here several hours, and letting our horses rest, we traveled southeast for quite a distance until night overtook us. We went into town in little groups, each man taking every horse with which he might come in contact. We all met later to transfer our newly gotten steeds to the common herd. We did not keep for ourselves what we had stolen for the band. We stood guard and herded the horses while the boys who had held the horses first went to enjoy the town air for a while.

We loved to go near the saloons and inhale the fragrance from the old beer bottles that had been thrown away. We stole all we could find to take some back. We spied a tent, and to that particular spot we all went. There, snugly couched in the arms of Morpheus, lay a man and woman. The tomahawk and scalping knife were brought into use, and two bloody scalps [soon] dangled from the belts of two warriors.

We seldom feared Uncle Sam's regular soldiers much because we knew that they would only carry us back to the reservation if we were captured. Also, we knew they had to consume a great deal of time in getting ready to take our trail. But we dreaded the Texas Rangers and the frontiersmen called the Minutemen, whose guns were always loaded and whose aim was unerring. They slept in the saddle and ate while they rode, or did without. When they took to our trail they followed it determinedly and doggedly, day and night.

Mason, Texas, at the time Herman was raiding the surrounding countryside

We stole horses here and there and started back to our headquarters on the plains. But one fine morning we found the whole country full of soldiers, and had a desperate fight with them. Several of our men were killed. We escaped and hurried northward and met some Kiowas and Comanches, but our resting place was not here. We were driven on farther into the Wichita Mountains of Oklahoma, but even there the red man, the one to whom this country and all of its wealth and riches rightly belongs, could not stop—not even among the mountains. He must bow to the inevitable. He must give up to greater numbers, superior skill, and improved firearms.

Through forced marches we had managed to keep most of our stolen horses. We camped with our new allies to trade, gamble, and run horse races. The sports continued for some time, but again we found ourselves in a desperate fight with the soldiers. Our squaws stampeded, in one of the fights, and over half of our women and most of our children were killed or captured. Ninety of our men fell victim to the white man's bullets. Our shields now seemed useless, for the balls went right through them.

We found our battles going against us, even when we were able to hold our own. One time, when night came on over the battlefield, the soldiers fell back to fortified camps and we made a charge on them. But it was to no avail. They could shoot faster, and seemed to know what we were hoping to do. The next day these soldiers retreated toward Fort Griffin and we followed at a distance, occasionally making a charge in hopes of stampeding their horse herd, but the soldiers were always expecting us, and therefore were ready, and we found our efforts fruitless, so we turned our weary way toward our camp.

Quanah Parker, of the Comanches, came out and persuaded us to come into the reservation at Fort Sill. Our men were rounded up and counted like cattle by the United States commissioners. Men came from all over Texas to examine our horses and claim their own which we had stolen. The white children in our possession were exchanged for the squaws and children of ours that the whites had captured. Carnoviste said that as he had not lost any squaw he did not propose to give me up, and truly, I did not want to go, for I had learned to hate my own people. So I kept hid in the Fort Sill camp.

But some other Indians reported at reservation headquarters that Carnoviste, the Apache chief, had a white boy in his camp. So the soldiers came to search for me. I was sitting in camp with Carnoviste smoking cigarettes when we saw the blue coats, brass buttons, and epaulettes of the soldiers, coming to search for me. I lay down flat and the Indians (there were several present) threw blankets over me and sat down on them—and me—and silently smoked while the officers searched the teepees. One of the officers stayed close by and talked; watched and smoked with the Indians while his men searched. My nose and mouth were in the sand and I was mashed as flat as a horned toad and nearly smothered. But the Indians would have killed me before they would have given me up.

Our chief got mad because that officer stayed so long and asked so many questions. The chief called his men together, as soon as the officers had left, and decided to quit the reservation.

22

OUR MEN were collected secretly, all the women and children came together; we stole all the horses we could find and all the guns and blankets, and under the cover of night we escaped Fort Sill.

The next morning, after a ride all night, we were many miles from the fort and the detested whites. We made for the plains as fast as we could travel, and soon we were in our old haunts.

Sometime about this period we engaged in an antelope roundup. The slowest horses and laziest riders were sent around on the wind side of the game to start them and run them a while. Then the swift-footed horses and the agile riders were to join the sport and rope the antelope—this being out on the open prairies where their fleet-footedness was their greatest protection.

I was stationed two miles along on the chase. My pony was in trim and my rope in readiness when the herd came by and I was soon going pell-mell over the plains in the dust of the antelope. After a half-mile's run I threw my lariat and missed. By then I had passed most of the herd, but one big old buck antelope was still in front of me and gaining on me. I gave a yell, hugged close to my pony, and sped over the ground at a renewed rate of speed. We had gone about three miles when I came in roping distance. My lasso was again in readiness, and one wild leap of the horse, I whirled the rope—and my horse stumbled and fell. But my rope had fastened itself around the neck of that king of the antelope family, and I picked myself up near the heels of the infuriated animal. Soon he was choked down, and my comrades were with me. By the time we got back, I was confined again to the tent for a few days.

There were huge herds of the musk-hog (or javelina), and they were very destructive to vegetation. When wounded they were very ferocious, and all the rest of the hog herd will fight for the wounded one. The whole company of twenty or more which I encountered were accustomed to back singly into a cave to sleep, the last one acting as a sentry. This one being shot, the others successively take his place, so if skillfully managed by the hunter, the whole number may be killed. But we hunted them with a dog, and at the slightest bark they seek the remotest caverns of their den and the dogs are too smart to go in after them. Once I volunteered to go and on this occasion there were at least twenty hogs. I boldly crawled through the first narrow place and was just getting up on all fours to move farther in when they smelled me and stampeded, running right over me, literally. Their toes were sharp and their tushes long, but they never stopped to attack me—which probably saved my life. I was somewhat bruised and be-smeared, but my comrades had killed enough as they left the cave to do us the whole season. We butchered these and hung some up to get a little tainted so they would be tender. (The Indians hated hogs such as the white men kept in pens that wallowed in the mud and stank. The wild ones ate berries and mast and ran free and were not lazy, fat and filthy. There was no excitement attached to a deer hunt.)

Some warriors made a raid into the interior of Mexico, once, and killed a large family, bringing back two Mexican children as captives: a boy and a girl. These children were well treated, for the Indians respected and were friendly with some of the Mexicans, those who helped us and traded with us. But still, occasionally the Indians would steal from them and fight them. The Mexicans trailed this bunch of raiders up and located them near our camp and wanted us to give them up. We argued for some time with the Mexicans, but one night before the diffi-culty was settled we ambushed and murdered these Mexicans, then hastily crossed the Rio Grande and took ourselves to our water hole on the Llano Estacado. but another Mexican party pursued us and we killed them on the plain.

It was not much honor to have a Mexican scalp on your belt for they provided us with arms, ammunition and many other necessary things, as well as good whiskey and mescal.

We needed horses, so a raid was ordered and a band of us went far down into the settlements, the haunts of my childhood. The first encounter we had was with two boys on the James River; one nearly grown, the other smaller. They fought desperately but were overpowered, killed and scalped. We stole many horses in that region, some of them, I afterwards learned, from my old neighbors such as Welge, Stone, Ellebracht, and Henry Keyser. We went to Fredericksburg that night and prowled around, stealing horses, but we avoided killing anybody for we were not anxious to be chased by the rangers.

We went from Fredericksburg on to Packsaddle Mountain country, robbing and stealing. On Sandy Creek we saw a man chopping wood, and grazing near him was a sorrel pony with a saddle on. The man saw us, jumped on the pony and tried to get away. We crowded him closely so that he quit his horse, dropped his axe, lost his hat, and made his way into a thicket. We started to surround him there but he ran to a house and entered. We didn't often fool around a house when we knew there was a man in it, so we contented ourselves with his horse and went on down the creek. Near there we found and drove away twenty head of horses.

There came up a drenching rain which wet our bowstrings and blankets, so we went into a thicket in the roughs and built a fire to dry them. We were standing around unusually talkative because we felt safe, when suddenly white men rushed in upon us. We stayed together and fought for a little while, but the Indians were falling all around, and we scattered. Going west, those of us who were not killed came together at a convenient place. Then we stole more horses and hurried on. We discovered that we were being followed by the rangers. They overtook us the second morning. It must have been near San Angelo. We had a hard fight, and our loose horses were taken by the rangers. One Indian was killed and several wounded, but we escaped. We made this fight so interesting for the rangers that they did not follow us any further.

We went to where we had left our people in camp, but no people were there. We found buffalo bones and on them pictures representing a fight with the white people; pictures of seven white men pierced with arrows, also a wagon burning up (we found the ashes and the irons), and finally bones arranged pointing northward—twelve of them representing a twelve day journey. By this time I had become quite a decipherer of Indian hieroglyphics.

We traveled on for twelve days in the northern direction, then we saw smoke a long ways apart, all in rows pointing westward. This we took to mean that the rangers were too thick and had made it so hot for the Indians that they were changing direction. It also indicated that they were closely pursued and warned us to be careful, as well as hasten to their rescue.

We went west for about a hundred miles. There was little water in that country, but we knew where there was a spring. The white men pursuing our squaws proved to be soldiers instead of rangers, and the Indians decoyed them off on a route where there was no water. We knew what the consequences would be, so we had filled our colons and hides with water and pursued the soldiers who were pursuing our people.

We began to find dead horses on the way, and then we came upon a man nearly famished for water. He was stripped, scalped, and cut to pieces. We followed on and found eight others in his same condition. They shared the fate of the first mentioned. These soldiers passed close to water, but it was in a deep hole and the Indians kept it covered up. We saw from the direction the troop of soldiers was taking that they would all perish on the dry sand, so we went back on the right trail of our people.

We found them at the spring, but in deplorable condition. All of their horses were jaded and worn out, killed or taken. Hundreds of widows and orphans were cut, wounded and bleeding and many of them were afoot and starving. Utter annihilation stared us in the face.

In this fight and retreat we saw our first Negro soldiers. We thought these Negroes came from under the water, from the fact that our shadow always appeared black in water. We called them "buffalo soldiers" because they had curly, kinky hair and heads like bisons. Our arrows would not penetrate their skulls. I remember hearing our chief instruct his warriors, at one time, that in fighting the buffalo soldiers never to shoot them in the head. He said: "Skull too hard; turn arrows, mash bullets, break spears, dull lances. Shoot him through heart; kill him easy."

We rested at this spring, killed game, creased mustangs and gentled them, mounted everybody and decided to move from the plains. We went up to the head of the Pecos River and on to the Rocky Mountains. Here we could take it easy and could lie down and sleep in peace. We were not afraid of the soldiers here.

BY THIS TIME, of course, the plains Indians in Texas were undergoing the final roundup. Colonel Ranald Slidell Mackenzie, Colonel Benjamin H. Grierson, General George Crook, were all pushing inward on them from all directions—although Herman's group, like most of the Indian bands, had no communication with other groups and no form of central intelligence to apprise them of this information. The same thing was happening to the Comanches, Lipans and Kiowas in other parts of northwest Texas, the Panhandle and the high plains. The end was near but they didn't know it, having no historians to warn them.

Herman brings up two more topics which need a bit of discussion in this chapter: the hardness of the Negro soldiers' heads and the creasing of mustangs.

Regardless of the chief's contention, shooting a Negro soldier in the head was just as effective a way of killing him as shooting a white soldier in the head. Despite some individual differences in the thickness of skulls, no Negro soldier's could "turn arrows, mash bullets, break spears, dull lances." This is another of the legends of the white world which Herman seems to have accepted and applied to the Indian world. Possibly the Indians believed it, but reality should have taught them rather quickly that it wasn't a fact.

Herman also speaks of creasing mustangs. This is one of the fondest legends of the American West, but several experts tell us it made a better myth than practice. I will not attempt to deny the Indians a skill with bow and arrow which allowed them to practice creasing, or nicking, with fair results, but I would like to introduce some words from Frank Collinson, the well-educated English frontiersman-rancher who knew the plains mustangs as well as any man. In "Fifty Thousand Mustangs"† he writes:

I HAVE HEARD a lot of talk about creasing mustangs—that is shooting them through the muscle of the neck, which will paralyze them for a short time. No doubt this has been done by men at times, but to talk of going out to catch horses this way is pure bunk. I have tried it a great many times and have broken their necks scores of times and never caught a horse that way and never knew anyone else who did.

George Causey, who was a buffalo hunter for twelve years . . . in the very heart of the mustang range, was one of the best hunters and rifle shots I ever saw. He had the reputation of killing thirty or forty thousand buffalo. I have seen him kill with a rifle a prairie chicken flying straight away from him. When asked if he had ever creased a mustang, he said, "No, but I have killed hundreds trying to."

And that had always been my experience.

---

† J. Frank Dobie, Mody C. Boatright, Harry H. Ransom (eds.), *Mustangs and Cow Horses*, Dallas, 1940, pp. 69–95.

23

AT FIRST game was plentiful as we reached the foothills of the Rockies, as we went on up into the mountains to get away from the soldiers game became scarce and our horses had no grazing. Finally horse feed had given out entirely. We cut holes in our youngest horses' ears and started them down the mountains to live but kept all the old skinned-up mules to feed ourselves. The first one we killed was an old gray mule, his back one solid sore; "set-fasts" and saddle galls were all over him. We ate him, then sucked his hide and bones to get out all the nutriment. The sores were the first parts we ate. That was sweet and tender.

It began to snow, and there we were, in the cold, bleak mountains without fire, food or shelter. To go down in the sleet over those steep places, where the least slip would hurl us into eternity, was almost too hazardous to try; to ascend any higher was impossible; to remain where we were meant starvation.

We killed and ate all the mules we kept, sucked and fought over the hides and bones like hungry dogs, chewed our moccasins, and sucked the blood from the palms of our own hands. In daytime our only covering was the canopy of heaven, for we were above the ordinary clouds. Sometimes a cirrus cloud, with its sparkling snowflakes, would fly right into our midst. At night we would lie down on the sleet and cover up with snow, and it was astonishing how snug, cozy and warm we kept.

Here we had not the tender-hearted soldiers nor the revengeful rangers with whom to contend, but freezing and starvation were more horrible. We started laboriously working our way down. The foremost man, the first time, slipped and we heard a splash as he went down the crags to the black stream below—and returned no more. Great abysses and yawning sepulchres of snow seemed to beckon to us, decoy us on and almost sigh for our blood to warm their bleak, cold sides.

Spring came at last—not to all our company, though, for I fear the cannibal had been there—to find frozen ears, sore noses, benumbed fingers, nail-less toes, and frost-bitten heels. We descended from our lofty place of "safety" and "refuge" and on our way down found an old horse frozen stiff. We stopped and made several meals of him. A little farther down we came upon another carcass on which we subsisted, until we reached the vale below and there we found that most of our horses, like sensible animals, were well fed and looking good. We managed to kill some game here and fared some better.

After spending some time in this foothills region we turned back to our old hunting grounds. We had undergone so many hardships in that mountain winter that most of the tribe had sickened of freedom and wanted to go back to the reservation. A council was held and it was decided to go back to the White Pine Reservation in New Mexico and give up. This we did, and the commissioners allowed us to move off some twenty-five miles from reservation headquarters and live in our own camp. As we had come in of our own accord we were allowed more liberties than those tribes who were forced to come in and surrender.

24

I HAD TO STAY out in the woods or be killed by my chief, for he would not give me up. One morning I was sitting on a log partially concealed by the undergrowth when I saw a black bear climb a tree and go into a hole. I was anxious to capture a grown bear alive, so I considered what to do about this one. I knew there was a young Indian, Snowbound, hard by, so I howled like a wolf. Snowbound answered me and in a few moments joined me. We had a consultation and decided on a plan. He sprang on his pony and rode into camp, procuring several buckskins and some good thongs. We made a bag from the hides and put a drawstring in the top and fastened the bag near the bear's hole in such a way that when bruin came into the bag the top would draw together and the bag would fall.

We built a fire in some cracks below and forced the bear out the top of the tree. When the bear came into our net it worked admirably. It closed up, and the drawstring being tied in a bowknot. it came untied from the tree. Down came bear, bag and all. We tied the thongs of leather around the top of the bag and made bruin a prisoner. Such scratching, growling and biting! Then we cut down the tree with an ax and Snowbound caught two little cubs. We traded them off for beer.

On this reservation it was easy to purchase whiskey of the most villainous kind from traders who would slip in and sell it to the Indians, despite the watchfulness of the soldiers. Present-day [1927] bootlegging activities are of similar character —and the liquor offered now is about on a par with the concoctions dispensed to the poor, simple savages.

When a quantity of this liquor was brought into camp it always produced rows and fights. A great many old grudges and feuds were brought up between different parties of our tribe when we were drinking, and when we were drinking a fuss or murder was sure to follow.

One of these drunken brawls resulted in the death of my best friend and master, Carnoviste, and made me a fugitive from the tribe for good.

We had a general carousal, and warriors of our party and a neighboring lot had a quarrel. We had quarreled before, and some men on each side had been sacrificed to the God of Discord. Our wives and their squaws had an altercation, just like their men, and how the hair did fly, but they, like all women, were more wind than water fighting among themselves.

One of the unfriendly bands came to where some of our warriors were and demanded firewater. A fight ensued in which one of our braves was wounded in the stomach. In a few days we retaliated by going to their camp and helping ourselves to some beer there. A real fight followed, and one party or the other would have been annihilated if the soldiers had not interfered. Our party being the aggressors, we expected to receive the greater punishment. Our chief called together all of our forces and we decided to steal horses from that other band and run away again.

But before we left, we got on a big spree, as some traders had brought us a good supply of liquor. That carousal was the worst I ever witnessed. Squaws fell out and literally cut each other to pieces. One squaw, while drunk, proved untrue to her husband publicly. He cut off her nose and made her go to the wigwam of the man who had taken advantage of her intoxicated condition, and had had illicit intercourse with her. This couple, for their outrageous public conduct, was estranged from the main part of our village, permitted to camp only on the outer edge. Several squaws died from the debauchery, which aroused the ire of their husbands and they began quarreling with the other parties.

All became quiet for a few days until some more beer was sold to us. Then the warriors took up the quarrel again. A band of us drove another band back toward where the soldiers were quartered, and then a few of us gathered up all the corn and beer and other belongings we could hastily find and made toward the plains. We had already concealed a great quantity of corn and beer in buckskin sacks and had horses stolen preparatory to just such leaving. By now corn to make beer and the firewater itself were the most precious things we could lay our hands on. We traveled a day and night and made camp in a nice, cool, shady place and began preparing for a real spree. We had learned how to make corn beer, so we had bought or stolen many large tin oil cans from the soldiers in which to boil our corn malt. Everything was moving admirably toward a Bacchanalian feast, when suddenly up rushed a dozen warriors from our own tribe, but our enemies. We would not double-team our own tribe, so a dozen of us volunteered to fight their dozen, but while we were preparing for the fight, the enemy killed one of our men and then ran back. Carnoviste ordered me to bend my shield and help drive away the cowards. He and I and several of our comrades mounted fast horses and gave chase. We ran them about five miles to where they had prepared an ambuscade, and very foolishly we went right into the trap.

Indians seemed to rise up out of the ground and fire at us. All our comrades were killed. Carnoviste and I turned and retreated slowly—making a kind of running fight—to within a quarter of a mile of camp. Two or three of the enemy came up to us and we had a hand-to-hand combat. Lances, daggers, tomahawks and spears flew lively for a while, but I was too busy to take much notice of what was going on around me. A warrior raised his spear to end my days, but Carnoviste, seeing the movement, reached his heart with a lance.

At the same instant a medicine man ended the earthly days of my master and chief, Carnoviste.

A medicine man thinks he can't be killed; that he is proof against his enemies so long as he refrains from eating swine. I thought, too, that he couldn't be killed. When Carnoviste fell, this medicine man came toward me with a Winchester, waving his shield. He said to me, "This is your last day, for now you die!" I ran behind a big rock and called to him, "You or me!" I had nothing but a bow and arrow.

The other warriors passed on to rout our camp, supposing the medicine man to be more than a match for me. He shot at me two or three times, his balls being deflected by my shield. I ran around and around that rock, the medicine man right after me, confident of victory. I had always hated this particular old devil, for all during the time I had been with the tribe he never lost an opportunity to torment me. I can see now his curled lip and hideous grin. All those years, I was just a helpless captive boy and could do nothing about his outrageous treatment of me. Now it was different, for my heart was filled with hatred that was unleashed by the killing of my chief. I became cool and collected, and as I ran around the rock for perhaps the fourth time, I suddenly turned and sent an arrow under his shield and through his stomach, then whirling away before he could fire. He fell and asked me not to shoot any more, saying he was killed. I was afraid that he was not quite so dead as he would have me believe, so I sent another arrow that pierced his heart, and he rolled up his eyes and died with a faint groan. The invulnerable medicine man was dead and Carnoviste was avenged!

I picked up his shield, took off his belt and buckled it to myself, made myself a present of his Winchester and cartridges, and felt that I could then whip all of the party which had attacked us. I knew the death of the medicine man would soon become known, but I was proud of my victory.

I went to a big rock and sat where I could see the warriors coming from our camp. I could tell by their yells of victory and the way they danced that they had killed or routed all our braves, and I could hear the shrieks and moans of our squaws. Finally I saw some of the enemy warriors go out and find the body of the big medicine man and then a howl went up. I knew my time alive was short, but I felt so proud of my victory that I didn't believe a bullet could kill me. I sat there and watched the warriors go back and bury the dead. I concealed myself among the rocks on a mountainside, and although they searched for me diligently, they did not find me.

Night came on, and with it the realization that I was utterly alone, without a friend or protector, a hunted and hated thing to be slain on sight. My friends were all dead. Where could I go?

25

I SAT ON A ROCK long after dark, waiting for destiny to put an impulse in my heart. If an Indian follows his first inclination he believes he is always right.

My horse had been killed under me in the day's fight, so I was afoot. The hill, or range of hills, which afforded me concealment swept around north of the main village, forming a half-circle. The scene of the battle in which Carnoviste was killed was nearly due west of the village. Knowing that search parties would, in due course of time, look for me, I bore away and followed the ridge to a point north of the village. There I waited until nearly midnight. My only hope lay in flight, but whither? At just that time the Apaches and Comanches were not on good terms; anyway, I did not know the Comanche language, and should I fly to them they might kill me. But I made up my mind to go, and at once. But before going I was determined to slip into the village and have a talk with Carnoviste's sister, Ete. She was young, handsome and winsome and had always been good to me and I had lavished all my love and affection on her.

I told Ete how Carnoviste had met his death, and how in turn I had slain his murderer. She said she thanked me and loved me for the ties of our childhood, and almost worshipped me for killing the murderer of her brother, but she urged me to return to white civilization if nothing else—but to fly from there. She gave me blankets, ammunition and provisions and advised me to get a certain horse that had been Carnoviste's—a gray horse on which I had won many races. For endurance and hardihood he was considered the best of any owned by the tribe.

She implored me to leave her dangerous quarters. I stubbornly refused to go unless she would go too. She argued that she was in delicate health and would be unable to make such a hazardous trip and would be an impediment to my progress so that we would both be captured and put to death. She said that she would not be well received among the whites (where she urged me to flee) while I would be perfectly at home.

With tears in her eyes and trickling down my cheeks, I drew her to my bosom and bade her good-bye. It was a trying hour to me to voluntarily tear myself from old associations and customs and enter upon a life that for five years I had been taught to loathe and abhor, but the hardest trial was to leave the girl that I had learned to love with all the fervor and simplicity of youth. A girl who more than

88

once saved my life and who had nursed me through severe spells of sickness. For a little while I held her in my fond embrace, our tears mingled. The parting kiss was given and our bodies dissevered though our hearts beat in unison and our souls remained united for long, weary months.

That was the last I ever saw of my Indian maiden, yet the sweetest memory of her still lingers.

Indian Girl—Herman's chief tried to get him
to marry a beauty like this.

This same woman is still living, or was two years ago (in 1925) when I got a letter written for her, asking me to come see her once more before she dies. She said she was almost blind. She lives on the Apache reservation in New Mexico among her tribe. You may wonder why I did not go to see her. As much as I would like to see this old woman again, I did not dare to go among that tribe, for there are yet living certain warriors who would not hesitate to avenge the death of the medicine man—fifty years later!

Before closing this chapter I want to say that one of the Apaches who stole me, Chiwat, a brother to Carnoviste, and who afterwards became a chief among his tribe, was not with our party when we had the fight, so he was not killed. He now [1927] lives among the Comanches at Indiahoma in Oklahoma. I met him in the spring of 1898 when I visited my old tribe for the first time, and he called me by my old Indian names. Pinero and Esacona also live there.

I GATHERED UP MY ARMS, provisions and supplies—including some nice moccasins and a beaded buckskin jacket Ete gave me which she had made—and crept out to the horse herd where the powerful gray was. It took nearly an hour before I succeeded in getting the animal away from the herd, but I would sooner have died than to have taken any other, for Ete's sake.

It required but a few moments to saddle up, mount and be off. I shaped my course eastward and rode without any sleep for the rest of the night. About fifteen or twenty miles out from the camp, I got down, smoked, made signs to the Great Spirit and worshipped. I went through all the signs and maneuvers of an Indian warrior. I waited His direction and when my impulse was to go southeast, I obeyed it. I was then somewhere near the head of the Pecos. I was many miles away when the morning sun came up.

I found myself on a vast plain with a low range of hills far to the north. This plain was wholly without vegetation except cactus and sagebrush. The soil was loose and sandy. I expected to be followed by the Indians and tortured to death if caught, so I tried, as only an Indian can, to obliterate all signs of my travel by often changing my course and following the trail of antelope or buffalo. During the day my horse and I suffered from the effect of thirst, but in the evening we came to a creek where an abundance of water was found. The sun was about an hour high when I reached this creek, and after having slaked my thirst I rode to a high ridge that lay a short distance east of the watering place. Just over this ridge I found grass in a small cove, and here I dismounted to let my horse rest and graze a few hours.

Leaving my horse there, I went back to the crest of the ridge to keep watch, as the elevation enabled me to see a great distance in the direction from which I came. The sun was low in the heavens, and I had not been on watch longer than half an hour before I discovered what I took to be horsemen; mere specks on the horizon far away to the west, and directly on my trail. Going to my horse, I hastily mounted and resumed my journey. That was the last I saw of my aforetime friends, the Apaches, for several months.

HERMAN tells quite a different story of his escape in the 1899 edition of his book. It follows the story related above until he is far from camp, then continues as follows:

FOUR DAYS AND NIGHTS I toiled on before I found water. I went then to where I had whiled away many happy hours with Willamina [the name he uses for Ete in this version] and then I began to feel my loneliness. The stillness and solitude of that evening was very oppressive. Not even the rustle of leaves or the chirp of birds. Everything was absolutely at rest. [Here he goes into a long and obviously appended reflection on how comforted he would have been by the Christian religion at this time if he had known the Christian religion.]

I went a little ways from the spring, tied my horse to my leg, partook of the last morsel of food that Willamina had given me, spread out my blankets and tried to sleep. Tired and worn out as I was from four days toil and travel, still old Morpheus refused to come. I would change my position; roll, kick and tumble, but my soul was so weary and my heart fairly bleeding for companionship. At last exhaustion overcame me and oblivion reigned supreme.

The next thing I knew the sun was shining in my face and my horse was pulling and snorting. I jumped up and looked around, and down toward the spring I saw the Indians coming. I threw my navajoes on my horse and darted off, just escaping a shower of arrows that were sent us as a morning greeting by our old friends and childhood companions, the Apaches; but this was rather too warm a reception for just four days' separation. I spun over the ground on my dappled gray, and behind me came the blood-craving savages, thirsting for vengeance. In my hasty retreat I had not forgotten any of my equipment.

I kept my shield behind me to ward off the poisonous arrows, and some of them came close. I kept my gun in readiness should they wound my horse, but as long as the gray was all right I trusted my all in flight. I leaned forward and the horse ran manfully, causing us to gain on the enemy. My horse and I had had a night's rest, but the Indians had trailed all the time. Farther and father apart we drew. Once the gray cleared a ditch that must have been twenty feet across and deep enough to bury the whole Apache tribe. We ascended a hill and looked back and far to my rear, on the summit of a neighboring hill, stood my former companions, signalling and making signs for peace. How I longed for peace and re-admittance into the tribe, and for a few minutes I gave it thought. I loved the Indians, for I knew no one else to love.

I motioned for one to approach. One old stealthy warrior that I despised stepped out from among the others and came serpent-like toward me. I knew from his manner that he meant me no good. He came closer and I recalled that he was the brother to the medicine man I had killed. I then glanced up the hill and saw the whole party coming. I knew that they were unfaithful, for I had seen their deception before. They considered it a virtue to decoy their prey and capture it without undergoing any danger themselves. My courage failed when I saw them moving, so I stooped down close to my faithful steed and he carried me away. They made a dash, but I was gone. I urged the gray up and got out of sight; I circled and came back on their trail. They lost my trail, spread out, and rode for noble game—but they never got it!

Poor Indians, they had taught me a few tricks and I had learned others. I outgeneraled them this time. I guess they are mad yet. I followed their tracks for many miles until I knew from their actions that they had given me up. Then I got off my horse and took a seat on a rock and wept.

I was so lonesome that night that I could not sleep, so I killed night hawks and whippoorwills and cut off their wings and put them under my head, as I had seen squaws do when their children would fret. When I did go to sleep I was troubled with nightmares and ill-omened dreams.

I painted up, smoked and worshipped every day. I smoked grass, leaves and dung. The odor of this mixture was extremely gratifying to the craving of the Great Spirit. We believed that the gods wanted something earthly. I traveled east and north and pined and nursed my own sorrows and dreariness. I came in sight of white men—two on horseback—but I was afraid of being scalped, so I kept out of their way, hiding like a wild varmint.

26

AFTER MANY DAYS TRAVEL over arid plains, rugged hills and deserts, during which time I came near perishing from hunger and thirst, I came to a deep, narrow canyon in which there was a small stream of pure, clear water and a growth of cottonwood trees along the margin.

My horse had become exhausted, and most of the day I had led the faithful beast. The walls of the canyon were almost perpendicular in places, and I experienced some difficulty in finding a spot to descend to the creek below. Finally I discovered a narrow trail leading down the declivity and when once in the canyon I found not only good water but also an abundance of good grass. Here I took up my abode.

How long I remained in this canyon I cannot say, but I must have stayed there six or eight months, perhaps longer. On my first coming I found deer tracks and the footprints of other wild animals, which made this little stream their watering place, and later I discovered that the game was quite plentiful. After a few week's stay in this solitude I became reconciled to my lonely life. I regarded all men as my enemies. In a friendly cavern in the walls of the canyon I found shelter and concealment at night, and as game came in to water near my place of hiding, I had no occasion to wander beyond the narrow precincts of the canyon.

But with all of this, there was a sense of dread weighing on my mind, a presentiment of evil to come, a racking fear lest the abundance of grass should attract the attention of my enemies and that I should be discovered and slain.

And thus the days and weeks and months glided by, until one bright night I was startled from my sleep by a strange sound, just what I could not tell but it seemed to have been that of a human voice. I went outside of my cave and listened, and in a few moments I heard a loud laugh! The moon was at its full and the canyon was lit up almost as bright as day. Going around a projecting rock near my cave, and looking down the canyon, I saw a large campfire not three hundred yards away. I could see human forms passing to and fro near this fire and could hear voices.

Taking advantage of a growth of willows which fringed the bank of the little stream, I crept up sufficiently near the camp to hear their conversation, and to my utter dismay I found that they were Apaches and I knew every one of them. They were evidently returning from a raid down in Texas, as they had a large drove of horses which was being herded below their camp in the canyon, having come in through the mouth of the canyon.

Returning to my cave, I gathered up a supply of dried venison, secured my horse, and going up the canyon some distance to a gap that served as an outlet to a level plain above, I struck out toward the east, not knowing where I was going any more than on the previous occasion when I had fled for my life from the same enemy.

I rode for several days and crossed a number of streams. On several occasions I saw men whom I took to be from the Texas settlements or Mexicans, but these I avoided, knowing that they would take me to be an Apache, the common enemy to all men. I was traveling southeast, keenly alert lest I should be surprised by white man or Indian. I was a wanderer on the face of the earth.

I came to a stream and spent awhile there. I would get beargrass and love-vine and boil these in water until they became a strong ooze, and with that I would wash my hair, which grew long, straight and beautiful. I was always careful to have all the oil worked out. I was never troubled with dandruff. I would lie down and watch my image in the water, and I would conclude that I was right pretty, but at the least rustling sound all the self-conceit would vanish and I would crawl away and hide, or seek refuge on the gray.

I had twenty-eight cartridges for my Winchester. Every ball brought down a deer, antelope or buffalo. The ammunition lasted me nearly three months, for in order to husband it I used my bow and arrow to kill game. When my cartridges gave out I carried the gun over between the Pecos and Rio Grande somewhere and hid it in a cave. I was afraid of the Mexicans, the Americans and everybody, but my gun was of no further use to me. I did hate to give it up, but then I knew where to find it if I ever needed it again. I never went back to see about it, so I guess it is buried in that cave yet.

I had gotten out of practice with the bow and arrow, and then the Mexicans, soldiers, rangers and Indians had recently been through the country; and the drouth had struck it, too, so game was scarce and wild. I ate all the food I had on hand quickly, then turned to cactus apples, sotol and other vegetation—along with bugs, insects and an occasional beargrass apple. These I fried, and they make a palatable dish. (You may wonder how I fried anything, or what I fried it in—I found a frying pan that buffalo hunters had lost.)

I went north and food and water gave out. I saw a drove of antelope, but could not kill any, so I went seven days without food and four without water. I was just ready to give up, to lie down and die, when a skunk ran at me and threw musk on me. But I killed and ate him for his trouble. I didn't cook him; I just cut him open and sucked what warm blood I could get, and then devoured him, but I was careful not to eat too fast or too much at once. I did not waste any part of him, for food was too scarce. I also found some muddy water. I put grass over it to keep from drinking flies and bugs, drank water, watered and rested my horse, ate more polecat, drank muddy water, and felt much refreshed.

I traveled on and found some buffalo. I selected a little calf and roped him. I jerked the little fellow down and let the horse drag him a short distance, then thinking I could manage him, I jumped down to cut his throat. But the little fellow jumped up, butted me down, and ran over me. I got up, but down he brought me again. I drew my bow but never tried to get up. I had fifty arrows; all these I stuck in that buffalo, but I was so weak I could not kill him and he kept butting and goring me. My horse had come up close to me, but I could not get up. I caught the fork of my saddle, but the little buffalo knocked me back. I made the horse leave me—it was still tied to the calf—and I got to my feet. I went on the other side of the gray and climbed on. We rode away with the young buffalo at the end of the rope. I knew I could only kill him by dragging him to death, so we went for many miles, until the hide was worn off his side, and he finally was so near dead that I could get down and finish him.

And right there I had a sure enough feast. I cut the calf open, and as usual ate the warm liver, and from his paunch drank the sour milk that I found there, then

93

took a good rest. I skinned and dressed this calf, ate more of the entrails, and prepared for cooking some meat. I got two dry sticks and rubbed and rubbed them together, cut new notches in them and rubbed on—but I was so weak I thought the fire would never come. By persistent effort I finally saw a little smoke. I blew on that and soon a spark was visible, then a blaze. I was very careful not to have much smoke.

When I cut the meat I was cautious not to offend the Great Spirit. If an Indian cuts or punches a hole in a piece of meat before, or while, he is cooking it, he has offended the Great Spirit and is sure to have some misfortune on the trip. If anyone in camp with an Indian pushes a stick through meat to cook it, he is immediately banished from the camp, if not killed.

I adhered to all the superstitions, for I believed in them as I was taught to do. I ate all I could, smoked, moved camp, smoked, ate, and moved camp again. At night I put my meat under my head and soon fell asleep. I did not tie my horse, for he would not leave me. In the night I heard him snort and run, then he came up close to me and squatted, as he was accustomed when I wanted to get on. I grabbed up my meat and other equipment and jumped astraddle and the gray galloped away. These night moves were nothing unusual for me. I was soon sure nobody was after me, so I dismounted and fell asleep. But again I was aroused. This time I saw what the trouble was. A big lobo wolf was smelling under my head for the meat. Of course I thought of Indians dressed in the skins of wolves to get close to me. I bounded up and let drive an arrow that ended the wolf's career, then turned around and shot another and another until I had killed five, and run several away. I skinned these wolves, replaced the arrows in my belt, and moved camp.

I could hear the night birds whistling, the coyotes yelping, the wolves howling, and I thought of the Indians and how we used to make these sounds after we had scattered from an encounter—and I wondered if these were real wolves and birds, or deceptive red men.

27

I SOON FOUND MYSELF on the buffalo range proper, and food was plentiful. Sometimes wild animals, at night, would trot around me and stir up the rattlesnakes, which were thick. They would sound their rattles and scatter their venom and make the air unpleasant.

The saddle I had been using—a forked stick—hurt my horse's back, so I concluded to make a better one. I tanned and dressed some hides and I had found a file and a piece of steel at an old camp. I cut a pole and fastened this steel on one end and set the other end of the pole in the ground. I rubbed the fleshy side of the hide over that steel until all the meat was worn away. Then I would put brains of the animal on the hide and that would make it soft and pliable. This was a slow process of tanning, but I had more time than anything else.

I cut down a willow tree, hacked off a fork and whittled out a saddle tree. I covered it with rawhide, padded it with buffalo hair, recovered this and then put on the extras. I bent a willow stick around, covered it with leather, and made exquisite stirrups. I then covered the whole saddle with buffalo robes and let them extend down as fenders. I measured my horse's back, and made everything fit. I was a long, long time working, changing and fitting this saddle, but my labor and perseverance rewarded me with a saddle that fit superbly and rode comfortably, and was indeed quite a curiosity.

I tanned hides, from the buffalo's to the black snake's, and made moccasins. The file I found served the purpose of an awl as well, and whit-leather, or sinew, was used as thread.

Texas hunters with their kill

I wound around over the country, constantly shifting my position, until one day I came in sight of a town (it must have been San Angelo) and I saw two men riding along. I moved toward them with the intention of giving up, but I saw that my dress didn't correspond with theirs, and I was painted like a warrior, and I thought they would kill me, so I turned around and rode the other way as fast as my horse would carry me.

I went out toward the Pecos, and one day I killed a bear, made a fire, and had a fine roast. I got a good greasy square meal that time.

I usually picked my camping grounds rather than just stopping at the end of a day. I stayed in rough places, but never where I could be hemmed up. I would study in my mind what would become of me. My mind was very active. I was in my seventeenth year and I thought a great deal about religion. I would lie at night spending hours watching the great celestial panorama. I would look at the great starry vault, this blue dome, and then at my shield, and I would see that each of the larger stars occupied the same position on my shield that it did in the heavens, and thus my shield served as a compass as well as a protector. Without that shield, how could I ever have found water?

I returned to the plains, our old haunts, and I would lie at a water hole and wait for antelope to come in to drink, and then I would kill them. My horse was pretty fat, for the grass was fine.

One night I could hear wild animals running, and the scream of something like a puma, but I was sure it was not a panther. It didn't sound right. Then the wolves began to howl, and they did not sound right. I was sure Indians were near, but the calls and imitations were not of my tribe. I lay perfectly still, but my horse came snorting and running up to me. The rattlesnakes seemed more numerous than usual, and I could hear them rattling all around. The whole animal world seemed disturbed. I filled my canteens with water, cut off what meat I could carry, threw my equipment on my horse, mounted, and stole away in the darkness. Next morning I saw many Indian signs. I must have been close to a large party. I saw a horse that belonged to them, but I had quit stealing. I thought, "What benefit would the horse be to me? There is no one with whom I can trade."

I rode out on the plains and worked away on moccasins; I got out of reach of water and my food gave out. I hunted for game and searched for water for four days. When I found the water I sank down exhausted at the spring and let my horse drink first, but I was careful that he didn't take too much. I bathed in the water and enjoyed its refreshing touch. I stayed at this water three days and was loath to leave it. I went up on a high point nearby and saw Indians coming. I gathered up my "traps," obliterated all signs, and got away from there without being discovered. We hid in the thick undergrowth some distance from the spring and a band of Apaches passed right close to us. They were very talkative. It was a band of young warriors, just back from a successful raid and they were feeling good. I believed I could whip the whole party, but I didn't care to kill the poor fellows for they were dogged by enough people anyway. They camped at the spring but left very early the next morning. They had a big herd of horses.

After they left we stayed at or near the spring long enough for me to poison a lot of arrows. I always kept a raccoon skin full of a solution of polecat and rattle-snake poison. I killed an antelope and ate enough to keep me strong. About noon the second day I made a fire and cooked some of the meat. I was more uneasy about rangers coming along than I was more Indians.

So I went back to buffalo country and visited all the old paleface camps I could find. I picked up all the pieces of iron or steel they happened to have left; these I would sharpen with my file and make arrow spikes, replenishing my arrow stock. I regained my strength and my horse fared sumptuously. I got so I could send an arrow clear through a buffalo. I would kill the big loboes, dress their hides, fill them up with grass and sew them and make fine pillows. I made jackets, quirts, leggings, lariats and anything I could think of from the buffalo hides. I worked all the time, for that was the only way I had to keep from getting too lonely.

I taught my horse many tricks. He would stand on his hind legs, squat when he saw me coming to mount, lie down and sleep close to me on cold nights. I would use his legs for a pillow, and I divided my blanket with him. At night he was my consort and companion, in daytime we were inseparable. Sometimes we would play hide-and-seek; I would slip off from him and hide in the tall grass, but he would trail me up and nicker when he found me. He was a fine scout, and a good sentinel. I could tell when someone, or even a wild beast, was around. I could lie down and sleep soundly, confiding in his vigilance. He would snort, move gently, or bite my arm if an enemy was around. He would lie perfectly still when I got up, give me time to arrange my equipment on his back, then he would kneel by me until I was saddled and well seated—then he would bound away and we'd defy the swiftest-footed animal.

At that time scouting parties, buffalo hunters, soldiers, rangers and Indians were numerous on the plains, and they were all my enemies, so I had to be constantly on the alert. Winter came on and we could have no fire at night lest we be detected.

We were away up north and it rained, sleeted and snowed a great deal. Horse food became scarce, covered up, but I would scratch away the snow so my horse could eat. We drifted south naturally. One morning we came in contact with a band of Indians, and once more the speed of the gray saved my life. He ran south through the blinding snowstorm and in this flight I lost most of my blankets. The ride over the sleet-covered ground was no fun. The wind blew from the north in a regular gale and we had nothing to eat. The snow changed to sleet and that is what saved us, as the Indians could trail us no farther. We fell exhausted, many, many miles from where we started.

How long I lay there I have no way of telling. The sun was shining and the gray was licking me the first I knew. The sleet had partially melted and my horse had excellent grazing. I found a covey of grouse hard by, so that day we rested and recuperated. My horse was stiff and sore, the old freezes and frostbites on my fingers and toes were reinstated, and my every joint was stiff. I was forced to be idle, and had no balm for my pains, no panacea for my stiff joints, but my body was easy compared to my mind. All the loneliness and desolation of my first exile seemed to come back to me, compounded.

I visited all the old camps, gathering up old hoops and wagon tires or such steel as I could handle, to replenish my arrows—but I could not drive my melancholy spirits away. They seemed to have come to stay. Faithfully I would work, cheerfully I would play with my horse, but somehow nothing was of interest to me.

I was tired of this lonely life, and I resolved at all hazards to make friends with somebody. Suddenly the thought occurred to me to join the Comanches. I had met them frequently when I was an Apache and I could understand enough sign language to get along until I learned their dialect. I wondered on what terms they were with the Apaches, what story I could tell, or how I could tell them anything. Fully a year had passed since I had left the Apaches, and the two tribes might be at peace—or they might be at war.

These were grave questions, and as I pondered I saw, far away to the northeast, a cloud of dust. It proved to be an immense herd of buffalo headed right toward us. They stretched for miles across the prairie. I knew nothing could stop them, and although my horse could stand a good, long race, how long would this one be? There was no time to be lost. I must either shoot my horse and get under him and risk being trampled to death, ride in a circle for no telling how far, or ride slowly and allow the beasts to pass me in their flight, risking being mashed or gored. Dangerous as it was, I took the latter course, and by that time the whole country was enveloped in dust and the animals were as far as I could see. I loved my horse, and as they crowded against us, I began shouting, whooping, shooting arrows, yelling and hanging on for dear life. I tried to clear a space around us. Soon we were enshrouded in darkness and in a thundering noise, but on, on we were forced by the herd. We passed over wallows, over prairie dog towns, over rough places where both horse and rider were blinded. To fall means annihilation. The very force of the buffalo bodies sometimes kept us upright.

I rode for hours until I thought I felt a fresher breeze and saw a bit more light. Soon the biggest part of the noise seemed to be ahead of me, then definitely began to recede. My great gray horse slackened his speed and I saw the mass of the furious animals was to the left of me, and gradually we rode out from them and were safe.

I got some of the dust out of my lungs, but I could not stop here for something had stampeded these animals. Buffalo hunters were thick in this country. I must seek a high point where I would have an unobstructed view of the plains.

This was the final event to make my decision. Whatever the state of affairs between the Apaches and the Comanches, I decided to risk my chances and join the first Comanche band I found.

28

ONE MORNING I located a party of Indians and discerned, by the split in the horses' ears, that they were Comanches. At a safe distance, and unobserved by them, I followed these Indians all day and watched them go into camp at night.

I selected an hour some time after dark for approaching the camp, for I intended making some sort of investigation before revealing myself to them, for I did not know what kind of a reception I would receive and I wanted to play it as safe as possible. So tethering my horse at a convenient distance from the camp, where I could easily get and mount him if I had to make a hasty escape, and taking my bows and arrows, I crept up close to the campfire and listened.

The Indians seated around were talking and laughing and seemed to be in high good humor. As a rule the Comanches are a fun-loving people and enjoy a good laugh, while the Apaches are morose and prefer to laugh only when someone is hurt or has had some calamity befall him.

These Comanche braves must have been telling some of their day's adventures, but I could not understand what they said. After remaining there within a short distance of them for twenty or thirty minutes, I mustered up enough courage to do a daring thing. I walked right in among them unannounced!

My sudden appearance caused consternation. Letting out loud war-whoops and yells, each brave sprang to his feet and darted off into the darkness, leaving me standing in the firelight. I must have been a vicious-looking Indian—long, dangling hair, uncouth and unkempt, with drawn bow. There I stood, wondering if they would come back and try to kill me. Soon they collected and came back in a charge, whooping and yelling, and I was surrounded in very quick time. I made signs for peace and tried to tell them I was a poor lone Indian without a friend, and hungry. The few squaws who were there were the first to approach me. One old woman, with a fierce countenance and only one eye, came up close to me and began to chatter in an excited voice, but I could not understand her.

I was wild, young, and timid, and I could not look that old she-devil in the eye, which came near to being my undoing, for I afterwards learned that she wanted them to kill me right there, saying I would bring trouble to them. However, a young warrior came close and began talking to me in the Apache tongue, and I told him that I was an Apache from force of circumstances, driven from the tribe; that I had killed a medicine man who had murdered my chief and master; that I was a white man by birth but an Indian by adoption; that I loved the Indian and hated the white man; that on my shield were the scalps of whites whom I had killed in battle, and that I was regarded by my race as a mortal enemy; that I was a petty chief under Carnoviste and had had a small band of warriors of my own, but they were all dead, killed in a drunken brawl; that I had forsaken the Apaches for good, and they were at that very moment seeking to take my life; that I wanted to become a Comanche and dwell with them and forever make war on the Apaches and the white people.

I told them many things of which they knew, and another brave came forward and said he had seen me with the Apaches at a certain time and that I had run a race with him and beaten his horse, and he knew Carnoviste and other Apaches.

After hearing my story in detail, and which I told truthfully and without exaggeration, they told me I was welcome to stay with them as long as I pleased and that I could accompany them to the main body of the tribe to which they were going the next morning, and they assured me that the big chief, Cotopah, would give me welcome there.

Accompanied by two of the young braves, I went out and brought in my horse. The squaws gave me plenty to eat, fixed me a comfortable pallet, and for the first time in many months I felt that I was among friends, and I lay me down to sleep with a feeling of security and contentment.

HERE, again, we have a story told two significantly different ways. In the 1899 edition, Herman makes a great deal more over his horse, Judge Jones (we must assume) having arbitrarily given the gray the name Rosanante. The seasons are also changed and a good bit of the detail. Frankly, I prefer the 1899 edition, except that I rather feel the 1927 version makes better sense. However, the reader may decide for himself, for here is the 1899 version taken up following the discovery of the Indians whom Herman thinks are. Comanches:

I WANTED to eavesdrop them, but I could not leave Rosanante to go to the Indians without him making terrible demonstrations. We had been constantly together for a year, and he was jealous of me. I carried him to the herd and thought I would leave him there, but pshaw! He wouldn't notice horses, but he stayed right with me. At last I took off my equipments, blankets, pillows, etc., and laid them down. I kept bow and arrows, dirk and other weapons and made Rosanante lie down by them.

The lights were out in all the camps except one. I crept snakishly up to that one and listened. The Indians were talking and laughing. I was sure that they were Comanches by the way they constructed their tents, by their location and general good humor.

Comanches are a fun-loving people. . . . These fellows must have been telling some of their day's adventures, but I didn't wait to hear much. I pulled the blanket down over the door and walked in unannounced, and my presence carried consternation. Such warwhoops and yells! There were four or five warriors talking and smoking when I entered, but they broke out like wild cattle through the tent, under the tent or anywhere else.

I must have been a vicious looking animal. . . . There I stood proud and defiant. Indians scattered at first, but soon collected— and such yelling and whooping! I was surrounded in less time than it takes me to tell it.

I made signs for peace; I was bashful and tired of being the center of attraction. My terms were accepted.

The squaws surrounded me, and such chattering, gabbling and yelling. I was wild, young, timid and even shamefaced. I could not look straight at anybody. I felt so tall that I reached the top of the teepee, and so gawky, awkward and uncouth. The squaws would come right up to me, laugh, talk, and pat me on the cheeks, raise up my head, jabber to me and grin; then they would hug me, embrace me and say all manner of nice things, but I would not look at them.

There was an old warrior who understood the Apache language, so I told him that I belonged to the Apaches, but was lost. I was afraid to tell the truth then, but afterwards I told him all.

He said if I had told them the true story at first they would have had a war dance. I was an impudent, saucy little booby. I would have fought the camp.

After laughing, talking and dancing around for some time, the squaws made me a pallet and soft pillows and I went to lie down, but Rosanante had been neglected long enough. He was making a mighty ado, so I went out and got my equipments and permitted him to come to the door of my teepee. He would not allow any Indian to come about me.

[At this point the two versions more or less converge again.]

The next morning my horse and I were the center of attraction. I showed off all his tricks, and some of the braves wanted me to run races with them. They tried to buy him or trade, but they didn't have enough property for that. They offered me several horses, saddles, ropes, guns, pistols, blankets, shields—and one chief offered me his daughter, but I remained firm in my resolve to keep my faithful horse.

We went to the main body of the tribe, which we reached after several days' journey, and I was given a cordial welcome by the whole tribe when my story was made known to them. The chief called his warriors together and they held a council, and after asking me many questions, through an interpreter I was told that I would be taken into the tribe on condition that I would always remain a Comanche, and that I would help them fight their enemies, and never surrender to the white man.

I made them a big speech in which I told them I was an Indian, I ate raw meat and I drank the warm blood of the wolf to give me the ferocity of that animal; that I poisoned my arrows with the venom of the rattlesnake to make sure they would kill the hated white man when they sped toward him. My talk pleased them, and sitting in a circle, we smoked the pipe of peace.

After smoking, we all stood up, and marching around, we placed our right hands over our hearts and then raised them toward the heavens. This process was begun slowly, but as we marched we struck the double-quick step, striking our breasts repeatedly and raising our hands very much like schoolchildren do now in modern calisthenics. This was kept up for some time, no doubt to see how much I could endure, and then I was led before the chief for a kind of obligation, in which I promised faithfully to perform all the duties of a Comanche warrior, to help provide for, protect and defend those with whom I was entrusted and surrounded, and to obey my chief in all things, in peace and war. Thus I was adopted into the tribe and became a Comanche. I remained a Comanche ever since, and those same privileges which were bestowed upon me in that solemn hour are mine to this day, and I am recognized by all Comanches as a tribesman, whenever I want to claim my tribe relationship. I was given a Comanche name, Montechena [Montechina], and that name appears today on the tribal records in Washington—Montechena Herman Lehmann.

I was allowed the privilege of selecting the family with whom I would live and of which I would become a member. I looked at them all and selected Cotopah, the Indian that could speak Apache, as my brother. I walked up to his teepee and bowed, touching my nose in the sand, stuck my dirk in the side of the door, hung my bow on the wall, and then the chief came and bumped our heads together. I enjoyed all the freedom, rights and privileges of the tribe.

I have never regretted my choice, for Cotopah proved himself to be a brother in many ways.

Comanche Indians—Herman's second Indian "family"

29

PROVISIONS were made for me at the camp and a portion of food supply set by in my name. A tobacco pipe of their style was prepared for me and I took an active part in all their festivities, whether social, carnal or religious.

Then we went out and had racing and gambling; I was not a greenhorn when it came to riding a pony race, and soon became one of their favorite jockeys.

The Comanches seemed to have accepted me in good faith right from the very start, for within a short time the chief in selecting a party of warriors to go on a raid to the white settlements directed that I go with them. He asked me if I knew the country where we were going and I told him that I had often been there with the Apaches. In fact, that was in the region where I had been captured; that there were many good horses to be obtained there, all of which he knew, for he said he and his people had dwelt in that region for many moons before the white men came and took those hunting grounds from them.

Before starting on the raid it was decided to move camp and go north some distance. The squaws tore down the wigwams, packed them up, tied them on travois poles and we moved along. We reached the Panhandle country going north, but scouts reported soldiers that way, so we turned south, traversed the plains, crossed the Pecos and Rio Grande, and came into Mexico.

We traveled leisurely along, killing game, tanning hides and drying meat. The Comanches kept out scouts, guards and sentinels similar to the Apaches, only the chief planned our routes, located suitable camping places, directed raids and fighting expeditions, and was general manager of everything.

When raiding parties were sent out, the best medicine men stayed with the squaws to care for the wounded when they were sent home for careful nursing, while the Apaches always took their best medicine men along.

We were moving along peacefully when one of the front scouts signalled back, "Prepare for trouble." No command was necessary; everybody understood the signal and Indians were ever ready to wage war, no matter with whom or what. We rode out in advance of the squaws, everything trying to be in front. We did not go far until we saw a Mexican train. A great many freighters go together and carry their families on a rawhide fastened to the coupling pole and axle under the wagon in all that dust. Sometimes one man has several large iron-axle wagons trailed to each other, two horses hitched to the tongue of the front wagon and two on each side of these, but their double-tree is attached to a rope or chain tied to the hind axle, thus working six abreast, five immediately in front of these, four next on, until there is one in front, making twenty-one horses under the control of one man. Several of these teams being together, is there any wonder they are called Mexican trains?

We were quickly discovered and we surrounded these wagoners, whooping and yelling and shooting. The Mexicans hastily abandoned the train and ran into a dense chaparral, and we captured two girls and one boy in the rout. These had to run the gauntlet and become slaves. We took several Mexican scalps and wounded others, then we examined the wagons and found them loaded with merchandise. We took all the tobacco, sugar, powder, lead, cartridges and guns we could find, as well as blankets and some clothing, then set fire to the wagons. We traveled rapidly from there for five days back into the United States and came upon a party of movers. They were pretty strong, so we did not attack them, but we stole all of their horses and left them afoot.

We then returned to the plains and our usual camping places. The scalps we had taken were placed on poles and we had a big scalp dance—the squaws going to the left and the warriors to the right; dancing, yelling and shouting continuing that day and night and part of the next day. Then the plunder was divided among the squaws, but the warriors divide their property as soon as it is taken, that is, each one keeps what he steals.

We hunted and killed an abundance of game and supplied the camp with meat, making things comfortable. Then the raiding expeditions were arranged. We divided up into small squads and started out in various directions. The band I was with came down the Colorado, crossed over to the San Saba, then over to the Llano, stealing all the way. Down near Packsaddle Mountain, in Llano County, we came up on a party of white men who hid under a bluff and rock and gave us a hard fight. Three of our men were killed and several wounded. Several of our horses were killed and some wounded, but we managed to keep the herd together and made our escape. We must have made it hard for the whites, for they did not try to follow us.

That night we passed a party of soldiers. [The 1927 edition says rangers or Minutemen.] They had left one old Negro to guard the horses and he was fast asleep. I sent an arrow through his heart and scalped him. [The 1927 edition says "We sent an arrow through his heart . . ."] We took possession of their horses, saddles and guns and never aroused the sleeping soldiers. We got about thirty-five good horses and hurried away from there before reinforcements could come. Riding in a run, day and night, never stopping to eat or to sleep until we were away up in the open country, we went back to camp, only to find it deserted. Signs left on the ground there told us that a battle had taken place in which some Tonkaways with soldiers had been in a measure successful; that the tribe had gone to the sand hills, followed by the Tonkaways and the soldiers. We were warned to be cautious, for our enemies would probably be between us and the tribe. The number of soldiers was pictured on the signal bone as legion.

From this camp to the next watering place was at least one hundred miles, so we filled up some cow paunches with water and hung them on our pack mules and set out over this dry country, but fortunately, it rained the next day. Late that same day we came in sight of a camp near a water hole—a special hole that always contained water, being about six feet down but the Indians had cut steps down to the water. We knew that whoever was camped there must be whites, for they had too much fire for Indians. Our spies investigated and reported that only a few men were there with a good herd of horses, and we decided to get those horses, too.

But we must also have water. Our water was nearly gone and it was sixty miles to the next water, so we had to water here.

We kept hid and very quiet until midnight and then we came together and cast lots to see who would go to the spring for water. The Great Spirit selected one of the warriors and me. We got our canteens (cow paunches) and, snake-like, we approached the camp. The men were still astir in the camp, but we had to have water. I went down in the well and drank, then filled up my canteen and climbed out. My companion did likewise. No one heard us.

We returned with the water and made plans to steal the horses. We sent one of the warriors on with the horses we already had and we remained to see what we could do. We rode up to the horses and found three men guarding them. When we fired on them they took to their heels, while the horses stampeded. Just about this time the soldiers in camp opened fire and it seemed that there must have been several hundred of them. We fired a few shots into the camp, but spent most of our time in collecting the horses.

There had been so much shooting, whooping, and yelling that the Indian who guarded the horses thought he was being pursued by the soldiers and he rode off and left us. We came in sight of him and spurred on our fresh mounts, but he hurried on, keeping a respectable distance ahead. We raced with him for many miles—to the next watering place—before he saw that we were not soldiers, but he had not lost a horse. We put the herds together and the twelve of us had nearly a hundred good horses, while our enemies were afoot. In three or four days we overtook the squaws and children with the camp equipage, and as soon as they learned that several of the warriors with our party had been killed, they set up a wailing and began gashing themselves with knives. We lost three braves on this raid. When we got back to the tribe we had no war dance.

I HAVE MADE a great deal of fun of some of the poetry which Judge Jones included in the 1899 edition of Herman Lehmann's story, and it is just about as bad as one can imagine. Either the verses themselves are mawkish and prolix or their sentiments are bewilderingly inappropriate to the text. And even when the lines carry some vague connection with the story (and I would emphasize vague), the style is often ridiculous. I would like to furnish one example so that the flavor of this bizarre compendium may be had.

While Herman is living alone out on the plains, before he joined the Comanches, he and his horse both fall victim to the cold and snow. He pictures himself as being almost disabled with frostbite. Then suddenly interjects:

This bit of experience brings to mind a little quotation from the Washington Star:

105

"It comes the sad season when bitter
    winds blow
And the shovel our lives must control.
When it isn't at work on the beautiful
    snow
It is frolicking free in the coal."

But at the foot of one chapter, a lengthy poem is appended which expresses a sentiment that must, surely, have been Herman's. The text declares that "we make slight changes in Labouchere's anti-imperialistic reply to Kipling's 'White Man's Burden,'" so perhaps some of this is original. Whatever is the case, it is the only piece of that injected 1899 verse (it is gone from the 1927 edition) which might be found interesting to most readers. So here it is:

Pile on the Indian's burden
To gratify your greed,
Go clear away the Indians
Who progress would impede;
Be very stern for truly
'Tis useless to be mild
With new-caught, sullen peoples
Half devil and half child.

Pile on the Indian's burden;
And if ye rouse his hate,
Meet his old fashioned reasons
With Maxims up to date.
With shells and dumdum bullets
A hundred times made plain
The Indian's loss must ever
Imply the white man's gain.

Pile on the Indian's burden,
Compel him to be free;
Let all your manifestoes
Reek with philanthropy.
And if with heathen folly
He dares your will dispute,
Then in the name of freedom
Don't hesitate to shoot.

Pile on the Indian's burden,
And if his cry be sore,
That surely need not irk you—
Ye've driven slaves before.
Seize on his towns and pastures,
The fields his people tread;
Go make from them your living,
And mark them with his dead.

Pile on the Indian's burden,
Nor do not deem it hard
If you should earn the rancor
Of these ye yearn to guard,
The screaming of your eagle
Will drown the victim's sob—
Go on through fire and slaughter,
There's dollars in the job.

Pile on the Indian's burden,
And through the world proclaim
That ye are freemen's agent—
There's no more paying game!
And should your own past history
Straight in your teeth be thrown,
Retort that independence
Is good for whites alone.

Pile on the Indian's burden,
With equity have done;
Weak, antiquated scruples
Their squeamish course have run,
And though 'tis freedom's banner
You're waving in the van,
Reserve for home consumption
The sacred 'rights of man'!

And if by chance ye falter,
Or lag along the course,
If, as the blood flows freely,
Ye feel some slight remorse,
Hie ye to Rudyard Kipling
Imperialism's prop,
And bid him, for your comfort,
Turn on his jingo stop!

Take up the white man's burden,
To you who thus succeed
In civilizing savage hordes
They owe a debt, indeed;
Concessions, pensions, salaries,
And privilege and right,
With outstretched hands you raise to bless—
Grab everything in sight.

Take up the white man's burden,
And if you write in verse,
Flatter your nation's vices
And strive to make them worse.
Then learn that if with pious words
You ornament each phrase,
In a world of canting hypocrites
This kind of business pays.

30

WE KNEW we could not remain long where we were, for the whites would hunt us down, and we believed that for every one we killed, seven would come to take his place, so we expected the soldiers to be reinforced to follow us; so we made preparations to flee to Mexico.

Scouts were sent out all over the country to collect as many men as could be found to protect the women. Seventy-five warriors came and we started south.

We were in no hurry, for we reasoned that the soldiers would have to send to the fort to get reinforcements and mounts, so we killed buffalo and traveled leisurely along, occasionally killing a buffalo hunter.

We had gone several days' travel when three warriors from a party of six came rushing into camp, almost exhausted, and told us that they had been surrounded and overpowered by thirty Tonkaways, who were well armed and equipped. In the fight the other three braves from our band had been killed before these three had managed to escape and bring us word of the attack.

We had more than three times the number of the Tonkaways, so we mounted and rode to meet them. We had gone two or three hours from camp when we located them in their camp, having a feast. The Comanches had been at war with the Tonkaways for a long time and had nearly exterminated the tribe. The hatred the Tonkaways had for the Comanches was fierce, for they blamed the Comanche for all of their misfortunes.

When we found those Tonkaways in camp, our chief gave a war-whoop and we all joined in one continuous yell and charged the camp. The Tonkaways fled at the onslaught and several of them were killed. We took possession of their camp, and what do you suppose we found roasting on the fire? One of the legs of a Comanche. A warrior of our tribe!

Our chief gave the cry for vengeance and we all joined in the chorus. We made another charge. No martial music fascinated our little band and urged us on to victory. But one look at those stern faces and drawn muscles would have shown that we meant to utterly annihilate the enemy.

The Tonkaways had collected in a canyon and reloaded their guns, preparing to receive our charge with a deadly fire. For a moment they checked our onrush; down would come a horse, over would tumble a rider, but on we came, in our frenzy. At first I was terrified, and it seemed like I could not face death that way, but I was in the front rank, and my comrades in the rear pressed me onward. Then I caught the spirit of vengeance. I became enraged, spurred on my steed, and fought courageously.

One of the Tonkaways rode out of the ravine where they were to challenge some of us to single combat. A Comanche made a dash at him but fell mortally wounded. Another went, and received a death blow. It seemed like human blood had made the Tonkaways bold, and somehow our shields would not ward off his bullets—but the third warrior to advance got him. At this single combat, by seemingly general consent, a cessation took place and at this recess every warrior loaded his gun and prepared for more battle.

The single combat was of short duration, and when the Tonkaway brave fell there went up a yell from both sides—exultant from us, a yell of rage from the Tonkaways. In a very few seconds we were in a hand-to-hand conflict with the Tonkaways, and they were soon vanquished. Those cannibals fought bravely, and eight of our men lay dying on the battlefield, while forty or fifty were more or less desperately wounded. But our work was not finished.

A great many of the dying enemy were gasping for water, but we heeded not their pleadings. We scalped them, amputated their arms, chopped off their legs, cut out their tongues, and threw their mangled bodies and limbs upon their own campfire. We put on more mesquite brushwood and piled the living, dying and dead Tonkaways on the fire. Some of them were able to flinch and work as a worm; some were able to speak and plead for mercy. We piled them up, put on more wood, and danced around in great glee as we saw the grease and blood run from their bodies, and were delighted to see them swell up and hear the hide pop as it would burst in the fire.

Some of the enemy may have escaped, but we never saw any signs of them. We had twenty-eight scalps, thirty-five split-eared horses, thirty long-range guns, some saddles, a number of blankets, many bows and arrows, besides a great quantity of ammunition and other trophies as a reward for our vengeance, which in some respects partly satisfied our bloodthirsty band.

The reason so many of our men were killed and wounded was because the Tonkaways had the advantage of position and equipment—also because our men were so enraged at the sight of our roasted companion that they became reckless and did not use their shields properly. I had four spikes and one lead mark on my shield. If a shield is in motion when a ball strikes it the bullet will glance off.

We returned to our camp with our wounded and dead, and also the scalps and other booty. Our camp turned into a sad spectacle. Such weeping, moaning, wailing, hair-pulling and gash-cutting. The squaws cut gashes in their faces and on their bodies and limbs which took months to heal. Besides, those squaws kept the places raw and the wounds irritated in order to make their rewards greater in the hereafter. There is nothing pleasant nor amusing about a funeral dance such as we had when we came back from the fight with the Tonkaways.

It was three months before all of our wounded recovered and we could go on another raid. We drifted north and another band which had just run away from Fort Sill joined us. This band was under Quanah Parker. Others came in from different quarters of the compass until we became about three hundred strong. We hunted for a while, replenishing our stock of buffalo robes, moccasins, wigwams and other necessities. The women did all of the work except to make bows and arrows, tomahawks and pipes. We robbed several buffalo hunters and left them naked, destitute and afoot out there on the plains, hundreds of miles from home, to die of thirst and starvation.

THE ENCOUNTER with the Tonkaways which Herman describes so bloodily well was certainly one of the last fights any tribe must have had with the Tonks. Never very large, the Tonkaway were slaughtered to fewer than two hundred in the middle 1860s by another Indian coalition in Oklahoma, so the total number of tribesmen could not have been more than a hundred or so by the time of this battle.

The Tonkaways were considered cannibals by both Indians and whites, but anthropologists feel their cannibalism was ritualistic—and not at all uncommon among other Indians. Herman, of course, mentions some cannibalism being practiced among his beleaguered band of Apaches during their Rocky Mountain winter, but he seems to excuse it under the circumstances. The Indians, like their white foes, could be selective in their various repulsions—hypocritical might be too sophisticated a word for it. One may read accounts written by soldiers, explorers and other western observers purporting to give eye-witness testimony about Tonkaway

cannibalism. Again, it is never stated that they ate other humans for sustenance. And, of course, to see someone take one bite of a human corpse is apt to make the observer so outraged that the eater might just as well have made a week's meals off the carcass.

The Tonkaways were once a fierce enemy to the Spaniards, in central Texas, but from before the Civil War they seemed to have gone over to the white world for protection and survival. They were the traditional scouts for the plains soldiers and the entire tribe was taken to Fort Griffin in the 1870s where the members lived in drunken degradation down along the Clear Fork River, the object of much high moral preachment by passing whites who might be going to or from lynchings, cattle rustling forays, or falsifying records at the courthouse. Eventually the Tonks ended up in Oklahoma, just a name on the map, their language and customs lost and their numbers a tiny, unverified handful. Despite their record of friendship with the whites, few tribes were as despised and rejected by the whites as the Tonkaways.

31

AT THE TIME of the Tonkaway fight about twelve of us went down near Fort Concho on a raid. There another Indian, Esatema, and I, both of us being afoot, were left behind by the rest of the band, all of whom were mounted.

Esatema and I came near a small town—it was Paint Rock or Eden—and discovered a tent and near the tent a horse was staked. I had a long-range gun and I told Esatema that if he would sneak up and steal the horse I would hold the gun in readiness and shoot the first white man that appeared, but he would not do it. He said we were there afoot, and he wanted a horse to ride, but if we killed a white man then we would have but little chance to get out of the country. Then I asked him if he would take the gun and shoot any white man who appeared if I would go and get the horse, and he promised to do so.

I sneaked around and approached the horse, which kept snorting and cutting capers. When I got hold of the stake rope I cut it and led the horse away. Esatema and I were able to ride off without being molested.

From there we went east, and late that evening we found a camp near which was a large bunch of horses. One of the horses had a large bell on. When the campers went to sleep that night Esatema and I shot arrows into the horse that wore the bell and killed him to keep him from running and awakening the campers. Then we silently rounded up the other horses, about twenty-five, and started in a dead run for our headquarters, away out on the plains.

We traveled for three days without seeing anyone or being bothered. We were going through a pass in the mountains, possibly it was Buffalo Gap, and ran right into a camp of white men before we saw them. Realizing that we had to act promptly, we put our herd into a run and went through that camp, yelling and shooting. It was just at daylight, and the sleeping men arose as one man and made a break for the brush, not taking time to get their guns. As we went through we picked up two of their horses and carried them along, but we did not tarry to find out how many men were in the camp, and as they did not follow us we made a safe getaway.

We soon struck the buffalo trails, which insured obliteration of our herd's trail, and reached our village with a good bunch of horses. The other ten Indians who had gone out with us met with many reverses and came back empty-handed.

Before getting back to the village, Esatema and I had killed a deer for meat, which we had not eaten for some time. We had lost our only knife and could not skin the deer, so we were quite perplexed as to how we could remove the hide. Finally we got hold of it with our teeth and pulled the hide off. As we had no way to cut up the venison, we threw the carcass on the fire and roasted it whole.

We stayed around the village some time, preparing to move to a safer region. We broke horses and roped mustangs. We had a thick leather belt around our saddles, also attachments around the shoulders so the jerks of the mustangs would not cut off our horses' wind. A young Indian was sent around the mustangs to stampede them and make them run toward us, and we would select the best and ride in among them and rope them—that is, those who had horses that could keep up with the mustangs. This time I roped a nice fat stallion. He was too much for my horse. He jerked my horse down several times and found that he could not get loose, so he turned back and made fight and would have killed my horse and me, too, if another Indian had not come to my rescue and roped him. We tied him down and tried for many days to tame him, but he would always pitch.

We killed a great many mustangs and roasted them. We would cut off a large slice, hair, hide and all, throw it on the coals and see it fry. After we thought it had cooked enough, we would rake it out and eat it. The part right under the hide was always nice and tender. Mustangs are very palatable, but an old fat jack tastes best—like good, fresh butter.

We felt somewhat disheartened, for we knew the white buffalo hunters were going to come in such numbers that the Indians would have no more hunting grounds on the plains. Our men were getting scarcer every day. War parties or raiders would go out and never return. We held a great council in which other tribes participated and pledged ourselves to kill all of the whites as they came into our territory, kill them as they destroyed our game, kill them as they killed our companions, our squaws, and our children. To follow them and kill them so long as any of us remained. On the strength of these bold expressions, we had a big war dance.

We set out going north, robbing the camps of buffalo hunters and killing them as we could. We found the plains alive with the hunters, and we came back, still fighting. Those were exciting times, for scarcely a day passed without a skirmish or a fight. We kept ourselves supplied with the finest of guns and an abundance of ammunition, saddles, and everything we needed, for these hunters were usually wealthy sportsmen "green" from the states.

But it looked like our warriors would all soon be killed. Down near the southeast edge of the plains we would leave our women, children and old men and go on raids. The country was getting so thickly settled and the rangers so bad we thought it best to divide up into pairs instead of staying in one large band. I had Esatema again as a companion, and he was a brave, daring fellow, very cautious and always used good judgment. We stole many horses and left many white men dead or wounded, scalped or lacerated. Once we fought the rangers, dodged them, then slipped back and stampeded their horses while they were burying one of their comrades, leaving these brave palefaces afoot.

Marco, a Mexican captive, and I went on a raid down east, and on a little stream we found some men camping. We withdrew a short distance and held a consultation, deciding on a bold attack. We primed our guns and started riding for their camp, whooping and yelling. Just as we got even with the camp we shot into their campfire. There were four of the white men, and did they scatter!

Their horses stampeded and we, of course, could not stop there long. We ran through the camp, with the frenzied horses, and off a steep bluff into a hole of deep water and both of us came near drowning before we could get out, for the water was freezing cold. Our ammunition got wet. I had a cap-and-ball pistol and had to bore the loads out. We finally rounded up the horses, captured nine, and pulled back for home.

On another raid, twelve of us came down east and met a four-horse stage near Kickapoo Springs. Several men were with the stage, so we had a running fight for several miles, but we drew off before the stage reached town. We traveled on, spending a great deal of time on high points or up on mountains watching. We killed several bulls and two yoke of oxen when we attacked a wagon. We burned the wagon, but I don't know what became of the driver.

We came on and met five palefaces and had a fight with them. But they hid behind trees and fought us after our own manner of fighting. These men took careful aim when they shot, and our shields were all that saved some of us. The battle was a stand-off and none of us were killed; but those fellows shot too close for comfort. I do not know how they fared in the fight, for we withdrew and they never followed.

Down near Smoothing Iron Mountain we took twenty-five horses, tore down some fences and left things like we believed the Great Spirit intended them to be —free and open. The Indians believed that if the Great Spirit had wanted the country enclosed He would have fenced it.

We came back by House Mountain and stole some horses and one old mule from Bob Moseley, who later became my boss, and we struck an air-line for the plains, for the rangers were after us. They overtook us and fought us, capturing all our loose horses. We scattered, drifting west and coming together near Beaver Lake. The chief said that the Great Spirit had told him that if we would follow the rangers and surprise them we would gain an easy victory.

Captain Dan W. Roberts' Ranger Camp

We located the rangers in a camp near the water's edge. We waited patiently, taking a good survey of the ground. We cautiously approached, but the rangers were not easily taken by surprise, for when we were fifty yards from them they fired on us, wounding one warrior and killing a horse. They were camped around a big live oak tree. We charged them, but they made us purchase with blood every foot of ground we gained. We formed in a single line of battle and covered ourselves with shields. While the fight was raging two of our warriors succeeded in stampeding their (our) horses and when they got them safely away we quit the battle and went to them, making our getaway. Several of our warriors were wounded.

112

We returned to the plains to train our horses, hunt, and enjoy life for a while. But we constantly waged war on the buffalo hunters. We had to be alert, for hardly a day passed but what we saw soldiers, or signs of them, and they seemed bent on forcing us onto the reservation.

One old chief had a fine black horse that everybody was afraid of, so he offered me a nice bay horse to break the black, but he said, "He must be gentle." The black had thrown several Indians, and I was not caring much about riding him, but I went and looked at the bay and he was a dandy. I borrowed the chief's saddle, put it on the black, blindfolded him, and jumped on. Such kicking, bucking, pitching and bowling around! The girth broke and away went the saddle and me, too.

My breath was gone, but I soon recovered, and the chief taunted me, asking, "Is the bay horse yours now?" I told him no, but he told me I could have the black. The next day we took the black into a lake of water and three of us got on him while three others were to keep him in the lake. They turned him loose and he started out across the prairie in a long run, stopping running only long enough to pitch us off. My nose was the first part of me that came in contact with the ground and was therefore slightly disfigured; one of the boys had his arm broken, and the other one was badly bruised. We went back and had a fight with the boys who turned the black loose.

I procured a fine, silver-mounted Mexican saddle and girthed him up tight and rode him. He got gentle and made the fastest horse among the Indians and we won everything that the Kiowas had with that horse. I kept him, and he was the favorite of the tribe and our boys always bet on him. When we surrendered at the reservation I gave the horse to Quanah Parker and he won several races on him. The Yankees brought down a noted race horse and Parker ran Black against him and won—but Black died the next day.

32

THE PLAINS were being thoroughly combed by the buffalo hunters who were killing buffalo for their hides alone. We would often see great wagon loads of hides being hauled away, and would find the carcasses of thousands of slaughtered buffalo. It made us desperate to see this wanton slaughter of our food supply.

One day quite a party of us came upon a hunter away from his camp, killing buffalo. He had killed several of them and about this time we saw two men in a wagon start out from the camp to go to him, presumably to skin out the buffaloes that lay dead upon the ground.

They saw us about that time and turned their team around and whipped it into a run, heading for a little brushy ravine some distance away, and when they reached it they plunged over the steep bank, abandoning the wagon and team and taking to the brush. We did not find them, and they got away safely. We went to the hunters' camp and destroyed everything we found there which we did not want to take away. We then went back to the body of the hunter we had killed and took two scalp-locks from his head, cut a gash in each temple, and thrust a sharp stick through his stomach.

One of the warriors took the hunter's gun and claimed it for his own. It was the longest range gun I ever saw, and every Indian wanted it, but it sure brought bad luck to the Indian who secured it. After we left there the buffalo hunters took our trail and followed us for a long time. Finally we got in a fight with them and the Indian who had the big gun was killed. Another Indian got the gun and claimed it for his own and he, too, was killed. Then it passed into the possession of the chief's son, and he fell with it in his hands. Then an Indian known as Five Feathers used it for a long time when he, too, was killed. The medicine man said the gun had an evil spirit and advised us to throw it away or hide it where the white men could never find it. So we buried the big gun and the two scalp-locks taken from the head of the buffalo hunter in the sand hills.

33

I HAVE OFTEN BEEN ASKED if I was ever wounded while I was with the Indians. I carry several wound scars which I received in battle. One of the scars is from a bullet through the shoulder, and another is a scar made by a bullet from a buffalo gun which passed through the calf of my right leg and laid me up for quite a while. This is what happened.

We had traveled south and had trouble with the buffalo hunters when we spied a big band of soldiers and Tonkaways. Our scouts watched them until they camped, and then we stampeded and captured forty horses. We moved toward the sand hills, but the soldiers drove us back.

About the middle of the plains we met a bunch of Mexican traders and swapped horses for sugar, meal, sun-dried biscuits, guns, ammunition, and trinkets. Sometimes we would give ten head of horses for one gun, and this time we gave twenty head of horses for one needle gun. But we had plenty of horses left.

We practiced shooting with our new guns, cleaned them up and killed plenty of game. We had almost forgotten about the soldiers. Just after daylight one morning, at a time when we least expected to be attacked, the soldiers fired on us. The Indians stampeded and scattered everywhere. Dabo and I were gathering the horses when the fight started and I stopped in camp only long enough to get my pistol. By that time the soldiers were right on us.

As soon as the fight started the squaws mounted and got our horses out of camp to prevent them from falling into the hands of the white men. We took refuge under a hillside and held the enemy, who were in the open, at bay for several hours. We were ordered to wait until the soldiers were real close before we fired. The soldiers fell back but came on again and again to get their dead and wounded. Four horses and riders fell, and among these was the American commander. When the bullet struck me in the leg I guess I was too excited to feel it, and I went right on fighting. But after a while the wound began to pain me considerably, and I had to lie down. One Indian was knocked senseless by a bullet, and we thought he was killed, but it proved to be only a scalp wound. Another Indian was shot through the arm and abdomen. The women had now returned from securing the horses, and they grabbed bows and arrows, guns and spears to help us drive away the enemy.

We were so well concealed under the hill that not an Indian was killed, but I think the whites lost several men. One Indian's horse was shot in the eye and the animal began circling around in plain view of the soldiers, but the Indian quit him and joined us under the bluff. Another horse became unmanageable and went to join the enemy but his rider quit him, too. My horse was killed. I dropped down behind him and fought there for a while, but it got too hot for me and I ran back to the bluff but in the run I was shot in the leg. I was using a long-range buffalo gun at the time and I think I hit the mark with it several times.

We made several charges but were driven back. The soldiers must have gotten afraid of us, for they sent scouts for reinforcements. Four soldiers left the battle and got a mile start on us. We had a long race and the first one we overtook was a big fat black man. He rode for dear life and yelled at the top of his voice. Two Indians knocked him off his horse and captured him. We brought him into our camp and he fell on his knees to beg for his life, almost scared to death. The chief had him stripped, then made him put on Indian garb and a war bonnet was tied on his head so securely that he could not get it off. Then the Indians made signs for him to run back to his white friends. He understood the signs and lit out. But when the white men saw him coming they thought he was an Indian and riddled him with bullets. He fell before he reached his friends.

Night put an end to the carnage. The soldiers withdrew and fortified their camp to await reinforcements, but we escaped. Some of the women did not come back and they had a number of our horses. It took us four days to find them and they were cut nearly all to pieces and some had died. They thought we had all been killed. One time during the fight a bullet struck my shield and knocked me flat on my back, causing others to think I was dead. The jar of shooting and holding the shields against the soldiers' bullets was so great that most of us were helpless for several days.

After we gathered our horses and women we traveled across the plains and met the Apaches. They asked me to rejoin them, but I would not, and while I was in their camp you can be assured that I kept my eyes open and was on the alert for any sight of treachery, or attack on me. One old Apache watched me closely and I was certain that, given the chance, he would make some attempt to avenge the

115

killing of the medicine man, but I was careful and gave him no opportunity.

The Comanches were watchful, too, and when they discovered what they took to be a plot against me, they became angered at the Apaches. The Apaches were afraid of being attacked that night, because of me, so they went clear away. That was the last time I came in contact with that tribe after I left them and went to the Comanches. I have met some members of the tribe on reservations in Oklahoma in later years, and talked with them, but they did not always belong to the band which had sworn to get me. Old Chiwat, who is still living at Indiahoma, Oklahoma, and now [1927] nearly one hundred years old, is an Apache who helped capture me. He has remained my lifelong friend. Chiwat is a pretty good old Indian. After the tribe was placed on the reservation he became a scout for the government and rendered good service in trailing marauding bands of runaways.

34

IN THESE DAYS of modern ways people get shot sometimes just about like they always have—there is usually a woman at the bottom of the trouble. And a beautiful Indian maiden was the cause of me catching an arrow in my knee, some time after I joined the Comanches.

One day while assisting a young girl skin a buffalo, I became infatuated with her beauty. Topay was her name. When her hand touched mine, lightning thrilled through me.

Well, I watched that girl, and when she went out from camp, I went also; when she stopped, I wanted to stop, too. But somehow her father did not look on me with much favor. He would scowl at me and, in fact, told me that he would kill me if I did not stay away from her and let her alone.

But she didn't want to be left alone, and I would court her on the sly. Many an evening walk we had taken together when the whole camp was in oblivion, but we did not content ourselves with these evening strolls. One night, by agreement, I went into her teepee after her parents, in another teepee, had retired and we thought the father was sound asleep. Now this need not shock the modesty of those who may read this, for with the Indian all nature took its course, and we had none of those petting parties now in vogue.

I told my sweetheart about the threats her father had made against me and asked her if we should not be more cautious, but she said he would not hurt me, even if he caught us, although he might try and scare me.

So the next night I had another appointment to meet her in her teepee (the tent for squaws was made of sticks), after everyone was asleep. The time rolled around and I was prompt, and crawled into my sweetheart's apartment and found her awake and ready to receive me with open arms.

116

I was whispering sweet words of love and encouragement to her and we were enjoying Elysian bliss here on earth, oblivious to the rest of the world, when suddenly I felt a rough kick on my exposed hinder part. I needed not a second hint, for I knew it was the toe of the girl's father's moccasin. Out I went, straight ahead, leaving a considerable hole in the tent because the old man filled up the door.

I went around the tent one way and he came around the other and as I came into his view he let fly an arrow which pierced me in the knee. I fell to the ground, unable to walk. The girl sprang from her teepee and gently folded me in her arms and rebuked her father for treating her lover in so brutal a manner. She said I was behaving nicely and that he should not have disturbed us. The old man weakened, forgave us for sparking on the sly, pulled out the arrow and showed his regrets in many ways. He even offered to let me have the girl if I would give him two ponies. But I shied off and have been cautious of women ever since!

The wound was very painful and I was lame from it for a long time because the spike was still left in my knee and it took a long and painful operation to extract it. But ever afterward I could get with my "jularky" when I pleased.

When an Indian chose a wife, in both the Apache and Comanche tribes, he had to purchase the girl from her parents with horses.

A brave would fall in love with a maiden and he would approach her father and make his wants known by offering him a certain number of horses for the girl. If his proposition was accepted he would deliver the horses, take the girl and conduct her to his teepee. There was no religious ceremony, no demonstration, no incantations or anything else to make the marriage impressive or of more than passing interest. The buck had procured a squaw and the squaw had found a master. Sometimes the father of the girl would make the first advances by offering his daughter to some warrior for a certain number of horses, in which event it was usually the prospective son-in-law's privilege to drive a good bargain.

Children were often born to Apache squaws who were on raiding parties. The Indians would permit their squaws to go with them on their raids, and if it so happened that a child was born the squaw would be left to take care of herself as best she could, or if another squaw was in the party and chose to remain with her sister in distress, she was allowed to do so. Within a reasonable time the squaw and her papoose would come into camp and there would be rejoicing if the papoose happened to be a male child, because that meant a future warrior. But if it happened to be a female no notice would be taken of the new arrival. I have known squaws to give birth to a child, abandon it immediately, and proceed on with the party with no apparent injury. I knew one squaw of the Apaches who gave birth to twins, and she became so angry because there were two children instead of one that she stamped her offspring to death and left their little bodies for the vultures to devour.

Comanche women were kinder to their children, and the births usually occurred

Comanche children on the
Indian Territory reservation

in the villages. A woman in delicate health was not allowed to accompany her warrior on a raid, but had to remain in camp until the looked-for event happened. They carefully nourished the newborn babe and bestowed upon their children, male and female, that motherly affection that was the child's due.

What we would now term illegitimate children were rare among the Indians. There was virtue among the Indians and, in their way of viewing it, it was rigidly maintained. Of course, there were times when a married woman "went wrong," in which case her nose was cut off, but it was seldom that an unmarried girl departed from the paths of decency and gave birth to a child.

Once, with the Apaches, after we had moved to another location, I had occasion to go back to the former site and found seven babies, deserted and forsaken by their mothers. No doubt most of them belonged to unmarried girls, for we had been a long time in camp, drinking whiskey and carousing at that time and many things happened which would not have occurred otherwise. I could not take the babies, so they were left there in the roughs to be devoured by wild beasts, or to starve.

118

One day two Indians, Watsacatova and Esatema, and I were down on the out-skirts of civilization on a raid for horses. We were afoot but had a pack mule along to carry our equipment, and we each took turns riding him. We were out on the prairie, not far from some broken country, when we discovered we were not a great ways off from a stream.

But we found some white people camped on the stream. We immediately thought of a fight; however, something had to be done with our mule. Northeast of the camp we saw a dense thicket, so we decided to conceal our pack mule in that thicket and make a raid on the camp. We led the mule there and tied him to a small tree obscure from the view of the palefaces. We then had to cross some open country in front of the campers, but fortunately the grass was high and a little ravine ran through the prairie just the way we wanted to go. We crawled down the ravine about one hundred yards when suddenly a wagon came rattling right up to us.

Watsacatova and Esatema had good needle guns and an abundance of am-munition while I had a fine pistol and at least one hundred cartridges—and we had our bows and arrows. The wagon contained three white men and they were leading a saddled horse behind the vehicle. The sudden appearance of the wagon caused us to act quickly. We rose up and fired a volley at those whites and I think some of us hit the spring seat upon which they were sitting, for away it flew out of the wagon and landed the whites on the ground on the other side. One man dashed back to the saddle horse, cut the rope, mounted him, and lit out for the camp. The other two men seemed stunned for a second but then they lunged back into the wagon, whipped the horses into a run, and also made for camp.

Within a short time we saw about a dozen armed men riding toward us with several bloodhounds, so we cut heel dust across the prairie. Esatema was young and agile, so he outran us. Watsacatova was big and fat, but he understood the situation and kept nearly a hundred yards ahead of me. We leaped over the ground ahead of those hunting hounds until we had measured off fully six miles, sometimes slackening our pace until the dogs almost reached us, at which time we seemed to get new inspiration to speed.

Watsacatova began blowing hard, running out of breath, and I overtook him at a critical moment when it seemed that the dogs had also received some of that inspiration we had been getting. They increased both their speed and their yelping.

"Don't leave me," Watsacatova pleaded. "Let us stop and fight. I can't run any farther."

I had noticed at first that he would have left me if he could, so I ran by him. By then the sound of the horses' hooves was right at us, but fortune was in our favor for there before us was a great bluff and beyond was a mighty, yawning deep. We dreaded not the leap from the bluff and the projecting rocks; the bullets of our white pursuers was what we were afraid of. Down the bluff we rolled, like a coon descending a tree and encountering grapevines. In rolling down, Watsaca-tova's long, dangling hair, done up in cowtail fashion, became entangled in some bushes, and in his hasty extrication the queue was jerked out, leaving him a bloody scalp. We reached the bottom scratched, torn and bruised, but still able to run. The dogs followed us down the precipice, but the horsemen had to go around. The dogs were not keen to overtake us when their masters were not near. I don't know why but I guess they had a second-sense that it was all very well to chase their retreating foes but not so well to catch them.

We found a river and plunged in, but instead of going straight across we floated downstream. The dogs lost our trail and we made good our escape. We still had our guns, but our other possessions were stored away on the mule, hidden in the thicket near the white men's camp.

We were tired, footsore and worn out. We checked our pace, stopped, found a bee cave, took some honey, mixed it with a little water, killed a beef, made some sauce out of water, honey, and tallow, and spread it over the meat after it had been well roasted. We had a feast. We cut the hide of the yearling and made some lariats and went on farther and stole three horses. The next night we found ourselves in the vicinity of a small town, and there we stole a bunch of horses and made a run for our headquarters. The fate of the pack mule and our supplies is still shrouded in mystery, and for all I know he may be standing there tied in that thicket yet. We never went back to see about him.

How Watsacatova's squaw did laugh when she saw her master's bald head! He looked as if he had been scalped, and the other Indians derided him for losing his topknot by running so fast. His hair never grew back, and he carried a bald spot on the top of his head to his grave.

One time, while I was with the Comanches, a band of warriors, including several Kiowas, was out on the Pecos and we discovered a large herd of cattle being driven by ten or twelve cowboys. We stampeded the herd and drove off the cattle. The cowboys at first put up a stiff fight, and then ran. Two of the cowboys were killed in the scrap, but we outnumbered them two to one, and if they had not sought refuge in some tall running, we would have killed all of them. We drove the cattle away out on the plains to our camp and killed some of them. The others were turned loose on the prairie and for a long time we would go out and slaughter them as we needed meat.

This fight took place near what is known as the Pontoon Bridge crossing on the Pecos, and years later I met a man who knew all about the fighting. He knew the two cowboys who were killed and said they were buried there on the Pecos River. He may have told me their names, but if he did I have forgotten them. So many incidents like that happened during my wild life that I never tried to remember the details.

We were all camped down near the southern border of the plains when twelve of us went down on the San Saba and Llano Rivers after horses. Several other war parties left at the same time, thus leaving the squaws almost unprotected. We came down the San Saba to where it empties into the Colorado and then crossed over the Llano and up it to Llano town, collecting the horses which the early settlers were kind enough to raise for us. It saved us a lot of trouble.

As we were leaving that region our scouts reported that we were being followed by the rangers, so we hurried along and gave them the dodge. When we reached our camp with all the booty, we found it had been attacked by a body of soldiers and some Tonkaway Indians and a number of our women were among the slain. Only ten remained, and all the men but two Indians and a Mexican who had married one of our women and been admitted into the tribe had been killed or captured.

These persons were hidden in the chaparral, and they came out and reported that the soldiers and the Indians had fought a desperate battle. They said that many of the women and children were roped, captured and carried away. They told us that they fought from ten o'clock in the morning until night put an end to the carnage. During the cover of night the soldiers left with their captives.

Just fifteen warriors were left and ten women. When the attack was made on the camp, most of the squaws ran away and hid, but five of them were killed while escaping. We arrived the day after the fight and found the dead bodies were still scattered about. I remember finding the body of Batsena, a very brave warrior, lying mutilated and scalped, alongside of him was the horribly mangled remains of his daughter Nooki, a beautiful girl, who had been disemboweled and scalped. The bodies presented a revolting sight. Nearby were a lot of empty Spencer carbine cartridge shells, telling mutely of the heroic fight old Batsena had put up in defense of his own. His Spencer rifle was gone, of course, but I have no doubt that it worked deadly execution before it was taken. Other bodies were mutilated, too, which showed the hand of the Tonkaway in the bloody battle.

Five of our women and several children had been taken by the soldiers to Fort Griffin. We buried the dead and followed the soldiers, but somebody stole nearly all our horses, and we failed to recover our women. We returned to the plains and stole out the camps of some of the buffalo hunters, killing the men and getting their guns and ammunition as well as their horses, but the soldiers were in after us all the time.

In our council we swore to take ten captive white women and twice as many white children as the soldiers had stolen from us. We swore to avenge the deaths of the squaws, especially Nooki. We vowed to kill a white woman for each year of Nooki's age—she was about eighteen years old—and that we would disembowel every one we killed. Some of the warriors were for going back into the settlements at once and starting in on our revenge, but we were so badly demoralized that we had to get our forces together and move to another part of the country before thinking about doing vengeance.

We wandered desperately, trying to find a place of safety. One day we met a company of soldiers but were not strong enough to fight them, so we dodged and went into the sand hills and on across to the Pecos and there met more troops and we were driven back onto the plains. There was no rest and no peace for us.

We killed meat and prepared for winter, and six of us went near Fort Griffin and stole a nice herd of the horses kept by the soldiers and as we came back we passed a ranch and drove eleven more good trained horses into our herd and we reached our camp with fifty choice animals.

We moved farther out onto the plains and met ten buffalo hunters and had a hard fight. We ran those fellows out of the vicinity, then we hunted, rode broncos and had a good time for a while.

We traveled into the mountains and found some gold. The old Indians had known where it was and the Mexicans had taught some of the Indians how to wash the metal. We gathered up a quantity and traded it to the Mexicans. We went into Mexico with our gold and got the guns, ammunition and horses we wanted. These Mexicans offered us fabulous prices to locate this gold for them, but this we refused to do.

We made a treaty with the Mexicans and attended a Mexican dance. We drank mescal and cheap whiskey and got into a row and had to flee the country in short order. The Mexicans offered us peace and protection again if we would locate that gold mine for them, but this we would not do.

We came back to the plains, only to find the soldiers camped at every water hole. But under the cover of night we would slip in and steal water—and we still remained the faithful fifteen.

We even crossed the Panhandle plains and went to western Kansas where we found a little rest, for there were not so many soldiers there. But the hunting was bad. We came back into the Wichita Mountains of Oklahoma, and five of us went over nearly to Fort Sill and stole Comanche ponies. We stole from our old tribe, but these Indians had given up to the soldiers so we felt justified.

We were run back onto the plains where we met tame Indians from the Fort Sill reservation and they tried to persuade us to come in and give up. They told us how many white people there were, showed us their government guns, and told us how much good firewater they drank, but the faithful fifteen did not go.

Some Mexicans stole many of our horses about this time and we, along with thirty-five tame Indians, followed after. Among the ones stolen was my gray, that wonderful horse that had saved my life so often and had been with me for years. In five days we overtook the thieves just below the Pontoon Bridge on the Pecos. It was early in the morning when we came in sight of them and they were eating breakfast. We made a furious charge and scattered them, but some of them made fight. The sides were nearly equal. We charged again, and by this time had killed ten. This routed them and some of us followed. Datee and I followed the man who was mounted on the gray, but he rode into the river and the gray's speed on the other side soon carried him beyond our reach. Of all the reverses I ever suffered, the losing of that horse was the greatest. For one moment the events of those stormy years I had him flashed across my memory and I silently shed a tear.

We bade our tame comrades good-bye, taunting them by telling them to go back to their masters and work. Once more they implored us to go with them and give up, but no; we wanted freedom.

Ranches and forts were being established everywhere and we had no showing. The soldiers were thick and game was getting scarce.

We went far up on the plains and Quanah Parker and four other Indians came to us and urged us to go on the reservation. The soldiers did not want to kill us, they said, so they had asked these men to come talk to us. Quanah told us that it was useless for us to fight longer. The Indians' old, wild life of freedom was over. The white people would kill all of us if we kept on fighting but if we went on the reservation the Great White Father in Washington would feed us and give us homes and we would in time become like the white men with lots of good horses and cattle and pretty things to wear.

He said the white men had us completely surrounded—as we well knew—and would come in on us from every side. Some of the braves decided it was time to go to the reservation, but some did not, so there was much disputing and arguing. Quanah remained with us about four days, promising us that if we would go to Fort Sill we would not be punished or hurt in any way and that all would be well with us. Finally our band agreed to go in, and when Quanah started, we went along with him.

There were several of us who went most reluctantly: myself, High Shorty, Cotopah, Esatema and Watsacatova. One night we saw an unusual number of signs of soldiers and became frightened, but Quanah advised us to stay, and all at once we were surrounded by the troops. Quanah raised a white flag and met the soldiers in consultation to convince them we were heading for the reservation. They withdrew and we went on without further trouble.

In a few days we began meeting white people everywhere and many other soldiers, but Quanah, who spoke English, got us along all right.

One night, after we had gone deep into white territory, High Shorty had a bad dream. The next morning he called all his men together and invited Quanah to come and told us his dream. The faithful fifteen had all come together, only a few weeks before, and taken an oath never to give ourselves up or submit to the domineering attitude of the whites. He told Quanah that he, High Shorty, was doing wrong by breaking that oath and he felt that he ought not to do it. He said: "Quanah, I am not afraid of you but I dread the white man."

Quanah offered him protection and a good time, but still High Shorty was not convinced. He trusted Quanah and believed he would do what he could, but he did not think Quanah could manage the soldiers. High Shorty would not move that day. He said to Quanah, "You were one of us . . . where did we lose our

123

Quanah Parker, great Comanche chief who adopted Herman

warriors? Did we lose them in battle? No, we weakened and submitted to the whites and they transported many warriors far away from their wives and loved ones. Shall we give up and be severed from all that is dear to us? You know how our comrades have been imprisoned and punished."

Quanah stood up and said sadly: "I have ridden on the black horse (the train) and seen white people by the thousands and thousands, and it would be the height of folly for you and fourteen others to try and whip them, and besides you know how hard it is now to hide from them for they have dogs that would trail you. You are too near akin to me for me to let the soldiers hurt you or any of your men. Come on and don't be killed."

High Shorty came, but sadly, and against his will.

We started on and Quanah sent scouts to notify the soldiers at Fort Sill that we were coming in and to give us protection. We were within fifteen miles of the post when I saw a cloud of dust and heard the soldiers coming. I was riding a black mare that was a pretty swift animal, and the fear was too much for me. I turned and rode for my life back toward the Wichita Mountains.

Quanah Parker took after me and ran me for three or four miles before he caught me. He told me there was no need to be afraid, that I would not be hurt. But I would not agree to go with him because of the terror I had of being captured by the soldiers. I wanted to die a fugitive rather than be turned over to the white man. Seeing my fear, and having a special regard for me, he told me then that I could join his camp on the reservation and not have to give myself up. His people had already been given their own lands and lived many miles from Fort Sill. He told me to go there now, and gave me direction, and we parted.

When he got back to the others the soldiers were there and had my comrades surrounded. All were disarmed and taken to Fort Sill where they were placed in a stockade and kept prisoners for some time. I followed Quanah's instructions and found his camp without being seen by the soldiers. I stayed with Quanah and herded his horses for him, hunted occasionally, and soon became somewhat reconciled to my situation. My comrades were made to work around the post and to do farm work, with which they were not familiar.

So that was the end of our Indian days, our free, roving times which we loved. We had looked everywhere but there was no longer a place for the Indian to escape. We were one of the very last bands to come in. Our world had ended.

HERMAN LEHMANN'S RECOLLECTIONS of his final days as a free Indian are rather precise. His two accounts are parallel to a large degree and even Judge Jones's bombast is toned down. The final surrender, which could have been an unequalled occasion for bathos, is handled with what amounts to disinterested detachment by Brother Jonathan.

I have left out a short chapter which appears in both books. It is a story of the second battle of Adobe Walls. Herman says he was not there, that he was down south with another Comanche raiding party, but that he was told about it by the Indians. I am convinced that his version of the battle came not from the Indians but more probably from white sources. It is a most routine telling, adding nothing at all to even the sketchiest history of that episode. And although it speaks of what the Indians did, the whole viewpoint is from that of the buffalo hunters. Besides, it is inaccurate and leaves out Isatai, the prophet, and all the religious motivation which was behind this last great collective effort of the plains tribes to oust the white hunters from their land.

Herman says he was a Comanche at the time of Adobe Walls, but this, too, is doubtful. The battle of Adobe Walls took place in June of 1874 and Herman, earlier in his story, has been quite positive that he was with the Apache band that fought the rangers on the Concho Plains in August of 1875. I suspect that on the Indian's uncertain time scale the Adobe Walls battle held a sort of floating position from which were measured, backward and forward, certain events and movements so that Herman was convinced it took place much later than it did.

I have also left out two other chapters from the 1899 book—although the temptation to include them for the sheer literary novelty of it was almost overpowering. As neither has the slightest connection with Herman or the Plains Indians, I reluctantly dropped them. One is titled "Musical Instruments, Etc.," which has an editor's note that it is "Clippings from old records." The other is even worse and is called "Silent Medium of Communication . . . Extracts from 'L.D.'" I feel I owe the reader one paragraph—the opening—from the latter:

"A pesky red man while wooing the dusky maiden, if by chance a hunting party, raid or exploring expedition was planned, and he chose to be one of the adventurers, he would have an understanding with his 'jularky' that at a certain time he would isolate himself from his companions, and she was to retire at the same hour to some secluded spot."

Actually, the entire idea, unless it was simply from whole cloth, seems to have come from the East Indians rather than the American Indians, although the author makes a feeble effort to attribute the "silent medium of communication" to the Apaches and suggests that if "some mesmerist or mind-reader were to go among the Apaches, win their confidence and learn this mode of communication, great things could be brought to light concerning the spirit."

As it stands, great things are brought to light concerning the honesty and integrity of Victorian journalism—but this is no place to get off into the pseudo-morality of that mock-pious age.

35

THE INDIANS, my companions, were made to grade the roads all around Fort Sill and then made to do farm work and promised these farms when they learned how to cultivate them. What did they care for farms? The Indians began to pine away and some died of a broken heart, but still the soldiers guarded them and forced them to work. I stayed with Quanah and would not work.

After we had been there about two weeks, two of our Indians, Esatema and Eschito, had to stand guard and watch the cattle which the government had given us. They allowed some of the cattle to get away. As punishment for this they had to chop wood. This so exasperated them that they planned to get away. One of the Indians asked his white boss for a chew of tobacco, and when the guard set his gun down and reached in his pocket for the tobacco the other Indian knocked him in the head with an ax. These Indians took his gun and ammunition and ran away. It was early in the morning. About five hundred soldiers and I don't know how many dogs were sent to catch these Indians, but they made good their escape and we never heard of them anymore.

I had not been with Quanah Parker very long before I discovered that there were a good many Apaches in the region who had been brought under control of the government, and among them were some of my old tribe in whose breasts still lurked the spirit of revenge. That they would make some kind of attempt to kill me I had no doubt, so I was on the alert.

One night I was riding along by myself, sitting sideways in my saddle and singing an Indian song. I had just come back from taking a bunch of horses out to grass. Suddenly somebody opened fire on me. It was dark, but I saw the flashes from the guns and knew where the shots came from.

I fell off my horse, then changed my place quickly and lay very still. They fired again at the spot where I had fallen, and I raised up and emptied my .45 caliber Colt's at the cowards. In a few seconds I heard somebody groaning.

I reloaded my pistol, jumped up and ran toward Quanah's camp. On the way I passed a big, black stump which I did not see until I was right near it, and thinking it was another assailant, I fired two shots at it is I went by.

I reported to Quanah what had happened and he called up all his men, but five were missing. We all scattered out and soon found four of them carrying the fifth, who was wounded. They offered all kinds of excuses and tried to pass it off as a joke to scare me. Quanah threatened them with the soldiers. They had an Apache horse and that was what gave them away. Some cowardly Apaches had hired these Indians to kill me. They acknowledged the whole scheme.

A few weeks after that we went out on a buffalo hunt, with the soldiers' permission, and I came home sick, I nearly died, and was certain, for a while, that I would. I was so weak I could not raise up my head. Yellow Wolf was a big medicine man who lived with Quanah Parker and he doctored me. He boiled a lot of herbs and kept me wrapped in poultices. He nursed me carefully, but I had to give him the best horse I had and a great number of buffalo robes. Poor Yellow Wolf, he died some years ago from asphyxiation while he and Quanah were stopping in a hotel in Fort Worth. Their room had a gaslight and they blew it out instead of turning it off. Next morning Yellow Wolf was found dead and Quanah was near death, too.

THIS GASLIGHT INCIDENT has been erroneously reported in almost every instance where it has been told—including Herman's mention above. The Indian's name was Yellow Bear, not Yellow Wolf, and he was reported to be an uncle by marriage of Quanah Parker. In December, 1885, Yellow Bear and Parker were visiting in Fort Worth at the Pickwick Hotel, the finest in town. Yellow Bear stayed in the room one night when Parker went out for a visit. When Parker returned Yellow Bear was already in bed asleep with the light off. Parker relighted the gaslight, changed his clothes and went to bed also, turning out the light but, as it developed, not quite turning off the flow of gas. The Indians did not blow out the gas. Both men had spent nearly a decade walking the white man's road and Parker, especially, had spent quite some time in the finest places the white world afforded. Gaslights were no mystery to him. Yellow Bear, when he had retired, had obviously turned out the light in a correct manner, else Parker would have discovered the danger when he came in and relighted it.

The error was created, like a good many more such stories, by a presuming reporter. Quanah Parker and Yellow Bear were not discovered until noon the following day and Parker was so nearly dead he could not talk. But a newspaper reporter, making a headline affair out of it, presumed this is what a wild Indian would do faced with the problem of turning off a gaslight and so he wrote it that way.

It appeared that way in the first day's edition, before Quanah Parker had revived to tell the real story. The next day both Fort Worth papers, the *Gazette* and the *Evening Mail*, carried the correct stories in interviews with Quanah Parker where he admitted it was his own carelessness that was to blame. The story was carried by most of the nation's important newspapers (the New York *Times* called the victim "Yellow Bag") because Quanah Parker was one of the most famous Indian chiefs of the day. Historian Ron Tyler, in 1968, tried to bring the "blow out the gas" story back in line with facts, but with an eighty-three year head start it appeared a hopeless job.

36

MUCH HAS BEEN WRITTEN about Quanah Parker, who became a great Comanche chief. Quanah was the son of Cynthia Ann Parker, a white girl who was captured at Parker's Fort in 1835 and retaken some twenty-five years later, in 1860, when the rangers under Sul Ross had a big fight with the Comanches on Pease River in which it has been reported that Peta Nocona, her husband, was killed. But Indians who told me of this fight claimed that Peta Nocona was not killed in this engagement but was killed or died some years later.

One old Indian of the Comanche tribe told me in strict confidence that Quanah was not Peta Nocona's son but was the son of Yotavo, a Mexican, who had been taken captive when he was a small boy and raised among the Indians. This Indian told me that Cynthia Ann Parker had been the squaw of this Mexican, but that Peta Nocona took her away from him while Quanah was a very small child and raised the boy as his own. I do not believe this, for I knew this old Indian was opposed to Quanah becoming a chief and I think he tried to discredit him in this way. I have talked to other Indians in regard to the matter and they assured me that Quanah was the son of Peta Nocona and Cynthia Ann Parker.

Quanah Parker became a great man among the Indians and was foremost in bringing about peace between the white people and the Indians. It was due to his persuasion that I was induced to come in to the reservation and submit to being restored to my people after all of my band had surrendered, and he greatly aided me in securing an allotment and headright from the government. I was put down as one of Quanah Parker's boys.

Quanah (fragrant) was, as stated above, the son of Nocona or Nokoni (wanderer), who was the leader of the Kwahadi band, said to be the most hostile portion of the Comanche tribe. Quanah was born about 1845 and grew up with the tribe. After the death of his father he rapidly rose to commanding influence.

128

Cynthia Ann Parker and her daughter, Prairie Flower

His band refused to enter into the Medicine Lodge treaty of 1867, by which the Comanche, Kiowa, Apache, Cheyenne, and Arapahoe tribes were assigned on reservations, and continued to raid and kill and pillage until 1874 when, in consequence of the intrusion of an organized company of white buffalo hunters, Quanah himself mustered the warriors of the Comanche and Cheyenne, with about half the Kiowa and some portion of the other two tribes, for resistance. In June, 1874, an attack led by Quanah in person at the head of about 700 confederate warriors was launched against some buffalo hunters who were strongly entrenched in a fort known as Adobe Walls on the South Canadian in the Texas Panhandle. The fight lasted all day and Quanah and his forces were compelled to retire with considerable loss.

The Indians were constant in their hostile movements until the next year when, being hard pressed by troops under General Mackenzie, most of them surrendered. Quanah, however, kept his band out upon the plains for two years longer, when he also surrendered. With keen foresight he recognized the inevitable, that the Indian had to give way before the superior force of the white man, so he set about to make the best of the new conditions and persuade his people to do likewise. Being still young and with the inherited intelligence of his white ancestry, he quickly adapted himself so well to the white man's ways as to become a most efficient factor in leading his people up to civilization.

Through his influence the confederated tribes adopted the policy of leasing the surplus pasture lands, by which a large annual income was added to their revenues. He encouraged education, house building and agriculture, and discouraged dissipation and savage extravagance, while holding strictly to his native beliefs and ceremonies. Polygamy being customary in his tribe he had several (seven) wives and a large number of children and a thirty-room house. All of his children have received a school education, and some of his daughters have married white men. For many years before his death he was the most prominent and influential figure among the three confederated tribes in all leases, treaty negotiations, and other public business with the government, and in this capacity he made repeated visits to Washington, besides having traveled extensively in other parts of the country.

As stated elsewhere, Quanah sent me to his camp where I stayed in fancied concealment. In the year 1877 I was adopted into Quanah Parker's family. I was seventeen years old at the time, but at that age a young Indian buck is considered a grown man.

Mr. Clarke, the government agent at that time, issued government rations to Quanah Parker for my maintenance as one of Quanah's children. I lived with Quanah's family for three years, or until I was brought home to my own people by the soldiers. I am still considered a member of Quanah Parker's family (1927) and am recognized as such by Quanah's squaws and children who bestowed on me all of the affection and kindness given a full blood brother.

Quanah Parker died February 22, 1912, at his home near Cache, Oklahoma, at the age of sixty-seven years.

Quanah Parker and one of his wives

THIS CHAPTER on Quanah Parker is in both of Herman Lehmann's books but in totally different form. The 1899 version is virtually useless, based mainly on an article in *Ennis' Review* "by Mrs. McQuirt." The article is mainly about Cynthia Ann Parker, not Quanah, and is shot through with errors.

The 1927 version is much more accurate, but I do not believe it was written by Herman Lehmann. Had he had anything to do with the writing he would have recognized the earlier error made concerning his status as a Comanche at the time of the second battle of Adobe Walls, as the correct date is given in this account. The other errors mainly involve the dates connected with Quanah

Parker's life. His tombstone gives the date of his birth as 1852, not 1845. Indian archival records indicate 1849 as probably the true year of his birth. Also, Quanah Parker didn't stay on the warpath as long as Herman's account says. Quanah wouldn't have been showing much of that "keen foresight" nor have "recognized the inevitable" had he stayed out until 1877 or -78.

The *Handbook of Texas* gives the date of Quanah's death as February 23, 1911, and his daughter, Neda Parker Birdsong, who wrote the inscription for his tomb, says he died February 21, 1911, "age sixty-four years."

37

ONE DAY, just after my convalescence, Quanah wanted me to go to the post with him. We went there and the soldiers surrounded me and called me "Charley Ross." As long as I was at Fort Sill I was called by that name. They wanted to keep me at the post. Quanah would talk to the general and then to me. He told me the general said my mother and my brothers and sisters were still alive and that I should be sent to them. I told him no; the Indians were still my people.

We stayed a long time and Quanah persuaded me to stay, but I got pretty mad at him and told him that he was no man at all to bring me there when he knew those soldiers would try to keep me. He said that he did not know it, and besides, he often went into Texas to see his white kin and always had a pretty good time. I got up and told him that if he was getting tired of me I was getting tired of him too, so I would leave him.

He and the soldiers carried me down to a creek nearby to talk to an old man and Comanche interpreter by the name of [Horace P.] Jones. About the same dialogue ensued with him. After we had talked for some time and I would not consent to go, he said that they would have to take me anyhow. At this remark I pulled my bow on him and fitted an arrow. You ought to have seen Colonel Jones crawling for a table out of the danger zone.

Quanah stopped me from shooting and told me that he would see that they did not take me by force, for he was going back to his teepee with me. I turned and was going to kill Jones anyhow, but he had fled. I never got another chance at Jones or he would have been a goner.

I went back home with Quanah and we talked over the matter a great deal, and finally he persuaded me to give up. I went back to the post and stayed one day. They were good to me and offered me sugar, fruits and many nice things, but I wasn't satisfied, so they went for Quanah again. But I was angry at him and would not go home with him. Finally they put me across the creek with my former comrades.

One young Indian proposed to me that we steal a girl apiece and run away. I went and talked to my old girl who nursed me when her father shot me, and she consented to go. We were to meet that night. My fellow brave stole another man's wife, two good horses and other necessities, and made good his escape. My girl was true to her promise, stole all the goods she could carry, and waited for me until nearly daylight. I started and nearly reached her when the soldiers, who had been watching me secretly, gave chase. I ran off of a bluff and fell into the river and came near freezing. Eventually I was driven back to camp and from then on so many soldiers watched me that I had no chance to escape.

For a few weeks hunting and the monotony of camp life was all I knew, but one warm day I was in swimming with two Indian girls and had some excitement. I caught one and hugged her and was trying to kiss her when the other girl came up behind me. They double-teamed on me and ducked me until I was nearly drowned—but I caught them off to themselves and one at a time I made them sorry they had ever immersed me, and don't you forget it!

About this time General Mackenzie saw my mother, down in Texas, and told her about me being at Fort Sill, although from the description he gave her of me Mother did not think I was her boy.

Adolph Korn, whom I had met once while his Comanche party was visiting my Apaches, had been back at his Texas home for several years and Rudolph Fischer had been sent back to Fredericksburg about three months before, so I was the only white boy left with the Indians.

General Mackenzie came back to Fort Sill and he and Quanah Parker began to talk to me about going home to my people. Quanah Parker told me how to find the way back to his camp from down in Texas and he promised to take care of my horses while I was gone. He said he would always be a brother to me and insisted that if I discovered this was not my mother and that I did not have any people among the whites that I should come back and live with him.

38

I LEFT ALL MY INDIAN PROPERTY with Quanah, and in company with five soldiers and a driver I started to Loyal Valley, in Mason County, Texas. We traveled in an army ambulance drawn by four mules, and went twenty miles the first day.

Four days' traveling brought us into a country where there was game. The soldiers would give me a gun and ammunition and say, "Here, Charley Ross, fresh meat!"

I would go out and bring in an antelope. The fifth day a soldier and I went hunting and got out of sight of the wagon. We killed prairie dogs for the sport of it and we sat down on a hill. I kept singing and making Indian signs. The soldier patted me on the head and motioned for us to go. I got up reluctantly and went with him. He didn't know that I was planning all the time to kill him and run away . . . but where would I go? All our old hunting grounds had been taken over.

I decided to give the soldier a good scare anyway. He watched me pretty close, but finally I got the drop on him and made him lay down his gun. He did not want to, but I soon convinced him that I was in earnest, and he put it on the ground and raised his hands in the air. I pointed toward camp and said, "Vamos!" He understood that and lit out for camp in a hurry. Once, at first, he stopped and looked back at me, but I levelled my gun at him fiercely, and before he got back to camp he was in a high trot. I had to lug both those heavy guns into camp, and he preceded me by probably five minutes, for I was about one hundred fifty yards to his rear. The soldiers motioned to me to come on into camp and when I got there they motioned toward the old soldier and we all laughed. He cussed and muttered and didn't like it at all, but they made fun of him all the way for letting an Indian boy take his gun away from him.

They kept my guns cleaned and always roasted my meat. I would not eat anything cooked in bacon or even in the same pan, but they petted and humored me or I would have killed some of them and run away.

I played all sorts of pranks on those soldiers. One morning I grabbed up a blanket, waved it over my head two or three times, and gave the Comanche warwhoop, and I want you to know those soldiers scattered. The driver even made the mules break loose. But they took it good-naturedly. They came back and laughed and said, "Charley Ross no good. Too much like an Indian."

We came to Fort Griffin and the five soldiers got on a big drunk, stole my money and all went to the guardhouse. A new outfit was selected to escort me. I was allowed to kill game for them, too, and do pretty much as I pleased, but they kept an eye on me at all times. We came to a big water hole and the soldiers caught some big bullfrogs and fried them in lard, but I would not eat them for it was against the Comanche's rule to eat lard. That was a violation of a sacred treaty that we had made years ago with the Carancahuas and therefore against our religion. I quit camp in disgust and would not eat with those soldiers anymore. I cut off meat and roasted it on an iron. Frogs and swine both were mud animals and too much for me.

The second day after leaving Fort Griffin I jumped down from the ambulance while it was moving and ran out and shot an antelope. One of the soldiers brought the little animal in and as he went to get on the wagon while it was in motion, his foot slipped, the mules jumped, he fell and the wagon ran over his leg, breaking it.

After this we traveled slowly, camped often and killed game, but gradually we neared the home of my childhood. We passed through Fort Mason and learned that my family's home was not far. We went on to the Llano River at the Simmonsville Crossing. Here we began to meet people who had come out from Loyal Valley to wait for us, word having preceded us that the captive boy was being brought home.

When we reached Loyal Valley we drove up and stopped at a place, and the soldiers made signs for me to get out. Quite a crowd of people gathered around. The captain said, "Charley Ross, get out and kiss your mother!" but I sat still in the wagon. I thought my mother was killed and all of my folks. The Indians had told this and nearly killed me because my mother shot one of them.

When my mother came out of the crowd I knew her, but I could not speak, and there were so many people I was afraid to try. The years of savagery which had passed over my head had erased from my memory all of the recollections of a mother's love and tenderness and to me in that hour which should have been a crowning event of happiness, my mother, although I recognized her face, was no more than a white squaw.

Curiously the crowd examined me and excitedly talked in a language which I could not understand, although it was my native tongue. At first everyone thought I was not Herman Lehmann. They looked for marks of identification and found a scar on my arm that was made when I was a little boy. Soon my brother and sister, Willie and Mina, came up to me and the dark curtain of oblivion which had been drawn so long began pulling back and to me there began coming some recollection of my early childhood.

I recognized my brother and sister as my playmates in that far distant past. Then somebody kept saying, "Herman . . . Herman" and the name had a familiar sound. It then occurred to me that it was my own name. Slowly but surely the mists began to clear away and I knew that I had found my people. But I was an Indian, and I did not like them because they were palefaces. And I wanted immediately to go back to the tribe.

DURING THE YEARS of Herman's captivity his family did not forget him, and his mother never gave up hope that he was alive and would be restored to her. For several years she had little cause to believe either fact, however. From time to time stories of captive white boys would be brought back to the settlements by Texas Rangers or soldiers, but the descriptions must have been those of other, known captives, for Herman never seems to have been recognized for whom he was, even in those rare instances when he was seen. As was stressed earlier, not many people had known Herman to begin with. Even when he became known to the Fort Sill soldiers as a white boy they thought he was another captive named Charley Ross, as he noted.

The first real evidence Herman's mother got that he had survived his capture came when Adolph Korn visited with her and told her that he had seen Herman with the Apaches a few years earlier.

Mrs. Buchmeyer (the family adopted that spelling in the '90s) wrote two accounts of Herman's homecoming; one of which appeared in the 1899 edition, the other originally published in *Hunter's Magazine* in 1911, and made a part of the 1927 book. John Warren Hunter, father of J. Marvin, Sr., was an intimate friend of the Lehmann-Buchmeyer family in Loyal Valley in the

nineteenth century, and when he became a magazine publisher it was only natural he should pay a great deal of attention to Herman Lehmann's story. Here, then, is the mother's account—a combination of the two versions which appeared over her name.

FOR FIVE YEARS after my son was captured I tugged on with my burden of sorrow and could not rest. I never could believe that he was dead. My friends would come to me and say, "Why do you keep worrying and thinking about that boy? He is dead long ago." But I would tell them that I would never believe that he was dead.

On the night of the 31st of December [1875] I had cried myself to sleep, and doubt seemed to have got the upper hand of me. It was a cold, bleak night and I wondered where my boy was wandering.

I dreamed I was walking beside a beautiful stream of water, clear as crystal, the green of summer on its banks. I lay down on the grass and looked into the clear waters and beheld some gold fish and some silver fish gliding through the waters and I said: "Why can't I be as happy as you, little fishes?" And as I spoke, a voice from behind me spoke and said: "Why can't you be?" I looked around and saw two men; one an old man with long, silvery locks that fell over his shoulders, the other a young man dressed in linen clothes and wearing a cap.

I told them that I could not be happy, for my son had been stolen by the Indians and for five long, toilsome years I had mourned his loss and ever since I had not known one single happy moment.

Then the young man said: "You will see your boy again." But the old man replied, "No, she will never see her boy any more." The young man responded: "She *will* see her boy again." The old man still held out that Herman was gone. The young man said "I will give you a sign as proof that you will see your boy again. If tomorrow, the first day of January, you see the sun, you will that surely live to see your boy again. Now, are you satisfied with that?"

I turned and looked at the old man and replied, "I am." At this I awoke. I was so impressed that I jumped up and rushed to the door. All was darkness; the earth was enshrouded in heavy, threatening clouds as it had been for three days, and it was misting rain. I dragged myself back to bed and cried myself to sleep. The next morning it was still cloudy and raining and I cried all the morning. My husband asked me why I wept so bitterly, but I would not tell him. He entreated me to share my sorrows with him so that he might comfort me. At last I yielded. He said: "Oh, that is only a foolish dream. Do not worry yourself about it."

That afternoon I walked out in the field near my husband's lime kiln and fell on my knees and prayed to God to give me some sign that I might see my boy, and as I started to the house the clouds parted and the sun came out beautifully, but only for a moment. My husband and children came running and shouting, "Mamma, did you see the sun?" I saw it and believed as surely as I'm alive that I would some sweet day see my boy again.

Time passed, oh so slowly. I increased my efforts to learn something about Herman. Some time in 1878 I heard that General Mackenzie from Fort Sill was to make an inspection of the frontier posts. He was to visit Fort Concho, Fort McKavett and Mason, thence to San Antonio. He would pass through Loyal Valley on his way to Fredericksburg. I made plans to intercept him, as I thought it would be a good chance to find out if there were any more white boys among the Indians that had come into the reservations

and given up. By some means he passed Loyal Valley before I could get to see him. I got my husband to hitch up and drive me to Fredericksburg. We followed the military party and within three miles of Fredericksburg we found the general camped. I was shown to his tent, and as soon as I saw him I recognized him. There he was, in the same dress and cap and all as the young man I had seen in my dream.

I told him when Herman had been stolen and said that as the general had just come from the reservation I thought maybe he could tell me something of my boy. He asked me to give him the age and description, as near as I could, of Herman. When I had done so he said: "There is one white boy there, but from your description I do not think that this is your son. He is not that old."

He dropped his head and studied for some time, then raised his head and smiled.

"Madam," he said, "I'll tell you what we'll do. We will go on to Fredericksburg and telegraph the soldiers at Fort Sill to bring him down. If he is your boy, I will be very happy for you to get your child back. If he is not your boy we will take him on to San Antonio and teach him a trade, for he has no business among the Indians."

General Mackenzie telegraphed the commanding officer at Fort Sill to start immediately with the white boy, Charley Ross, to Loyal Valley, but received the reply that Charley Ross had gone on a buffalo hunt with the Indians and the soldiers out on the plains of Texas and would not be back in the reservations for three months.

These were the longest three months I ever spent. I could not wait more than two weeks until I would go to the office and telegraph to know if he had returned from the hunt. Think of my anxiety and joy, mixed with doubt and fears. At last a telegram came saying Charley Ross had returned and, with an escort, would start for Texas immediately.

I counted the days, and many little things brought up misgivings. I trembled at everything; I was wholly unnerved. If this is my boy I can once more enjoy the happiness of this world. But I knew that the general had said this boy did not sound like my boy. I inquired of everyone who passed from the way the soldiers were coming to know if they had seen or heard of them. I obtained no tidings. But one morning the mail carrier told me he had passed the soldiers between Mason and Loyal Valley who had charge of the white boy and they sent me word that they would arrive that night.

I walked the floor, only stopping to listen for the ambulance they were driving, but I could hear nothing but the patter of the rain against the window panes and the low, murmuring wind. As we were eating supper a large crowd of two dozen or so came and said: "Mrs. Buchmier, we have come to take you out to meet your boy."

Mr. Buchmier objected to my going out in the rain, saying:

"No, you must not go out in the weather. It is too bad, and besides, you can't hurry them any." I knew that he was also thinking that it might not be my son, and the shock might hurt me.

A school teacher who boarded with us [probably J. Warren Hunter] told the crowd: "Boys, you go on and meet Herman. The night is too disagreeable for Mrs. Buchmier to go, and I don't know what she would do if she were to meet him on the road."

The boys left our house then and went toward Mason. They met the soldiers about three miles out where they had camped for the night. The boys asked the soldiers to hitch up and drive on into the valley that night, and they did so.

In the meantime, Mr. Buchmier and the school teacher had made me sit down, and they were holding me there. Friends had come from all around to see the meeting and, if my boy, to share with me my joys. There were three hundred people present. My heart, already pounding, beat wildly as I finally heard the sound of the soldiers' carriage, as the wheels of the ambulance came closer and closer and my heart beat faster and faster. Was that ambulance bringing me my boy?

I heard it drive up to the door, but my husband still restrained me. When the wheels stopped I tore loose from his grasp and ran out to the boy who stood between the soldiers, threw my arms around his neck and wept.

I then led him to the light, and when the rays of the lamp fell on him I cried out, "Great God!" I thought it was not Herman. The boy stood motionless and said nothing.

Then my daughter Mina ran to him and looked him over closely, then exclaimed, "Mamma, Mamma! It is Herman. Don't you see that scar on his hand? Don't you remember? That is where I cut him with our little hatchet."

Sure enough, a closer examination proved it was Herman. Imagine the joy, the happiness, the bliss that that assurance brought to me!

I shall ever be grateful to General Mackenzie for having my boy brought home.

(The remainder of the story is told, we must assume, by J. Warren Hunter):

Those who witnessed this happy meeting add a number of facts not mentioned by Mother Buchmier. Numbers of them have told me that it was near the noon hour when she received word that the escort would be at Loyal Valley that night. She immediately began preparations for a great feast. She found willing hands among the villagers to aid her. She started runners in every direction to call in friends, far and near. Every oven and stove in town was kept hot, baking bread and cakes; beeves and muttons were slaughtered and a pall of smoke ascended from pits of barbecued meats.

A slow rain began falling in the evening, but that did not retard preparations for the feast, nor did it lessen the attendance. Everyone loved Mrs. Buchmier; knew how she had prayed and trusted, and now that the lost son had been found and was nearing home, they hastened to join in the general thanksgiving.

When the boy arrived and she made sure that he was her son, those present relate that never before had they heard such shouts of praise and thanksgiving to God for His Goodness and Mercy. The good mother was a devout Methodist, and her righteous soul became full to overflowing and she gave way. There was no dearth of tears of joy that evening; feasting, singing hymns of praise, German and English, and prayers of thanksgiving occupied most of the night.

All the day following the feast was kept up for those who remained, and those who continued to come. During all this time Herman maintained a haughty indifference akin to Indian stoicism. He had forgotten his mother tongue, German, and could not speak

137

English. He sought on every occasion to shun the company of others, and when assigned to a clean feather bed in which to sleep, he refused, preferring to sleep on the ground with only a blanket for a covering. When the escort left he wanted to return with the soldiers and was with difficulty restrained.

One of his brothers became his constant companion, teaching him his forgotten language, and preventing him from running away. It was a difficult matter to induce him to wear clothing, and oftentimes he would doff the suit furnished him, paint himself, and with leggings, breech-clout and feathers, appear among the guests in all the barbaric panoply of a Comanche warrior.

So the lost son was home, as this episode has been described in such Biblical flavor. But the captive boy was still a captive—just as much a prisoner of this new world as he had once been of the Indian world. He not only did not speak the language, he could neither read nor write, of course, and had no conception of how white society operated. His story, while amusing, turns ironic, and even from the standpoint of decades afterward, has a deep strain of tragedy running through it; the tragedy not just of a man wrenched out of his time and place, but of an entire culture turned upside down in one sweeping moment of decision.

Herman, the captive, was restored, but for the remainder of his life would be more Indian than white; happier remembering the one than being the other.

39

MOTHER WAS KEEPING A HOTEL on Happy Hill, in Loyal Valley, and had several boarders, including some traveling men. All the family and most of the people of the town gathered around me: some laughing, some crying, and all talking. I did not approve of such conduct, so I broke away from them and started back to Quanah's, but they caught me and brought me back.

The soldiers told Mina how I liked my food, so she fixed it as near to my whim as was possible for a civilized person to do. In fact, everyone did all that could be done to please me, but I didn't like any of them. That night I would not sleep in the house, although they prepared a nice feather bed for me and arranged everything for my comfort. I made a pallet of my own blankets out on the ground.

Herman and old trail-drivers in San Antonio in the 1920's

138

Next day, when the soldiers started to go, I was ready to go with them, but they made me to understand that they were coming back for me and I should stay. But no, I was going with them anyhow. They had to slip away from me or I would have gone, too.

My folks fixed up a big feast for me and Mina came to invite me to the table. I pretended not to hear or understand her but lay on a blanket, singing an Indian song. She motioned me to come on, but I would not notice her. I was homesick and was planning, scheming and contriving to run away. I would much rather have gone back to the plains as I had been that lonely year with the birds, the wild animals and my gray horse. But finally Mina induced me to go to the table— which turned out to be a mistake.

I went in and was just ready to sit down when I saw a fine swine ham smoking hot on the table. I kicked over everything in my reach and made for the door. They stopped me and entreated me not to do that way. I pointed to the pork and made them understand that if they would remove that I would eat. It was removed and I sat down and tried to eat, but the food did not suit me and the thought of having to eat with these hog-eaters choked me. I wanted my meat roasted over a flame and I didn't care for anything else. All those sweetmeats and delicacies disgusted me and I despised so much effeminacy.

I sat around and smoked cigarettes. One thing I did enjoy in the white world was the good tobacco. I went down to the creek and found suitable wood to make me a bow and a great many arrows. I sang all the time like a Comanche, and I waged war against the hog family. Whenever a shoat came in sight I would kill him, no matter to whom he belonged.

My mother started me to school but I came back the first day and made them understand that if I had to go back there I would tear down all the latticework over the windows so I could see out. I was never made to go anymore.

I would saddle up my Comanche pony and go out hunting. Somebody gave me a Winchester and my step-father furnished me with cartridges. Willie always went with me to watch me and to teach me the ways of the white man. I wanted to steal calves, or to kill them for our food, but Willie made signs to me that it was wrong to do this with other people's animals. Even more than with the calves, I insisted we take all the horses we saw but Willie would not allow that either. I was mad all of the time because these ways were so different from my Indian ways and, in fact, nothing pleased me.

When I met children I would give a yell and draw my bow on them just to see them run. For a while that was all the real fun I had.

I would kill deer, put them on my pony, ride up to the gate, dismount and leave the horse and deer there. If anybody wanted the deer they had to go skin and clean them, I would not. Somebody had to stake and feed my pony, too, for I thought work of that kind was for squaws. I was furious if they failed to roast me the short ribs or tenderloins, but my people tried to do everything to please me

139

for several months and I began to learn how to behave. Willie tried to get me to learn the golden rule, saying it was the white man's way: "Do unto others as you would have others do unto you."

I would run away but Willie would bring me back, and the women would cry around me and entreat me not to do that way. I had a horror for tears.

At last the kindness, tenderness and gentleness of my good Christian mother, the affectionate love of my sisters, and the vigilance of my brothers gradually wove a net of love around me that was as lasting as time itself. I began to understand that everyone was not my enemy.

Crowds would gather around to see what they called "the Indian boy." I would jump on the wildest horse as he ran by me without either bridle or saddle. I would cut many capers to delight them: dance, yell, shoot my bow and arrow.

One day while I was amusing a crowd of spectators, I noticed that they did not seem to take so much interest in my performance as usual and were gradually leaving. The center of attraction seemed to be down on the creek.

I could hear speaking, shouting, singing, crying and other sounds, and I noticed everybody was wearing different clothes from their everyday garb.

The whole time seemed like a holiday. Men and women with fine clothes would come and go, and several long bearded men passed me wearing black coats with cloth enough in them to make a whole suit. Everyone respected these fellows and I decided they were the medicine men there to hold a consultation as in the Indian tribes.

I resolved to see what was going on down there, so I slipped through the bushes and watched them. (A crowd of men and boys, headed by E. "Ship" Martin, paid no attention to the other doings but watched me.) I saw one of those who I thought was a medicine man get up and speak something out of a book. Occasionally he would look at his people, then upward, and I wondered why he did not smoke, as this was the way the Indians worshiped, blowing smoke toward the Great Spirit or the sun, and down at the earth, our mother. I concluded, therefore, that this was a council of war. But then I realized there were too many squaws there for that.

Several other theories ran through my mind as the scenes changed. The people rose and sang, then they all got down on their knees and covered up their faces. Some groaned while others wept, some sighed, one man made supplication or mumbled something, then they also got up and sang another song. Then the most important medicine man came to the front and everyone listened respectfully as he went through a long talk and made many gestures, everyone watching him carefully except for those in the crowd who were eyeing me.

The sober looking medicine man with the long coat mumbled something at first but gradually grew louder, and began singing off his speech, waving his hands while teardrops trickled down his cheeks and his face wore a sad faraway expression as his eyes turned up.

140

His people seemed to lean forward and drink in every word he said, longing for more. He kept talking and then all the people arose and mingled their voices in a mighty chorus while the melodious strains floated on the breeze and reached my ears as a balm to the pains of my own heart.

Then shouts of laughter, shrill screams, merry faces and sad-eyed spectators mixed. Some shouted, others with cold, dark scowls on their brows, still others with heart-breaking wails, all rushed to the center of the arbor and began dancing, shaking hands and creating general confusion. It was, of course, a sure-enough old-fashioned Methodist shouting meeting, but I did not know this. I thought it must be a new kind of war dance, a rain dance or some kind of religious ceremony.

I saw my mother and sisters taking part in these activities and I was so moved by the sight that I raised up, gave a Comanche yell, and cleared several benches at a leap—regardless of the nicely dressed matrons and timid looking young girls sitting on them. A few leaps landed me in the middle of the revival.

My manner of worship did not suit those white people, and they stampeded. The long-coated medicine man said a few words in a quick and jerky manner and soon I was left monarch of all I surveyed. I gave a few more whoops and a little dance and looked around to see what had become of all the council, and I saw the big medicine man tearing along with his coattails flapping as he headed for my mother's hotel. Mother, Mina, Caroline and a dozen others were pulling at me to leave. Everyone else was gone except for a few idle spectators who seemed to admire my way of doing things up.

My people took me home and never permitted me to go back to church until I could understand their language and ways better so that I could behave myself. True, I broke up the meeting that day, but I was just as earnest, just as prayerful, just as candid and sincere as the most sanctified among them. Only my mode did not conform to their theories.

I have seen just as much earnestness and less hypocrisy among the Indians in their worship as I ever have since among the whites.

I amused myself by making blunt arrows and it was fun for me to plug men away off who dared me and thought I could not hit them. One day John Davis, a young man at Loyal Valley, was off about one hundred and fifty yards when he dared me to shoot at him. He yelled, "Herman, you can't hit me from there." He turned his back and tucked his head between his shoulders and, Zip! My arrow took him right between the shoulders and Mr. Davis plowed up sand with his nose. In a few minutes there was a great blue spot where the arrow struck.

A few days later August Jones, another young man, was about a hundred yards away and gave me lief to shoot at him. This time my arrow had a spike on it. He turned in the same manner as Davis and I blazed away. I made a mistake in the distance—aimed a little too high—and plowed a furrow through the top of his shoulder, the arrow passing on. That put an end to this kind of fun, for the people seemed to be afraid of my shooting after that.

141

Plugging hats became one of my favorite pastimes. The boys would put their hats off about a hundred yards and bet me the drinks that I could not hit them. I would win the drinks every time. The crowd would laugh and applaud; the boys would have to get new hats. The hat trade became quite good in Loyal Valley.

Nearly every stranger and every drummer who came along would stick up his hat and let me shoot at it. The arrow would go through so quick that I could often win treats for the crowd after I had shot, for the owners would not believe the hat had been hit until they went to get it, then on the opposite side there would be a larger hole torn out.

One old fellow had a fine white Stetson hat which he thought he could use to fool me. He doubled it up in a small wad and put it, still wadded up, on a stick about fifty steps away and said that was what he meant when he said he bet I could not hit his hat. I whizzed an arrow at it and it went clear through, making not just two holes but as many as there were folds, completely ruining his fine hat. But that fun soon played out, too, and I was left to be the terror only of the traveling men.

40

I WOULD NOT WORK AT FIRST, but seeing everybody else labor, and having been taught that it was wrong to steal, I began to want to possess property like other people.

The first work I did was for Mrs. August Jones. I scoured and whitewashed her house for a pair of pants. I stayed there for some time, washing dishes and doing the chores for my board. I hired out to a Mr. Dossey at fifteen dollars per month, helping to build a church and other heavy rock work. I worked for Dossey for a month and it rained a great deal. At the end of the month I asked for my pay but he said he could not pay me more than seven dollars and fifty cents for my work.

I would not take that, so I went back to Loyal Valley and my brother Adolph went to see Dossey and Dossey promised to pay me twelve and a half dollars. I loaded up my Winchester and presented it to Mr. Dossey muzzle first, demanding full pay. I told him that I was working by the month and I could not help the weather. I drew back the hammer of my gun and Dossey said "Yes, I'll pay you," and he did too, and gave me fifty cents extra.

I dug a well for Mr. Bogusch. I was to work for him for a month. I stayed there and worked hard, doing menial services for three weeks, and he insulted me and I quit him. He would not pay me because I had not worked out my month. I herded sheep for Mr. Lehmberg for fifteen dollars per month, and there I was treated kindly and given a place in the family as one of the children. He would tend to the sheep every other Sunday and let me go to church. There I got a pretty good start. If there ever was a true Christian, then it was Julius Lehmberg.

I came back to Loyal Valley, bought some stock cattle and worked around home. The country was all open then and I had a good range for my stock and they increased fast. I lived very economically, for my wants were few, and I soon became what people call "well-to-do."

I hired out to Henry McGee, and his house caught fire and burned my clothes and what money I had on hand, and here I was beaten out of some of my hard-earned wages. I went to him with my Winchester and he pleaded that he had no money but would pay me as soon as he could get a check cashed. I guess he has not cashed it yet.

I cow-hunted and made a crop at home. I loved beer and other strong drinks, and when a man did anything I didn't like I never quarreled with him, I would fight it out with him. So Loyal Valley, Fredericksburg and other neighboring towns were often the scenes of my little fracases.

My sense of honor, justice and integrity was very acute. I believed in people practicing what they preached. I would not tell a man a lie or do anyone an injury intentionally, and when I had anything against someone I went right up to his face and told him of it and then we would settle it in friendly fashion or fight it out. I didn't care which way and we would be the very best of friends afterwards until some other trouble arose.

I went up the [cattle] trail with Henry Deering, worked for Bob Moseley and other good stockmen, and when my work was done I got my pay and attended to my own cattle. I settled down to a white man's life as near as I could do so.

One of Loyal Valley's school girls stole my heart, eventually. I was thrown with this girl a great deal, for I drove her father's team to San Antonio on several trips.

On one of those trips to San Antonio I took too much beer and made the mules run through the narrow streets. Several police halted me and tried to stop my team, and out near the bridge one daring fellow succeeded in checking the wild stampede of my wiry mules and demanded the cause for such recklessness. I told him the team had run away with me and thanked him for stopping them.

He didn't seem to believe me and wanted to carry me back to headquarters for trial. I talked to him for a while, called his attention to something on the opposite side of the street, popped my whip, knocked him down, and my mules soon carried me safely out of town.

The girl and I began seeing quite a bit of each other. We would go walking on Sunday evenings and converse about the subject that absorbed my whole thoughts —her. One such evening a crowd of us young people went walking and I, as usual, was with Miss Burks. When we were by ourselves I proposed to her and she hummed and hawed and asked for more time. She said she would answer me the next time she saw me.

I was still bashful, but the next time we met I asked her what she had decided about our hitching up for better or for worse, and she said it was all right with

143

her, but I had to ask her parents. I rode over several times before I could sum up courage enough to mention the matter to the old people. When I did her father, who got along with me pretty well, said he had no objection to our marriage but that his daughter had a terrible temper and he was afraid we would not get along. I was not afraid of that, of course, because I was in love and thought we could have nothing but happiness.

The wedding day came. We married at her home and had a big infare dinner at my mother's place. All my friends and relatives were there. I thought this the most happy time of my existence. I loved my pretty young bride and in her I had implicit confidence.

We lived with my mother, who was keeping the hotel. From the first my girl wife seemed to care but little for me. She flirted with every other man she met and ignored me as her husband. One day she told me she didn't love me and never had. She said she loved another and her parents had made her marry me.

This nearly broke my heart. I told her that such a complaint was too late now and that if she had told me sooner I never would have married her. We moved across the street in a house to ourselves, for I was very jealous of her and did not like having her around all the traveling men in the hotel. She was quite pretty and always attracted the attention of the men wherever she went.

I was working for Mr. Rountree and was away from home a great deal, but I provided well for her and gave her anything she asked for. But she would take care of nothing. Wastefulness and extravagance was the acme of her delight. I would give her large sums of money and never know where or how she spent it. Even worse, she would act imprudent everywhere she went, flirting and saying shocking things, and therefore she became the subject of every gossiping old woman in the vicinity.

One night there was a ball in town and she expressed a desire to attend. I was a member of the Methodist church and did not approve of dancing, most especially of married women dancing with others. I told her I would rather she not go, but if she must that I would come home and escort her. She promised me that she would not go.

The night of the ball came and a gallant young fellow, X, came for my wife and she accompanied him, danced and flirted around considerably while I was out of town. When I came home everybody was talking about her. It made me mad, for I still had confidence in her. But her ring was missing and she told me she had lost it. We looked all over the place for it but never could find it. A certain old lady told my mother that my wife had given X her wedding ring as well as thirty dollars in cash, and that she, the old woman, had three letters from my wife to X, fondly recalling several acts of illicit intercourse with him, mentioning the ring and the money, and also an elopement they had together planned. (Meantime the young gallant had run away with two of his cousins, thus wrecking more homes than mine.)

144

I had as much as I could stand. Believing it all to be a lie I went to see this old woman and told her to establish what she had told or be prosecuted for slander. She presented the letters—letters that my wife had written and no mistake about it.

I went home and asked my wife to come with me and help clear up this slander and if she were innocent I would protect her with my life. She didn't want to have anything to do with it at first, but I insisted, and pale and trembling, she came and she was proven guilty beyond a doubt.

Mr. R. offered us a room in his house, pasturage for my cattle, and twenty-five dollars per month in salary to work for him. I told her that we could go over to the ranch, away from her seducer, and that I would forgive her and we might yet be happy. But no, she would go nowhere with me.

My property had been decreasing and my whole world going wrong ever since I had been married. I had only five dollars in my pocket but I wanted to get away. I saddled my pony and rode back to the Comanches at Fort Sill, spending several weeks with Quanah Parker. I hired out and worked for wages there with the tribe for several months and my domestic troubles seemed to have completely left me. One day, however, thoughts of my cattle in Texas came into my mind, and being governed by the first impression, as of old, I sold my pony, bought a railroad ticket to Lampasas, mounted the iron horse and was soon in Mineral Springs.

I hired a livery rig and rode for Loyal Valley, arriving there at 9 P.M. I settled with and dismissed my driver and went to the house that had once been my home. But Mrs. Lehmann, my wife, was not there. I walked around town to a house I knew of and there I found her sharing it with another man. This time there was no way to mistake her character for I caught her in the very act.

I carried her to her mother and told the mother I would rather be separated than live with such a woman as her daughter. Several hard words passed but I left her there, never to see her again.

I gathered up what few cattle she and the thieves had left me and sold them, only realizing about four hundred dollars from my once flourishing herd.

I bought a four horse team and wagon and went to freighting. Everybody looked down on me and treated me as they would a dog. I drank some and fought a great deal. I gambled and ran horse races and was turned out of the Methodist church. I worked hard to drown my troubles and made money fast but spent every cent of it.

Once in San Antonio I saw a drunken Mexican strike a little boy, and I knocked him down with my fist. He got up and came at me with a knife. This was in a wagon yard and there was a stick nearby which some fellow had to prop up his wagon tongue. I picked that stick up and knocked the Mexican down. He lay there trembling and right then a policeman placed irons on my wrists and marched me to the station. But he having been a witness, I was only fined five dollars and the costs. I don't know what became of the Mexican.

145

I kept a beer saloon at Cherry Springs in the Free State of Gillespie and made money easy, but I drank so much I got too fat, so I sold out there and soon spent the money.

HERMAN kept in close contact with his Indian peoples and, as evidenced above, often in his times of trouble he would flee to them for comfort or refuge from the harshness of the white world. The sad story of his first marriage, by the way, is not included in the 1927 edition. He apparently was still bitter at his experience at the time of the 1899 book, even though he was remarried, and happily so.

During those early years when he was trying to adjust to a new environment, Herman and his brother Adolph went on an extended visit to the Comanches in Oklahoma, and in a separate chapter of the 1899 version, Adolph tells about it:

WHEN HERMAN CAME HOME I was away and was the last one of the children to meet him. But when I did see him he offered me his paper and tobacco to make a cigarette.

I was with him a great deal. Once I went with him to Austin and there we played many pranks on Herman, all of which he took in a good humor. But then I went with him to the Indian Territory and he got even.

We went to a blacksmith to get a coffee pot mended, but the blacksmith said, "I work for no white man; I am here to do jobs for the Indians." Herman raised a row with him and I had to separate them and we moved on.

So many Indians visited Herman that I got tired of cooking for them so one day I killed a young wild turkey and fried it in lard. Herman had told me that the Indians could not eat anything with lard used in it so I thought this might get rid of some of our hungry guests.

One of the Indians who came to dinner with Herman asked if I used any hog grease in cooking and I told him no. He ate a big mess of the turkey and that evening he nearly died. He said that he knew I had used lard and lied to him and that he would settle the matter with me when he got over the sickness. That frightened me, so we moved on, but the Indians continued visiting Herman and eating all the bread and everything.

One day we were at a settlement store and the Indians began to come in thick. I asked Herman what was the matter and he said, "The Indians act like they are going to kill the whites and break out." That evening about dark they began shooting and I could hear gunshots from every direction. I could not see anything, but I was scared and begged Herman to let us leave there, but he almost fell off the wagon laughing. The Indians had received several hundred beeves from the government and were killing them.

At another time an old squaw came up right close to me and her papoose was squalling for life. I looked at the little fellow and it was all bound up so that I could just see a little bit of its face. The squaw threw the child down and put a big red handkerchief over the child's face. I said aloud but to myself, "Old gal, you'll kill that child." Herman overheard me and again he nearly broke his side laughing. This was the way all Indian babies were handled. He told the squaw in Indian what I had said, and they both rolled and laughed.

While we were there the Wichitas visited the Comanches and they had a big war dance. I was acquainted with a settler's wife and daughter who had recently moved there, so these ladies invited me to be their escort to the war dance. We went down near the place and here came the nearly naked Indians with lances, riding in a half-circle. I became intently interested in the dance until Herman came to me laughing. I looked around and my female company was leaving a blue streak as they crossed the glade going home.

The drums and bells started; the chiefs were seated in a half circle in an amphitheatre; two braves danced. Near the opening of the arena was a log covered with the hide of a buffalo. A warrior would ride down a straight track in a run, stop suddenly, and stick his spear in the buffalo robe, and then the music and dancing would cease, and this warrior would rehearse his experiences and hardships. After he made his speech his horse was carried away and he joined his

146

comrades in the half-circle. The drum beat, the bells rang, and the dance was continued by the same two braves and the next warrior rode up and went through the same performance. But the same couple did all the dancing. This was kept up for two or three days and nights.

While there, one Indian caught and handled a very vicious looking rattlesnake. Herman stayed with Quanah, and I found employment, so we spent several weeks up there, but I was always afraid of the Indians.

Herman's 1899 book ended with his brother Adolph's recollection of their trip to the Indian Territory. In his 1927 edition we can sense that the unhappy period of adjustment he went through back in the 1880s must have seemed remote and embarrassing, for he does not mention any of it: his drinking, his fall from grace in the community and all the reckless things he did. It is interesting to note that the "Credentials and Testimonials" which appear first in this present volume were added as a sort of appendix to the 1899 book. He felt a real need, it is evident, to justify his past and assure his fellow citizens that he was not just a good fellow now but a responsible citizen of the Anglo-American world. By 1927 this incumbency had mellowed with time.

He says, looking back in 1927, "In due course of time I learned to talk the English and German languages and became friends with everybody in the community. The fear the little children had toward me gave place to friendship, and the older ones began to regard me as an equal in the social scale. I learned to work, and would often be hired by ranchmen and farmers there. I knew all the old settlers; Ship Martin, the Moseleys, William Kidd, the Marschalls, the Keysers, the Langes, and others and was related to a great many of the settlers."

By 1927 a great many things had changed not just for Herman but the society in which

he lived. Few changes were more profound than the way people looked at the Indians. Where, in the 1860s and 1870s, they had been bitter enemies, little better than wild beasts to be exterminated, despised, feared, by 1927 they were a historical curiosity; a harmless but fascinating survival of a remote period of time that had no connection with real life. So swift and total had the changes been that even persons like Herman, who had lived the life, felt the social and hereditary impulses of this society, could not really bring themselves to admit how important it had been to them. The savagery of the hatred of white for red and red for white, lost its point in such fashion that its memory was more dream than emotion. The white world did not so much forgive the Indians as forget them. By 1927 not only was there no bitterness left against the Comanches and Apaches who had burned, scalped, and murdered all along the Texas frontier; there was no feeling left at all. The fact that Indian tribes had held a form of domination over those parts of the state was as alien to modern times as the fact that an ocean had once rolled over the parched hills and prairies of the Permian Basin—and much less important, for the Indians left nothing commercially exploitable. Indians? Something the movies had invented to create suspense in certain badly written and poorly acted film dramas.

But people like Herman still lived, of course; people who not only remembered what had been but who had been part of what they remembered. If by 1927 most of the people around him no longer recalled flames in the night or the loss of fathers, sons, and mothers, part of Herman's life could never change and could never forget. One of the things he kept an interest in was the others like himself who had undergone captivity, who had been "Indianized" and could never scrub it from their minds and hearts. So in 1927 he included this section called "Other Captives":

41

I HAVE OFTEN BEEN ASKED if the Indians had other captive white children while I was with them. It must be remembered that I was with a comparatively small band of Apaches during my captivity in that tribe, and when I joined the

Comanches I was thrown with a small band also. These two tribes operated in bands and it was seldom that all of them ever came together in a large body. But nearly every band had white and Mexican captive children. There were many white children and women captured in South and West Texas. I have met some of these captives since I was restored to my people. Today there are men and women among the Indians in Oklahoma whose identity has never been established, who are classed as Indians but are of white parentage.

Jeff and Clint Smith, former Indian captives

Some of the captives died among the Indians, some were purchased by their people. Clinton and Jeff Smith, captured near San Antonio, Texas, were kept by the Indians about five years. Jeff was sold to the Apaches and was recaptured in Mexico. He now lives in San Antonio. Clinton was taken from the Comanches at Fort Sill and sent back to his father. Dot Babb, who now lives at Amarillo, Texas, was a captive of the Comanches for several years. Frank Buckelew, now living at Medina, Texas, was a captive of the Lipans for over a year and managed to escape from them. Adolph Korn was captured in Mason County and spent six years with the Comanches. He died at Mason about 1902. Rudolph Fischer was captured by Comanches in Gillespie County and after spending several years with them, was restored to his people, but he was not content to stay. He returned to the Indians and is with them yet and has grown quite wealthy.

Mrs. Mahala McDonald, now living at Melvin, Texas, was captured near Harper, in Gillespie County, when she was quite small and was kept for a few years by the Indians. Malinda Cordell was captured in Llano County many years before my capture and was kept for several years. She was finally purchased from the Indians and in 1891 was living at Menardville.

There were hundreds of captives in the various tribes.

AT THIS POINT Herman reproduces a chapter from the book *Andele, or the Mexican-Kiowa Captive*, written in 1899 by the Rev. J. J. Methvin, adding "some of the incidents of which I am quite familiar." Here are some of the incidents mentioned in the narrative:

42

UNDER PRESIDENT GRANT'S PEACE POLICY, Laurie [Lawrie] Tatum, a friend [Quaker], was appointed agent for the Kiowas, Comanches, and Apaches, and on July 1, 1869, undertook the duties of that office, with agency headquarters near Fort Sill.

At that time there was one band of Comanches, the Quo-ja-les (Kwahadi), who refused to report at the agency at all. They ridiculed the other Indians for submission to the white man and, continuing their marauding expeditions, they formed a nucleus for other Indians who were warlike and restless under the white man's rule. They sent Agent Tatum word that they would never come to the agency and shake hands till the soldiers came out to fight them and then, if they were whipped, they would come.

They thus set at defiance all authority till [some years later] when General Mackenzie surprised them and took one hundred of their women and children and carried them away prisoners. Soon after the Quo-ja-les reported at the agency, acknowledged their defeat and asked that their women and children be returned to them.

"But," said Agent Tatum, "you must first bring all the white and Mexican captives you have in your band."

Perry-o-cum, the Quo-ja-les chief, did not expect such a demand, and stood in stolid silence for some minutes, but seeing the determined look on Tatum's face, he gave instruction to his band to bring in the captives.

In a little while they brought in Adolph Korn and Clinton Smith, two Texas boys, and two others who had forgotten their names and every word of English. They remembered some incidents of their capture, and taking these as a clue, Agent Tatum advertised in the Texas and Kansas papers and at last found their parents. Their names proved to be Temple Friend and Valentine Maxie. Twelve captive Mexicans were also thus rescued, and one case, that of little Presleano, was of special interest.

There was an air of superiority about him. He was bright, talkative, quick to apprehend, and sprightly in movement. He seemed to have been a pet in the home and heart of old Perry-o-cum, the chief, and the boy loved the chief. Perry-o-cum knew that and felt sure if it was left to the choice of the boy he would not be forced to give him up. So Perry-o-cum spoke up thus:

"Agent Tatum, I am willing to give up all these other prisoners. It is right that I should, and you have a right to demand it, for they belong to your nation. But this boy is a Mexican, captured in Mexico, and he does not belong to your government and you have no special right to him. I love him as my own son and he loves me. If you will not force him away, but leave it to his own choice, I shall be satisfied."

Tatum watched the intense anxiety of Perry-o-cum as he spoke, and waited a little while before he replied . . .

"Perry-o-cum, what you say is good as to giving the boy his choice, and if you will let him remain here till afternoon we will find out what is his choice." This was readily agreed to, and the chief went away, leaving the boy in the agent's office.

The agent had a good dinner prepared, of which the boy partook with much relish, and while he was feeling particularly comfortable from the surroundings, and the kindness shown him, the chief was summoned to the office again. A Mexican interpreter had been secured and after petting the boy for a while, Tatum began talking to him about his father and mother, not knowing they were dead, and that the little boy had no memory of any father and mother save old Perry-o-cum and his wife. So when he put the question, "Do you wish to remain with Perry-o-cum, or do you want to go back to your own people?" to the delight of Perry-o-cum, he said he wanted to remain with him.

"But don't you want to see your brothers and sisters? Don't you want to go to them?"

The little boy dropped his eyes in thoughtfulness a moment. The memories of home began to dawn upon him, and when he looked up again he said slowly and with a serious look upon his face, "I want to go home."

"Then I will send you," said Agent Tatum, and as he looked across the room at Perry-o-cum, he saw the tears chasing each other down his otherwise stolid cheeks, but he was caught in his own proposition and he felt he must submit. The boy was returned to his people in Mexico through General [C. C.] Augur, commander of the military post at San Antonio.

On July 10, 1870, a band of Kiowas went to the home of Gottlieb Koozer, in Texas. Mr. Koozer was not aware of the Indians' approach till he saw them in the yard, and being defenseless, he decided it was best to show a friendly spirit toward them, so he went out to meet them and offered his hand in friendship. Two of them took hold of his hands at the same time in apparent friendship, while another, stepping a little to one side, shot him through the heart. They scalped him and then went into the house, destroyed what they found therein, dresses, feather beds and many other things. They took Mrs. Koozer and her five children—one a young lady, one small girl, and three boys—and also a young man by the name of Martin Kilgore, who was about fourteen years of age, and started back to their reservation.

As soon as news of this outrage was received at Fort Sill, Agent Tatum determined to rescue the prisoners and find out, and punish if possible the depredators. He announced to the Indians what he had heard and declared that he would never issue any more government supplies to them till they brought the prisoners in. The Indians demanded a ransom, for two years before they had been paid $1,500 each for some captives. He sent a letter to Mrs. Koozer by the hands of a trusty Indian on the 7th of August, 1870. On the 18th of August the Indians, giving up any idea of fighting, went to the agency with their wives and children.

Whenever Indians are not expecting to fight, they take with them their wives and children everywhere they go, but when war is expected they send them all away together in care of the old men. When, therefore, women and children are in sight there is assurance of peace.

They had two of the Koozer family, Miss Koozer and her little sister, with them. The little one, who had not seen her mother for several days, began crying but was forced to hush. Indians do not allow their captives to cry. The soldiers became indignant and stepped forward to take the captives, but in an instant the Indians pointed a dagger at the heart of the girls. The soldiers did not proceed further, for it meant sure and instant death to the girls.

The Indians took them away, but seeing they could not change Agent Tatum from his purpose to withhold all government supplies till the prisoners were delivered, by 11 o'clock the two girls and two boys were brought in and delivered to him. A Mexican Kiowa had the mother and he was stubborn and insisted upon a ransom, "a mule and a carbine."

Having delivered the above four, the Indians called for the supplies, but were informed that all of the prisoners must be brought in first. Very soon Mrs. Koozer and the other boy were brought in, but they had left young Kilgore at their camp out many miles upon the reservation. Agent Tatum then paid the Indians $100 apiece for the captives, lest in the future they should kill all they found on their marauding expeditions instead of taking them captive. He then issued them the usual government supplies, with the understanding that he would issue no more till M. B. Kilgore was delivered to him.

The Koozer family were a pitiable sight. Nobody can describe what Mrs. Koozer and her daughter suffered till they found some protection and relief from an Indian woman who seemed to have more than the usual influence of a woman among the Indians. Mrs. Koozer was appropriated by a Mexican Kiowa as his wife, and he was very cruel to her, trying twice to kill her, but she was each time protected by the chiefs.

Three days later Colonel [Benjamin H.] Grierson sent a detachment of soldiers to conduct Mrs. Koozer and her children to Montague, Texas, from which place she reached her home in safety.

These were the last captives for whom any ransom was ever paid. Soon after this another trial was made to extort a ransom for prisoners that utterly failed. It was about the time of the arrest of old Santanta [Satanta] and others. Old White Horse and six other Kiowa men and one woman went to Texas, murdered Mr. Lee and his wife and took captive their three children; Susan, aged sixteen; Millie, aged nine; and John, aged six. As soon as it was known at Fort Sill, Agent Tatum suspended all government issues to the Indians till the captives should be brought in.

This was delayed by a proposed council in which delegates from the civilized tribes were to be present. These civilized tribes hoped by their delegates to persuade the wild tribes to quit raiding and be peaceable. This council was set for July 22, 1872, at old Fort Cobb, but the Kiowas did not go there till ten days after.

White Horse was stubborn, and declared that he did not want peace, but said that he and his young men would raid when and where they pleased. Lone Wolf said they would return the prisoners in their possession when Santanta and Big Tree were returned from the penitentiary [Huntsville] and all the military posts removed from the reservation, and their reservation extended from the Rio Grande to the Missouri River.

The delegates of the civilized tribes and Kicking Bird tried to pacify White Horse and Lone Wolf and other war-like Indians, but they could do but little. Agent Tatum adhered to his purpose to issue no more rations till the Lee children were brought in and about a month later they delivered the two girls to Agent Richards at the Wichita Agency, and they were sent under care of Caddo George, a trusty Caddo, to Agent Tatum at Fort Sill. The boy was brought in two weeks later, and on the same day an older brother arrived from Texas and took them home.

These were the last captives the Kiowas ever took. It became unprofitable and exceedingly dangerous for, as Texas became more thickly settled, the people determined to put a stop to Indian raids and they were ready to exterminate the war-like tribes, if necessary, to accompany that end. The government, too, was proceeding by legal process to punish those who were guilty.

THE LAST PARAGRAPH stating these were the last captives the Kiowas ever took might be open to historical question. As we can recall from Herman's recollections, the Indians continued to take Mexican captives even after they may have given up the practice on the Anglo-American frontiers.

Herman (or his editor) adds a brief account of the so-called Wagon Train Massacre of 1871 and the trial and subsequent tragedies in the affairs of Big Tree, Satanta and Satank. As Herman was not a part of this episode and had no connection with its later details—and as it is quite well documented in many frontier histories—I have not included the story. Herman's version, whatever its origin, seems accurate.

Satanta

Big Tree

Kicking Bird

Lone Wolf

43

THERE MAY BE SOME PEOPLE who think I am an imposter, or that I have never been a captive, so I am giving below a letter written by the Commissioner of Indian Affairs at Washington, D.C., in 1901 to the United States Indian Agent of the Kiowa Agency, Oklahoma, which established my identity and caused me to be enrolled as a member of the Comanche tribe, the same as if a member by blood. This should set at rest all suspicion that I may be an imposter. I have other documents to prove my identity and I have living near me at Grandfield, Oklahoma, many old Indian comrades who regard me as a blood brother.

The letter follows:

Department of the Interior,
Office of Indian Affairs,
Washington, September 30, 1901

Lt. Col. J. F. Randlett, U. S. Indian Agent;
Kiowa Agency, Oklahoma.

Referring to your communication of the 25th ultimo, and to previous correspondence relative to the application of Herman Lehman [*sic*] for enrollment by adoption and full tribal rights with the Comanche Indians of the agency under your charge, you are informed that this office is now in receipt of a letter dated the 26th instant from the Acting Secretary of the Interior who decides that the said applicant is not entitled to an allotment of land with said tribe, but adds "as the Indians in 'business council' through their chiefs and headmen voted 'that he be enrolled with the Comanches, with full rights as a member of the Comanche tribe,' the Department authorizes the enrollment of the said Herman Lehman, or "Montechema," [*sic*] as a member of the Comanche tribe, entitled to all the benefits of money conferred by the agreement of October 21, 1892, the same as if a member by blood, this being the only right that the Indians could confer on persons adopted or enrolled after the cessation of their lands under the above mentioned agreement.

For your full information in the premises, I enclose herewith a copy of said decision of the Department, and you will in accordance therewith enroll the said Herman Lehman as a member of the Comanche tribe of Indians, and advise all persons interested of your action in the matter.

Mr. R. N. Richardson, the atty. in the case, has this day been informed of the action of the Department, and furnished a copy of said decision.

Very respectfully,
A. C. TONNER,
Acting Commissioner.

I have now given the reader the story of my life, which has been eventful. There are many little incidents and details which have been omitted, because if they were all told it would require a book many times the size of this volume. Enough has been told, however, to give the reader an insight in the manners and customs of the Comanche and Apache tribes of Indians. I was one of them and I have told the story truthfully.

In 1890 I was married to Miss Fannie Light at Loyal Valley, and to us five children were born, two boys and three girls, and they are now grown and occupy places of usefulness in the world. My oldest boy, Henry, died in a U.S. Army camp at Houston, Texas, during the World War.

My career has been rather checkered; I have lived as a savage and as a civilized man, and while I still love my old Indian comrades, the refining influences of civilization have wrought a great change in me. When I was a savage I thirsted to kill and to steal, because I had been taught that that was the way to live; but I know now that that is wrong. I would not take human life, now, nor would I steal. "The way of the transgressor is hard," is a saying that is true.

I am an old man now. I will soon reach the total of three score and ten years allotted to man, if death does not claim me—seventy years of wonderful experience. I have seen many changes since I came into this world, the oxcart gave way to the horse-drawn vehicle, and the automobile has surpassed that mode of travel. Speeding railway trains, flying machines, radios, and many other wonders have come to pass. We are living in a fast age. I am glad God has spared my life and permitted me to live to see these wonderful changes. I gave reverence to Him in the only way I knew how when I was an Indian; I worship him now after the manner of an enlightened white man.

When I look upon these great changes I marvel and wonder how it can be so. Of many of these things I am yet in ignorance. I cannot understand how the human voice can be wafted over the radio thousands of miles without the aid of wires, but it is done, for I have heard it. It is as much a mystery to me as the first telegraph line I ever saw.

A party of Indians were coming down into the settlements on a raid when, at a point in the vicinity of Fort Concho, we came upon a newly constructed telegraph line. We stopped and considered it, and wondered what it meant. Each Indian had his own notion about what it was intended for, but we were all wrong. The chief said he believed it was to be a fence to be made so high that the Indians could not get through, and so we proceeded to cut it down. Coming on down into the settlements we stole some horses and went back that way with the drove, and we found the line had been rebuilt and the wire was in place again.

And the puffing locomotive and railway train were also objects of wonder, when I came back to civilization and beheld them. The first train I ever saw was while I was with the Indians, and of course we did not know what it was, and in consequence got a scare that almost drove us frantic.

155

We had come far down into the settlements on a raid—it may have been near Austin—and one night while we were waiting in a secluded spot in a little ravine for the moon to come up, a train came suddenly around a curve from behind a mountain and was right on us before we had time to mount our horses.

That hideous monster, belching smoke and hissing steam, and with glaring lights, bore down upon us at terrific speed, and we ran, scrambling over rocks and through the brush, to get away from it. It followed us for a little ways, but we thought it had lost our trail, as it went rushing on away from us.

We were somewhat scattered when things became quiet, and I was uneasy for fear the awful thing had caught three of our comrades. But when we gave our agreed assembly signal, the Indians came forth from their hiding places and we held a consultation. We decided to leave that region at once and not attempt to steal any horses there, for that monster might return and catch us.

It was generally agreed among us that it was the Evil Spirit that was aboard, and was seeking to devour all mankind, the white folks included. When we went back to camp and told what we had seen, the Indians were greatly alarmed, and the medicine man warned us to stay out of that region.

44

MY MOTHER died at Castell, Texas, April 15, 1912, at a very old age. My brother Willie, who was captured by the Apaches at the same time I was captured, and who escaped from them a few days later, lives near Loyal Valley, Texas, yet, and has a good ranch property there. Another brother, Adolph Lehmann, lives in Menard County, Texas, and is in good circumstances. My sister, Mrs. Mina Keyser, lives at Loyal Valley, and my sister, Mrs. Caroline Dye, lives in Dallas.

To the dear old mother, and to these noble brothers and sisters, I owe all for my restoration, for if it had not been for them I would today be an Indian still.

Conclusion

HERMAN LEHMANN was a famous figure in Mason, Llano and Gillespie counties all his life, being called on to entertain with his Indian skills on numerous occasions, right up to his last years.

But he never quite became like his neighbors. He was always an Indian, and from time to time he had to go back and live with "his copper-colored brothers."

J. Marvin Hunter, in his Introduction to *Nine Years*, in 1927, said, "I have known Herman Lehmann personally and intimately for thirty-five years. When he was brought back from his captivity my father, the late John Warren Hunter, was living at Loyal Valley, the home of Lehmann's mother, and I have heard him relate amusing incidents of Lehmann's Indian ways, and how the savage boy would scare the children of the village. My own mother used to tell me if I was not good 'that Indian' would sure get me.

"For a long time he dressed in his Indian garb; he did not like the white man's clothing; he wanted to be alone, out in the woods; he kept aloof from everyone. Finally . . . the wildness gave way to a kind and noble nature, and he became a white man again. But he never forgot his friends, the Indians.

"Years afterward, after he had married a splendid girl at Loyal Valley, he was granted a headright in the Indian Territory, through a special act of Congress, and he went there to live upon his claim, and among his tribe. Yes, his tribe, for he was still a Comanche in the eyes of his copper-colored brothers, and he still possesses all of the tribal rights and privileges even unto this day."

Many Texans saw Herman perform. Nearly forty years after his death there were people in Loyal Valley and Cherry Spring who remembered his "Indian shows" and his stories vividly. Fred Gipson, the well-known Texas writer who also came from Mason County, remembered sitting beneath a rail fence at a rodeo where Herman rode down, and killed with bow and arrow, a steer. He drove the animal right toward the place where young Gipson huddled, dropping it at the last instant with his well-placed shafts and leaving the boy wide-eyed with fright and admiration.

A Loyal Valley woman said that she, as a little girl, sat at Herman's knee, listening to his tales, and that often, just as he reached some particularly suspenseful part, he would, without warning, give a wild-Indian yell, "chilling us down." Another woman points out the site of the grounds where Herman entertained the townspeople so often, and tells of the arrows he gave her two sons—which they still had—telling the boys that the arrows had killed men, red or white.

What everyone seemed to remember about Herman Lehmann was his sense of humor. He was good-natured and refused to take life with the seriousness one so

Herman Lehmann and his family, 1899

often found among his German contemporaries. This got him the reputation of being irresponsible. In the first few years after he returned to white society and decades after his death there were those who, while remembering him with affection, still retained the opinion that he was "wild" and never truly became civilized.

But Herman got along well with everyone and, oddly enough, seemed to have an especially close relationship with the old Texas Rangers and cattlemen whom he had fought with or robbed while a tribesman.

He was lean and hard of body all his life, and he rode a horse with ease and grace, right up to the months before his death. In his last decades Herman's thick and abundant hair turned snowy white, which added to the impressiveness of his person, especially when he was wearing the warrior's trappings of the Comanche.

Herman spent a good portion of his last thirty years in Oklahoma, and most of his children eventually settled there. Willie remained at Loyal Valley, and his ranch house still sits in a hidden valley less than two miles from the little community. It was here that Herman spent much of his time, and it was here he died of pneumonia on February 2, 1932. Willie lived until 1951 when he died just one month short of his ninetieth birthday.

Loyal Valley, like so many other little Texas towns, fell victim to the automobile. Today it sits off on a narrow loop of road which curves a mile or so away from U.S. 87. The post office was closed years ago and not even a service station carries the name.

158

Herman Lehmann

But the landmarks are rather abundant, if you stop and talk to the few persons living in Loyal Valley. Mrs. Buchmier's hotel is now a two-story, thick-walled residence; the little schoolhouse, where Herman returned for one day of class, still stands, its ancient log walls covered by plaster. John O. Meusebach's outdoor bathtub and its water supply cistern are to be found at his former two hundred-acre nursery. Traces of the settlement's forting-up place, the municipal well and trading square, and the hotel's livery stables can all be located, and a few hundred yards along a well-kept dirt road is the old home of the Kidd family where the Apaches stole a herd of horses at the same time they captured Herman and Willie.

But the most important landmarks are those found on the mailboxes around Loyal Valley, Cherry Spring, and Castell, which is just a few miles northeastward in Llano County. Here are still found the familiar family names which Herman knew, some of which have been on the land since it was colonized in 1847; Kothe, Kothmann, Keyser, Crenwelge, Grenwelge, Moseley, Kidd, Leifeste, Marschall, Lange, Nixon and Evers.

Loyal Valley still draws historical attention from time to time because of its two most famous residents, the Baron Meusebach, and Herman Lehmann. Meusebach, who died in 1897, is buried in the neat, rock-walled Meusebach-Marschall family cemetery a mile east of Cherry Spring. Herman lies in the small Loyal Valley burial ground between his mother and Willie. His modest, brown stone makes no mention of anything but his birth and his death.

He was the last white captive to be released by the Comanches, but more than that, he remained a voluntary captive to their way of life for the remainder of his many days.

THE END

Bibliography

Texas State Gazetteer and Business Directory 1884–5. Volume II. R. L. Polk & Co., St. Louis, Mo.

Indian Depredations in Texas, by J. W. Wilbarger; Austin, 1889.

The Comanche Barrier to South Plains Settlement, by Rupert Norval Richardson; Glendale, Calif., 1933.

Six Years With the Texas Rangers 1875 to 1881, by James B. Gillett, New Haven, 1963.

Indian Wars of Texas, by Mildred P. Mayhall; Waco, 1965.

A New Land Beckoned: German Immigration to Texas, 1844–1847, Compiled and edited by Chester William and Ethel Hander Geue; Waco, 1966.

John O. Meusebach, German Colonizer in Texas, by Irene Marschall King; Austin, 1968.

The Indian Tribes of North America, by John R. Swanton; Washington, D.C., 1968.

"Apache Captive Tells Thrilling Story," J. Marvin Hunter, *Frontier Times.*

"Herman Lehmann, Indian Captive," Uvalde *Leader-News;* March 7, 14, 1941.

"Reunion Marks Capture," by Ruby Olivia Montgomery, Houston *Post*, March 5, 1933.

"Mason Vet Recalls Captivity," Mrs. A. C. Bowman. Reprinted from San Angelo *Standard* by Graham *Leader*, September 15, 1932. (Interview with Willie Lehmann.)

"Recalls Early Castell," San Angelo *Standard*, May 3, 1934. (About Mrs. Wilson (Johanna) Hey, and Mrs. Minnie Ringenot, sisters of Adolph Korn, and family life.)

Mason County Scrapbook and Obituaries; University of Texas Archives.

THE AUTHOR wishes to thank Mrs. Jimmy Byerley, of Loyal Valley, and Mrs. Clara Kidd, of Fredericksburg, for their information about the town of Loyal Valley and their recollections of Herman Lehmann.

Typesetting by
G&S TYPESETTERS
Printing by
CAPITAL PRINTING COMPANY
Paper supplied by
LONE STAR PAPER COMPANY
Binding by
CUSTOM BOOKBINDERS
Design by
WILLIAM D. WITTLIFF